CHANNEL FOUR
Television with a Difference?

STEPHEN LAMBERT

BFI Publishing

First published in 1982 by the British Film Institute
127 Charing Cross Road
London WC2H OEA

Cover: Larry Smith

Cartoon on p. 31 copyright © John Kent 1972

British Library Cataloguing in Publication Data
Lambert, Stephen
    Channel Four.
    1. Channel Four—History
    I. Title
    384.55'4'0941   HE8700.9.G7

ISBN 0 85170 124 8

Typeset by Sprint, Beckenham, Kent
Printed by Garden House Press, London NW10

Contents

Acknowledgments

My thanks are due to Anthony Smith and Ed Buscombe, who were responsible for commissioning the book and have read and commented on the manuscript; to Jeremy Isaacs and Justin Dukes, for their co-operation and helpful comments; to my two supervisors at Oxford, Dr David Butler and Mrs Mary Warnock, for their advice and encouragement; and to the Social Science Research Council, whose financial assistance made the work possible. I would also like to thank the following for generously helping me with time and information: Rod Allen, Lord Annan, Lord Aylestone, Peter Batty, John Birt, Kenneth Blyth, Paul Bonner, Sarah Boston, William Brown, Iain Bruce, Rob Burkitt, Anthony Butler, Chris Dunkley, David Elstein, David Glencross, Christopher Griffin-Beale, Godfrey Hodgson, Michael Jackson, Roy Lockett, Barrie MacDonald, Ian MacDonald, Paul Madden, Kenneth Miles, Sara Morrison, Geoffrey Nowell-Smith, Richard Paterson, Tony Pearson, Lady Plowden, Vincent Porter, John Ranelagh, Merlyn Rees, Bernard Sendall, Colin Shaw, Brian Tesler, Michael Tracey, David Wheeler, Phillip Whitehead and Lord Windlesham.

I am very grateful to David Barlow for his interest and criticisms, and to Felicity Gray, who typed the manuscript and has given me much help during the book's composition and preparation.

Introduction

In terms of wavelengths the fourth channel already exists. It is the empty room of British broadcasting, awaiting only furniture, fittings and an occupant. (*The Annan Report: An ITV View*. A Response by the ITV companies to the Report of the Committee on the Future of Broadcasting, June 1977)

The empty room of British broadcasting was finally occupied on 2 November 1982 when, after more than two decades of debate, the fourth national television service went on the air.

The new channel is a novel addition to Britain's television system. By Act of Parliament it is required to encourage innovation and experiment in the form and content of its programmes. Although financed by advertising, it is not directly dependent on the income earned from the sale of its advertising space. Unlike any other television service, it does not make its own programmes; it commissions them – some from the ITV companies, but a substantial proportion must, by law, be obtained from independent producers. In brief, Channel Four has been charged to provide a 'distinctive service'.

In the late 1950s the then Independent Television Authority first unsuccessfully argued the case for a second commercial television channel. Since then there have been ten different holders of ministerial responsibility for broadcasting, four changes of government, and two major committees of inquiry into broadcasting. The industry itself has undergone a multitude of changes during those twenty years and nearly all have had a bearing on the evolution of the new service. This book aims to provide an account of the complex history of motivations and pressures that brought about the establishment of the Channel Four Television Company Ltd.

The technical capacity for a fourth UHF national television channel has existed for years. All sets since the late 1960s have been equipped to receive it; many manufacturers have pre-emptively labelled the appropriate button 'ITV2'. The social and political question of how to use this technical capacity has taken a long time to resolve. So long, that some now wonder whether Channel Four, the last component in the public service broadcasting system, is perhaps already obsolete. The future belongs, perhaps, to the pluralism of the new media made possible by the technologies of optic-fibre cables, satellites, and video-cassettes. The era of regulation, of two broadcasting authorities responsible for three – now four – channels, is drawing to a close. The present Government, especially the Department of Industry, is keen to encourage the development of electronic media technology. Already Direct Broadcasting by

Satellite has been authorised to begin in 1986, and following the recent publication of the Hunt Committee Report it is likely that a decision to introduce national cable television will soon be made.

However, there has been talk of an imminent technological revolution in broadcasting for well over a decade. What will eventually come may not necessarily happen as quickly as some interested parties would like. In the meantime, Janus-faced, Channel Four will attempt to straddle broadcasting's past and future.

While the BBC/IBA duopoly remains intact, the new channel will attempt to fill the gaps in the public service already provided, by aiming to cater for those groups of people who until now have not been adequately served by television. Looking ahead, Channel Four will stimulate television production by independent producers in Britain, for it will give them, for the first time, a significant home market. And if television's future belongs to the new technological hardware, it also belongs to those who can supply the required software; the programmes that will be shown via the new media. By encouraging the development of an independent sector before then, Channel Four will help to give Britain a stronger basis from which to compete in any forthcoming international production explosion.

Because television sets are already designed to receive the new service, Channel Four has had the opportunity to address nearly all its potential audience from its first day on the air. No other television channel has had this advantage. Indeed, one of the reasons that it has taken so long to decide how to use the fourth channel is the fact that its arrival will not lead to the sale of any new domestic television equipment. Vigorous and effective lobbying by television equipment manufacturers preceded the introduction of Britain's first three television channels in 1936, 1955, and 1964. On each occasion the manufacturers wanted a service that would give the public an incentive to buy the equipment needed to receive it. The absence of a similar hardware dimension in the case of the fourth channel meant that the debate about its utilisation was conducted solely in terms of programming philosophy. There was no reason to employ the vacant channel until its programming objectives had been articulated, discussed, and agreed upon; something that would obviously take time. Such lengthy prior consideration contrasts markedly with the breakneck speed with which cable and satellite television seem likely to be introduced.

Essentially a descriptive rather than a critical account, this book is intended to show how Channel Four's programming objectives have evolved. It is an attempt to bring together in a continuous narrative the disparate published and unpublished documents and statements through which the Fourth Channel Debate has been conducted.

Although now widely forgotten, the ITA's original requests for a second commercial television channel were for one that would compete

2

with ITV1. Chapter One traces the factors that led to an abandonment of this policy in favour of a complementary conception of ITV2. The opposition to ITV2 that emerged in the early 1970s is considered in Chapter Two. A number of alternatives were put forward and one in particular, for a television 'foundation' that would 'publish' work from a much wider variety of authors than the three existing channels, gained support and eventually received government endorsement. A change of government in 1979 nullified this endorsement, and Chapter Three explores the compromise that was ultimately reached. Finally, Chapter Four examines the two years of preparation that have preceded the launch of the new service. Obviously Channel Four's execution of its stated programming ideals cannot yet be reviewed, and thus this chapter must remain open-ended.

1 ITV2: Competitive or Complementary?

In 1971 the Independent Television Authority submitted a document to the Minister of Posts and Telecommunications entitled *ITV2*. It proposed that the vacant fourth television network be used to introduce a second commercial service, complementary to ITV1. The two channels, it suggested, should be jointly planned and scheduled to prevent the same kind of programmes being shown at the same time. To ensure competition was avoided, the ITA argued that the existing ITV companies should provide the programmes for the second service and that no new contractors should be appointed. The document was the first formal declaration of a major change in policy that had occurred within the Authority during the late 1960s. Previously the ITA had assumed that any additional commercial channel would compete with ITV1 and be run by different people. This switch from a competitive to a complementary conception of ITV2 must be seen as part of the maturation of independent television, and to understand this development it is useful to recall, even if only in the barest outline, the evolution of British broadcasting policy from its origins in the 1920s, with particular reference to the arrival of commercial television in the 1950s.

PUBLIC SERVICE BROADCASTING: 30 YEARS OF BBC MONOPOLY

In Britain, the foundations of a *public service* conception of broadcasting were formulated by the Sykes (1923) and the Crawford (1926) committees, and realised in the shape of the British Broadcasting Corporation through the guiding vision of John Reith, its first Director-General. Reacting to what they saw as the vulgar, mass entertainment approach of the film industry and the popular press, Reith, the politicians, and the civil servants involved were determined that broadcasting should not follow the commercialised pattern of the United States. The waveband, said the Sykes Committee, 'must be regarded as a valuable form of public property . . . the control of such a potential power over public opinion ought to remain with the State.'[1] Direct governmental operation was thought to be undesirable, for the relevant ministry would always be open to accusations of partisanship. So, a public corporation – the BBC – was established; subject to ministerial advice but free to use its own judgment in respect of its day to day programming. With regard to financing, it was agreed that the Corporation should receive public funds; not from general taxation, but from revenue collected through the sale of licences to radio users. In this way, not only would those who used the service pay for it, but also such an arrangement would reaffirm the BBC's independence from direct governmental control. However, the power to decide whether, when, and by how much the licence fee should be raised remained with government.

In talking of *public service* broadcasting, Reith and his colleagues were openly embracing an educational model of broadcasting's social role. The radio was seen as a potential instrument of mass edification in the spirit of Arnold and Ruskin. Asa Briggs explains the ethos by quoting from Reith's *Broadcast over Britain*:

> The BBC, in brief, was to be dedicated to 'the maintenance of high standards, the provision of the best and the rejection of the hurtful.' Reith had no sympathy with the view that it is the task of the broadcaster to give the customer what he wants. 'It is occasionally indicated to us that we are apparently setting out to give the public what we think they need – not what they want – but few know what they want and very few what they need . . . In any case it is better to overestimate the mentality of the public than to underestimate it.'[2]

Light entertainment, popular music, and sport, which all featured in large measure in the BBC's weekly programme, were seen as something of an unfortunate necessity; they were there as 'groundbait' (a term still used in the 1960s by BBC Light Entertainment producers to describe their contribution).[3] Reith's high-handed cultural dictation reflected the values and standards of the professional middle classes. Raymond Williams points out that when radio arrived Britain, unlike many countries, already had a national press and, more generally, a clear idea of its national culture. He goes on to suggest that it was only because of this, and the fact that Britain possessed an unusually cohesive and compact ruling class, that public service broadcasting could be understood and administered by an organisation independent of detailed state supervision.[4] The more typical arrangement in Western European countries of the same size was direct governmental administration of broadcasting.

Once the BBC was established Reith endeavoured to consolidate his organisation's long-term survival. He encouraged it to become a very close institution with its own traditions, codes, and rituals; there was no question of making the airwaves available to those outside the broadcasting profession. The universities and churches, for instance, were denied a *right* to broadcast respectively the programmes on education or religion, or to determine how they should be broadcast. Only in the case of news did those outside the Corporation have a direct influence over content, for during the BBC's first twenty years its bulletins were merely résumés of the news agencies' daily reports. Yet even here it was a résumé prepared and presented by broadcasters not pressmen. In restricting broadcasting to a few professional voices, the BBC constructed its own picture of the nature and interests of the audience it served. And it is worth noting at this early stage that it was the assumptions and practices of the BBC and ITV as broadcasting institutions, rather than the legal restrictions contained in licences or charters, that were to become the subject of critical attack in the 1970s debate on the fourth channel.

Despite occasional complaints against the Corporation, the BBC enjoyed its monopoly status for thirty years. It was a period of remarkable growth; by 1950 the original single radio service had expanded into three domestic radio programmes, an overseas service, and a television channel. Its wartime achievements earned it worldwide admiration and with the return to peace its position seemed assured.

IN FAVOUR OF COMPETITION

Ironically, it has been suggested that the war, from which the BBC gained so much respect, also contributed to the ending of its monopoly. Already in 1938, the ISBA* and the IPA† had examined the popularity in Britain of foreign broadcasts transmitted from Luxembourg and Fécamp. They had concluded that these commercial stations – many sponsored by British advertisers – attracted a considerable share of the national audience, especially during the dour Reithian Sundays when the listening figures ran into millions. The war dramatically increased the British public's exposure to, and thus potential demand for, alternative forms of broadcasting; not only was the American Forces Network available to British civilians, but also many ex-servicemen returning from overseas brought with them their generally favourable experience of commercial radio.

Perhaps even more important was the fact that the inevitably close wartime relationship between government and broadcaster raised in the minds of many, who until then had supported monopoly, the question of how appropriate it was to have so great an accumulation of cultural and political power under one roof. In 1946, Sir Frederick Ogilvie wrote a letter to *The Times* that was to become an important text in the debate about the continuation of the BBC's monopoly. Sir Frederick had succeeded Reith as Director-General but had resigned during the war after objecting to the increasing governmental control of the Corporation. He shocked many supporters of the BBC by warning of the dangers of continuing its monopoly:

Monopoly of broadcasting is inevitably the negation of freedom, no matter how efficiently it is run, or how wise and kindly the board or committees in charge of it. It denies freedom of employment to speakers, musicians, writers, actors, and all who seek their chances on

*Incorporated Society of British Advertisers (trade association of major advertisers).
†Institute for Practitioners in Advertising (trade association of advertising agencies).

the air. The dangers of monopoly have long been recognised in the film industry and the Press and the theatre, and active steps have been taken to prevent it. In tolerating monopoly we are alone among the democratic countries of the world.[5]

There is no need for us to consider here the detailed history of the campaign for commercial television. A number of excellent accounts exist already.[6] What is important is an appreciation of the spirit of the 1954 Television Act and the assumptions made at that time about how independent television was likely to develop in the future. Following its 1945 defeat, the Conservative Party reviewed its policies and with the General Election of 1950 a large group of young new Conservative politicians entered Parliament. Many of the more able formed themselves into a loose association known as the One Nation Group. Committed to a vision of the mass consumption society, free of wartime rationing and recent Labour nationalisations, they were united in their support for free enterprise and opposition to monopoly. Broadcasting presented itself as one area where swift, sweeping change was both feasible and desirable; for in conflict with the Reithian ethos, they saw broadcasting as essentially a commodity like any other, its purpose being to satisfy the wants of consumers. In an ideal world, a proliferation of channels, resembling the multiplicity of the newspaper industry, would give the consumers sovereignty.

But the Party leadership needed to be convinced and thus the introduction of commercial television hinged on the ability of a substantial body of backbench opinion to persuade its leadership to accept a policy of change. Sensibly they confined their lobbying to the relatively unknown and immature field of television, accepting that the BBC's prestigious international radio reputation was likely to prove too formidable an opposition. With the BBC's Charter due to expire in 1951, the Beveridge Committee of Inquiry had been appointed by the fading Labour administration in 1949 to consider the future of the Corporation. In the BBC's favour, Beveridge recommended the continuation of a single broadcasting outlet, although the Committee felt the broadcasters had too much power and that greater authority should be given to the Board of Governors. One member of the Committee dissented, and in his minority report Selwyn Lloyd argued the case for introducing commercial broadcasting. The new Conservative Government agreed with him and in its May 1952 White Paper suggested that 'in the expanding field of television, provision should be made to permit some element of competition.'[7] There then followed a seventeen month interlude before the Government published its detailed proposals. It was a period of fierce public debate between the defenders of monopoly, represented by the National Television Council, and the proponents of commercial television, who had formed the Popular Television Association. The latter concen-

8

trated on stressing that advertising on television did not have to entail American-style sponsorship; advertisements could be separated from programmes and responsibility for programme content would remain with the television stations, not the advertiser. The Government shared this view in its second White Paper. But to the disappointment of the ISBA, IPA and some Conservative back benchers, it believed it would be necessary to have a supervisory authority to regulate the conduct of the new stations and ensure that commercial broadcasting was not run solely for profit. The authority would be a public corporation; it would own and operate the transmitting stations and rent its facilities to privately-financed companies, who would supply the programmes and draw their revenue from advertisements. The public service conception of broadcasting was thus substantially maintained in a compromise that mediated between the State's claim to regulate and the claims of free enterprise. The Government congratulated itself with the thought that such a combination of effective control on the one hand, and greater freedom on the other, was 'a typically British approach to this new problem.'[8]

ITV: REGULATED AND LIMITED COMPETITION

The second White Paper also dealt with the shortages of available broadcasting frequencies. VHF Band I (41-68MHz) was just wide enough to accommodate the stations needed by the BBC to give full national television coverage. Three additional bands had been earmarked for future television development: VHF Band III (174-223MHz), UHF Band IV (470-582MHz), and UHF Band V (582-960MHz). However, techniques for using the latter two bands were not fully developed, so any immediate additional service was restricted to Band III and even here there were only enough channels readily available to provide a single network with national coverage. The memorandum gave no clear indication of how additional channels would be used when they became available; it merely remarked that the proposed arrangements for the first commercial service would not in any way prejudice future developments. All essential features of the White Paper survived the Parliamentary debates and in July 1954 the Television Act became law.

Within its first month of life the new Independent Television Authority expressed its concern to the Postmaster-General that in allocating the Authority so few frequencies the possibility of arranging competition between programme contractors was ruled out. Although it would have been possible for the ITA to use its available channels to introduce direct competition in certain areas, this could only have been done at the cost of leaving other areas without any commercial service. But on this matter, public service had clear priority over competition – coverage would have to come before diversity. In May 1955 the ITA formally asked for control of all eight channels in Band III so that it could introduce two national, directly competitive commercial services.[9] The request was rejected. In a written reply to Parliament, Charles Hill, the Postmaster-General, deferred consideration of any additional television service until at least 1958. The need to assess both the initial performance of the first commercial service, as well as future technical developments such as colour, were given as reasons for postponement.

Despite these initial failures the pioneers of independent television continued to assume that their confinement to a single network would be only temporary. Bernard Sendall, Deputy Director-General of the ITA for its first twenty years, confirms this in Volume One of his history of independent television:

> It never entered the heads of the Members of the Authority that successive governments would so allocate frequencies as to preclude all freedom for the ITA to cover the country with more than one station in any one area. Monopoly had at last been broken: they can hardly be blamed, in view of all that had been said, for assuming that it was to be succeeded by genuine plurality and not mere duopoly. They were not to know that in later years the notion of competition, except in terms of competition between the BBC and ITV, would lose favour; and that even between these two organisations competition, as distinct from planned co-existence, would come to be increasingly deprecated.[10]

Although the ITA was limited to only one station in any one area, the Television Act had charged the Authority to secure 'adequate competition' in the supply of programmes. In its first annual report the Authority explained how it had attempted to comply with the spirit of the legislation through the introduction of networking. By appointing at least one contractor per station, the ITA envisaged competition between the companies to sell their programmes to the network. With the cost of programme production so high, there was every incentive for the companies both to export their own programmes to other stations and to import programmes where this was cheaper than producing their own. In fact, in an attempt to maximise competition the Authority appointed four contractors for its first three stations covering London, the Midlands, and the North. By splitting the week between the five working days and the weekend, the ITA constructed a mosaic-like arrangement whereby each area was supplied with programmes from two of the four companies in the course of a complete week – thus, Associated-Rediffusion was the London weekday contractor, Associated-TeleVision supplied London at the weekend and the Midlands during the week, ABC Television was the contractor for the weekend in the Midlands and the North, and Granada Television supplied the North during the week.

All the evidence suggests that there was a commitment within the Authority in its early days, especially in the case of Robert Fraser, the ITA's new Director-General, to initiate as much competition as possible.

10

In one of his first memoranda to Sir Kenneth Clark, Chairman of the Authority, Fraser stressed that the network would have to be optional, otherwise it would not be competition but a cartel or market-sharing.[11] Fraser went on to suggest that perhaps another level of competition could be introduced if the ITA were to insist that the companies obtained a certain proportion of their programmes from sub-contractors. But this idea of an ITA-imposed quota of sub-contracted material was never taken up. Nevertheless, during the early years of ITV, when the companies' production capacity was not fully developed, many semi-independent producers were in demand: film series, quiz shows and advertising magazines were bought as programme packages. In the main, these were attempts by American-style producers to introduce American programme forms into British television. By the mid-1960s, however, the ITV companies had expanded to the point where they were able to reject many of these approaches from outsiders and, more importantly, the ITA had changed its mind about sub-contracting. Keen that the companies should become omni-competent broadcasting organisations producing their own programmes in all fields, the Authority increasingly discouraged the practice of buying programmes from outside the ITV system. This tendency for the companies to produce nearly all the programmes on ITV is something we will consider in greater detail when tracing the origins of the opposition to ITV2.

The initial financial performance of the companies militated against the Authority's plans for a competitive network. As a new advertising medium, television was slow to develop. The companies experienced greater financial difficulties at first than had been expected and, in response, the ITA went so far as to ask the Government for an assistance grant of £750,000 – for which provision had been made in the Act. By the time the money was available revenues had begun to rise and the grant was never given. However, while the Authority believed the prospect of company collapses to be imminent it could raise no objections when an agreement was made between the companies. Rather than compete with one another, each would be responsible for providing an agreed proportion of the network's total output, exchanging programmes between themselves at terms settled in advance. This agreement, later to be derogatively referred to as 'the carve up', continued after 1956 when the era of high profitability – characterised by Lord Thomson's notoriously frank 'licence to print money' comment – had set in. As the ITA's technical coverage of the country expanded a second tier of programme companies joined the network – but not on equal terms with the original four. The function of these smaller, regional companies was to provide programmes suited to the tastes and interests of their particular localities and not to enter into competition with the 'Big Four'. The monopoly-based prosperity of the ITV system meant, however, that these companies developed production facilities in excess of those required for a purely

11

local operation. But it was an excess they found hard to exploit; for, in general, they were unable to sell anything more than the occasional programme to the network. During the 1960s the regionals increasingly resented this exclusion, although it would be wrong to assume unanimity on this matter. Anglia, for instance, built up its *Survival* team at great expense and was most successful in selling these natural history programmes to the network. It consequently opposed any attempt to introduce a fixed network of regionally produced programmes, knowing that this would probably reduce its own contribution in favour of other regionals. But what is important to realise is that there was some resentment, especially on the part of the regionals' programme-makers, and that this led in the 1970s to an element of disagreement between the ITV companies about the arrangements for ITV2.

The ITA's *1957-1958 Annual Report*, published two years after Hill's postponement, gave a clear indication that the Authority was confident it would soon be allocated a second commercial service. The report revealed the existence of an option agreement that had recently been sealed between the ITA and the four central companies. The broken-week contracts for the Big Four had only been introduced, repeated the report, in an attempt to drive as much competition into the central areas as the single network would allow. The Authority did not think it was ideal and, in fact, all the regionals had been awarded contracts for the whole week. If a second service was introduced the mosaic would be broken up and in each of the central areas there would be two competitive companies with seven-day contracts:

> However, it would be most unfair first to deny the early applicants, who were taking all the initial risks and who would be building the system, the right to seven-day contracts, while offering that right, at a later stage and over their heads, to newcomers who would be entering television only when it was established ... The Authority therefore promised ... that, on the opening of second stations in London, Midland and Northern areas, the four existing companies serving those areas would be given first refusal of seven-day contracts there.[12]

But despite attempts such as the option agreement to precipitate a governmental authorisation of a second commercial channel, the new Postmaster-General, Ernest Marples, remained uncommitted. In March 1959, he declared that a third television service would have to wait until a decision had been made about the line definition system to be permanently adopted in Britain. The Government was considering a switch from 405 to 625 lines. In 1936, the United Kingdom had decided to transmit television on 405 lines but this had proved to be an example of Britain standardising too early. Most of the rest of Europe had subsequently chosen the technically superior 625 lines standard and, as a result, British television equipment manufacturers were cut off from

12

the Continental market. It was felt that if there was to be change, the third service should be transmitted on the new standard as it would provide an incentive for viewers to buy the new television sets needed to receive 625 lines. In the event, the Government decided that with the BBC's Charter due to expire in 1962, it would be useful to have the opinion of an independent review body on the future of broadcasting in general, and the question of additional services and the line standard in particular. In July 1960, the industrialist Sir Harry Pilkington was appointed chairman of a Committee of Inquiry.

COMPLEMENTARY TELEVISION: PILKINGTON AND BBC2

Despite the ITA's efforts, a second commercial channel in competition with ITV for advertising revenue had still not been introduced by 1960. Nevertheless, the arrival of a single commercial channel had, of course, instigated one form of competition within television. The BBC's income through its licence fee was secure; its appeal to the audience, however, was not. The Corporation had been thrown into disarray as it had watched the figures for ITV's share of the audience rise between 1955 and 1958 to 70 per cent. In his colourful description of the impact of commercial programmes on the Corporation's staid output, Peter Black, former television critic of the *Daily Mail*, noted the success of ITV's American-style quiz shows:

> Until ITV arrived the public had never seen a newsreader who exploited his personality instead of carefully neutralising it. They had never seen Sunday night variety, or an American drama series; most important, they had never seen anyone earn a pound note for correctly distinguishing his left foot from his right, or a wife win a refrigerator for whitewashing her husband in thirty seconds starting from NOW. And if any single programme innovation can be said to have won the mass audience it was the giveaway shows.[13]

A survey published for the ITA in 1958 found that, among families with both BBC and ITV, the most popular programmes for family viewing were *Emergency Ward 10, Popeye, Robin Hood* and *Sunday Night at the London Palladium* — all ITV productions. Under pressure from ITV, the Government had agreed to abandon the 'Toddlers' Truce', the early evening curfew between 6p.m. and 7p.m. In the glowing words of one enthusiastic supporter of commercial television, this was all achieved 'by the sort of instinct that makes capitalism work – an instinct for sensing what the majority wants, or would want if it were available to them.'[14] It was also an instinct that knew how to make money; by 1960, £100 invested in the non-voting stock of one of the four original companies in 1955 was worth £1,200.

The BBC's response to ITV's success revealed an ambiguity in its own aims and obligations. In theory it was possible for the Corporation to ignore ITV and continue within its own tradition as the national instrument of broadcasting, choosing to place its cultural priorities wherever it saw fit. It was not, after all, competing with ITV for the same source of revenue. However, in practice the BBC was inevitably drawn into competition. A corporate orthodoxy was established: unless the BBC could hold about half the national audience, government would be reluctant to grant adequate increases in the licence fee for fear of suffering political unpopularity. Some people have criticised the BBC for choosing to base the weight of its claim for more public money on the size of its audience rather than the quality of its service. But it has to be appreciated that the financial history of the Corporation since 1960 has been a continuous struggle to persuade government to keep the licence fee income in pace with dramatically increasing operating costs. It seems unlikely that government would have found such claims more convincing from a less popular BBC. Besides, BBC programme-makers in the late 1950s were frustrated with making programmes that the public were not watching. So, under the leadership of Sir Hugh Greene, the BBC fought back to audience parity with ITV by 1962. In Greene's own words: 'I told the television service they must aim at increasing our share of the television audience from its lowest ratio of 27:73 to 50:50 by the time the Pilkington Committee reported.'[15] Thus arose the great flowering of young talent that was to become such a feature of broadcasting in the first half of the 1960s. Tom Burns explains how the BBC believed it improved its audience ratings by quoting from Gerald Beadle, at the time BBC Director of Television (although notably Burns feels the need to add a sceptical rider):

> It was regarded by the BBC as accomplished by expanding the range of entertainment (*Steptoe and Son, Z Cars, Maigret, TW3* and so forth) and by the new-look news and current affairs. 'In my view,' [wrote Beadle] 'BBC-TV's new management achieved the same end by the more subtle means of infusing new life into output, so that, still clearly distinguishable from the output of ITV, it was in its own way just as entertaining.' All the same, it has to be remembered that the biggest regular audiences commanded by the BBC during the early sixties were for the *Billy Cotton Bandshow* and the *Black and White Minstrel Show*.[16]

In short, although the BBC was not prepared to imitate the programme forms of independent television, it did recognise that it would have to be more successful in its attempts to entertain than it had previously been.

But the guardians of the heritage of the Reithian mission to provide an enlightening public service were unhappy with the effects of competition. As the BBC explained in its evidence to Pilkington, in conditions of competition 'it is inevitable that the problem of scheduling for one

14

network only leads to a situation where cultural programmes suffer most.'[17] Increasingly, the Corporation felt that while it was limited to one channel it was unable to fulfil all the requirements of its Charter. In fact, the BBC was highly self-critical: 'It does not inform enough; it does not educate enough; its ability to experiment in order that it may entertain better is very strictly limited.' Already, in 1956, in its Annual Report the BBC had argued that competition, whatever its virtues, did not tend towards diversity of choice but rather a choice between programmes of the same kind. Only planned alternatives could give the genuine choice that the public had become used to in sound broadcasting. If the BBC was given a second service, it told the Committee of Inquiry, it could balance serious drama against light comedy, and thought and opinion against light entertainment. This complementary programming could only be implemented, it believed, by a publicly funded organisation that was free of the pressure to sell advertising space. Pilkington agreed.

Inspired by the views of one of its members – Richard Hoggart, historian of popular culture – the Committee's report, published in June 1962, praised the BBC and condemned ITV. Those who had opposed the introduction of commercial television had been right. Television, believed the Committee, had far too great an influence on the values and standards of society to be given to privately owned, profit-seeking companies to operate. The report accused the ITA of underestimating the effect of the medium and consequently scaling down its responsibilities; it was too passive, acting more as an advocate than a controller of the programme companies. There was no alternative but to radically change the existing arrangement for independent television. In future, a far more authoritative ITA should act as programme editor and salesman of advertising time while the companies should be simply programme-makers with no relationship to the advertisers and no control over scheduling.

In political terms the severity of the report's condemnation was a mistake. ITV was far too popular for its destruction to be politically contemplated. Besides, the same Conservative Party that had introduced commercial television was unlikely now to mutilate it, and certainly unlikely to increase drastically the powers of a State watchdog. The 1963 Television Act did strengthen the ITA's power over the planning of schedules but the structure of ITV remained the same.

Although Pilkington's general approach was not palatable, its particular recommendations on additional services and the line-definition did prove to be more acceptable. The definition standard in the United Kingdom, said the report, should be changed from 405 to 625 lines. This should be achieved by the 'duplication method'; that is, the existing BBC and ITV services transmitted on 405 lines in the VHF Bands I and III would be duplicated on 625 lines in the UHF Bands IV and V. Both sets of transmissions would continue until all the existing 405 lines television sets had been replaced by the public sometime in the future. The report

15

went on to explain that following the 1961 Stockholm European Broadcasting Conference, the United Kingdom had been allocated sufficient frequencies for six national network television channels; two in the two VHF Bands and four in the two UHF Bands. While the line definition change was being implemented, four of these networks would therefore be occupied, leaving two in the UHF Bands free to be used immediately. The question was obviously, should they be used, and if so by whom? Given the Committee's general outlook, the BBC's request for a complementary channel was favourably received. The BBC took great care to impress Pilkington; Greene described it as an 'exercise in psychological warfare'[18] and the Corporation prepared and presented its evidence with almost military precision. The ITA's case for an additional commercial channel, separate from and competing with the first, was much less attractive to the Committee:

'The master consideration,' the Authority stated, 'is that the third service should be independent of the first and second.' It offended good constitutional principle that programme production for two television services should be in the hands of a single organisation. . . 'the variety needed is not to be found in the simultaneous offer of different programmes by the same producer' – that is, of course, by the same producing organisation – 'but in the offer of the same classes of programmes by different producers.'. . . On the BBC's case for a second complementary programme, the ITA observed: 'In the Authority's opinion this would be a vice in a restricted broadcasting system, not a virtue. . . in a free society, control of the means of communications should be diversified not centralised.'[19]

But Pilkington disagreed. At least while the companies were monopoly sellers of advertising time they had some freedom to realise 'the purpose of broadcasting', reasoned the Committee, but with two competing commercial services it would be even harder for them to provide programmes not aimed at the majority audience. It was diversity of programme output, not ownership, that the Committee believed was paramount. The result of competition for advertising revenue would, as the ITA seemed to admit, be sameness of programmes rather than variety. In concluding, the report recommended that the BBC should have one of the two unallocated UHF channels but the other should not go to independent television while it remained constituted and organised as it was at present. Pilkington did not believe, however, that the fourth channel should remain permanently vacant:

If, however, our recommendations to reconstitute and reorganise independent television are adopted, it would in our view be advantageous if independent television were in due course authorised to provide a second programme. The advantages would be: first, that it would offer the reconstituted Authority the opportunity to provide complementary services and so to extend the range of interest of both; second, it should help to promote competition of the right kind between independent television and the BBC – that is, competition in realising the purposes of broadcasting.[20]

The Government's 1962 White Paper on the Pilkington Report authorised BBC2. It agreed that a second ITV channel might prove to be desirable but it was not prepared to introduce it yet. In response to Pilkington's fear that a second service would lead to greater sameness in programming, clause 13 of the 1963 Television Act stipulated that if a second channel was introduced the ITA would have to ensure that, as far as possible, the same kinds of programmes were not broadcast at the same time. But it was still taken for granted by the Conservative Government and Party that a future ITV2 would be supplied by separate, competing and new contractors.[21] In the Parliamentary debate on the subject, the Postmaster-General, Reginald Bevins, under pressure from Conservative MPs, told the House that the Government hoped to issue a licence for an 'ITA2' during 1965.[22] The reason it was being delayed was not because of Pilkington's criticisms of independent television; after all the Government was not accepting the need for drastic change. The objection, explained Bevins, was a financial one. A second commercial service would have to broadcast in UHF on 625 lines and until a reasonable proportion of the audience had sets capable of receiving the service, it would be unattractive to advertisers. Bevins suggested it was largely because so few viewers were able to receive ITV when it started that the companies had lost so much money in 1955. By 1965, he estimated, half of London's viewers would have the new sets and a second competing commercial service would be viable, at least in the capital and other areas with large populations. In the light of Bevins's promise, John Rodgers withdrew his amendment to clause 13, proposing that a second channel must be introduced by 1965. He agreed with Bevins that the timing was all-important and that there should be some room for manoeuvre, in case there were still financial or other obstacles at that time. If the Conservatives had stayed in office, the fourth channel would probably have been allocated to the ITA within the first few years of the new Parliament.[23]

But this was not the case. In October 1964 after thirteen years in Opposition Labour returned to power and Anthony Wedgwood Benn was appointed Postmaster-General; the plans for ITV2 turned cold and were to remain on the shelf for the rest of the decade. In its 1966 White Paper on Broadcasting, the Labour Government noted the Conservatives' intention to introduce a second ITV service, but concluded that the additional channel would make a large demand on resources and it could not be afforded a high place in the order of national priorities. Moreover,

17

the Government was not satisfied that the case for any new service had been fully established, and there was also the possibility that the fourth channel would be required for a specialised service of educational television forming part of the structure of the new Open University. It ruled that no authorisation would be given for at least the next three years.[24]

MAINTAINING THE DUOPOLY:
THE CHANGE TO A COMPLEMENTARY ITV2

In their evidence to Pilkington, the ITA had told the Committee that it could not defend the ITCA* companies' high profit levels. It agreed that they were without parallel in present times but suggested that they were the inevitable result of monopoly. Until there was a second commercial service, the buying of advertising space on television would remain a sellers' market; the problem could be effectively solved if the Government sanctioned the Authority's request for a competitive ITV2. In Parliament, Bevins accepted the logic of the ITA's argument, but as we have seen he did not believe a second commercial service could be introduced at the same time as BBC2. In the meantime, it was felt that something had to be done about ITV's remarkable bonanza. Since 1959, when the House of Commons Public Accounts Committee had examined the finances of independent television, the Treasury had been aware that ITV represented a significant potential tax source. They therefore successfully pressed the Government to introduce in the 1963 legislation provision for the payment by the companies to the Exchequer of a 'levy' – designed to reflect the fact that the State had conferred upon them the sole right to operate a commercial television service within a given area. In its first year of operation, the central companies paid £18 million in levy and the regionals a further £3½ million.[25] The companies squealed. Norman Collins, deputy chairman of ATV, claimed that the introduction of the levy would mean his company would go out of business and would not apply for a renewal of its franchise. On both these points he was proved wrong. The introduction of the levy did, however, undermine one of the central strands in the ITA's case for a competitive ITV2. For once the companies' super-normal profits had been taxed away from them, they were to find it much easier to defend their monopoly to both Government and the Authority. As we shall see, it was only those who complained they were suffering from the direct effects of monopoly – the advertisers and the advertising agencies – who were to continue into the 1970s lobbying for a competitive channel. The second development that contributed to the ITA's change of policy on ITV2 was the financial crisis

---

*Independent Television Companies Association – a trade association formed in 1958 to represent the ITV programme contractors in their relations with outside groups.

18

that occurred within ITV between 1968–70 following the reallocation of contracts in 1967.

When ITV began the programme companies had assumed, like the ITA, that competition with separate contractors in each area would be fairly quickly introduced. However, during the 1960s they began to entertain the possibility that an additional competing service could, and should, be indefinitely delayed, for its introduction would undermine the financial stability of independent television. Once again, it would be wrong to suggest a greater unanimity than actually existed. Some of the original campaigners for commercial television, who had vigorously opposed the BBC's monopoly, did not subsequently find it as easy to defend the companies' advertising monopoly as those who joined ITV after it started. In their evidence to Pilkington the smaller regional companies were particularly worried about the ITA's policy for a competitive ITV2. Anglia suggested that another channel would kill regional programming and Ulster Television argued that an additional service in its area would make it impossible for any station to survive. This opposition to a rival ITV2 markedly increased during the last third of the decade when it became apparent that the ITV system was more financially unstable than had been thought.

In early 1966 the ITA had agreed to extend the existing contracts until July 1968 because of the uncertainty of future developments: the Authority did not know whether it was going to be given a second service and it was not clear when the line-definition conversion of ITV would take place and whether it would be in colour. Once these matters had been clarified by the Government's White Paper – it favoured the immediate introduction of 625 lines and in colour – the Authority invited all interested parties to tender bids for the new franchises.

What followed has been likened to a gold rush. New companies were hurriedly formed, many involving celebrated personalities both within television and public life in general, and many boasting high programming ideals. The most notable was London Weekend Television, which was to find its hopes shattered during its first year of operation. In a significant step away from its advocacy of competition, the ITA abandoned the broken-week arrangement for all areas except London. The programming benefits of the more coherent 7-day contracts were deemed to outweigh the advantages of the 5:2 day split competition. Pilkington's recommendations might not have been implemented, but it seems likely that the Report's castigation of the Authority influenced the ITA's conduct during the 1967 enfranchisement process. Moreover, the chairmanship of the ITA by the strong-minded Lord Hill, former Postmaster-General, counteracted Sir Robert Fraser's continued enthusiasm for competition. When the new franchises were announced Hill euphemistically emphasised the need to introduce new blood into ITV; companies were to be dispossessed 'pour encourager les autres'. Rediffusion, the London weekday contractor, was required to merge with ABC Television, who although supplier for the weekends to the North and Midlands had its headquarters and production facilities in London. The new company was named Thames Television. ATV Television was given the contract for the Midlands, but Granada's franchise for the North was divided and a new major network company, Yorkshire Television, was given the area east of the Pennines. The 'Big Four' thus became the 'Big Five'. In addition to Yorkshire, two other new companies were appointed – London Weekend, and Harlech, which replaced the deposed Welsh contractor TWW. It was hoped that all the new franchises, including the five central companies, would place a greater emphasis on their regional connections.

The financial problems of the companies began as soon as the new contract periods started. The realisation that the transition from the old to the new companies would mean redundancies for some technicians and producers led to a national strike by members of the Association of Cinematograph, Television and Allied Technicians (ACTT). This benefited the BBC, who were making a strong drive to improve their audience share; by October 1968, ITV's figures had fallen in six months from 58% of the total audience to 47%.[26] In the spring of 1969, advertising revenues slumped and in the year ending July 1970 there had been a dramatic drop of over five per cent in advertising receipts.[27] In addition, the two new network companies experienced serious teething difficulties. During its first few months on the air Yorkshire's transmitting mast collapsed, while LWT, one of the most idealistic of the groups contending for the franchises, discovered that its programming philosophy was not proving viable in the face of fierce BBC competition. Senior executives were sacked and, in protest, others resigned. On the point of insolvency, the company received a saving injection of new capital when Rupert Murdoch's *News of the World* Group stepped in and bought a large proportion of the share stock. (The crisis at LWT, and the criticisms of the ITA's handling of the affair, is a subject we will return to in the next chapter.) Finally, two other factors greatly exacerbated the companies' already weak financial position. First, the introduction of colour television in UHF 625 lines required them to undertake a major re-equipment of all their studios and post-production facilities. Second, the 1969 Budget increased the scale of the levy. Both the companies and the Authority objected to this and argued it was unfair; for since the levy was assessed on income not profits, it made no allowance for programme costs and ignored the fact that a company might be making a loss. An increase was thought to be crippling; William Brown, Managing Director of Scottish Television, explained to the Select Committee on Nationalised Industries a few years later that during 1969-70, although his company was making a loss, it was required to pay £750,000 in levy.[28] Following frantic lobbying from the ITA the Government agreed to a reduction. At the same time, in March 1970, it instructed the National Board for Prices and Incomes under Aubrey Jones to examine the financial system of ITV.

The Board's report, published in October of the same year, confirmed the belief that the financial outlook for some years to come was likely to be unpromising:

> To summarise, the ability of commercial television to attract advertising would appear to have diminished, partly because of a much slower rate of growth of the audience, partly because of the loss of audience to the BBC. Recent trends in the food industry, both manufacturing and retail, may also have contributed to the fall in this year in ITV's advertising revenue. The decline in advertising would appear therefore to reflect certain permanent factors – e.g. the cessation in the growth of the TV audience – but also certain temporary factors some of which it is within the power of ITV to combat.[29]

ITV's main requirement, said the report, was a sense of stability. In future, contracts should be automatically renewed unless a company had been warned twice by the Authority that its performance was unsatisfactory. The NBPI also identified a problem of excess capacity: in favouring both regional programming and multiple sources of network production, the ITA had been forced to encourage the duplication of studio facilities, equipment, and staff within ITV. The creation of a fifth major contractor in 1968 had aggravated this situation and the report reckoned that the companies were only using 65%-70% of their resource capacity. A reduction in the number of contractors should be considered and a relaxation in the restrictions on broadcasting hours would also help. On the question of a second commercial channel the report noted that a competitive service with new and separate contractors would clearly not alleviate the problems of the existing companies. The NBPI went on to consider the alternative possibility of a complementary ITV2 run by the ITCA companies. This would employ much of the spare capacity and, in effect, would be similar to the extension of broadcasting hours that the Board had already proposed. But the report concluded that although net profits might be raised as a result of this, the financial outcome was too uncertain for it to be recommended as a sensible course of action. However, the Board did concede that it had received no detailed financial estimates for a complementary ITV2.

It would be wrong to attribute the Authority's eventual support for a complementary ITV2 simply to the contingency of financial gloom. Across the other side of the broadcasting fence, the growing success of BBC2 was making the benefits of a complementary service very apparent. BBC2 had opened in April 1964. There had been tremendous pressure from the television equipment manufacturers for an early start – they needed the public to have an incentive to buy their 625 line sets – so the service had begun only in London and without the construction of its main studio completed. The initial programming policy, known as 'Seven Faces of the Week', devised by Michael Peacock, tried to give each night of the week a particular emphasis: one evening it was drama; the next education; then features, repeats and so forth. This arrangement was claimed to be more creative than simply planning the schedule against BBC1, but it also helped camouflage the fact that because of the early start, there was a shortfall of programmes. The policy was not popular and after a few months on the air 'Seven Faces of the Week' was abandoned. Both BBC's television services, it was felt, should offer a complete evening's viewing with a wide range of programmes, jointly planned, and with several synchonised starting times, known as 'common junctions'. The main problem for BBC2 was to overcome the audience inertia which inhibits the breaking of established viewing patterns. The fact that many people had, out of curiosity, sampled the new channel's original and off-putting output and resolved that it was not for them did not help to overcome this inertia. To win an audience, BBC2 had to contradict the chief programming aim of the Corporation's pre-BBC2 years, which had been to ensure that, above all, viewers did not switch channels. Cross-channel presentation on the two services obviously helped and, under the controllership of David Attenborough, BBC2 slowly began to acquire an audience as its geographical transmission coverage expanded. It also began to prove that it was invaluable for the Corporation's television collectively. It became a nursery ground, a place for experiments that, if successful, could be repeated on the main channel. Many BBC successes were to start life on BBC2 – comedy series like *Morecambe and Wise* and major drama projects such as *The Six Wives of Henry VIII*. The financial advantages of cross-channel repeats were significant bonuses. And, perhaps most important of all, the existence of 'quality' programmes like *Civilisation* on BBC2 quelled the objections of those in the Corporation who had felt uneasy about the effects of competing with independent television. In fact, as Peter Black points out, many of the programme forms that flourished under monopoly and were dowsed by competition – e.g. literary panel games, natural history films, classical serials, science features – returned with BBC2 to peak-time viewing; 'sometimes with their old producers happily back in the sun after years of wandering in the shade.'[30] By 'sharing' some of its public service responsibilities with BBC2, the main channel felt that much freer to compete with ITV1 for the majority audience. As we know, the BBC made a successful attempt to boost its audience figures during ITV's 1968 franchise problems. ITV had lost many of its veteran audience winners – such as *Sunday Night at the London Palladium, Double Your Money*, and *Take Your Pick* – and the ACTT strike gave BBC2 a breakthrough exposure from which it continued to benefit when ITV returned to the screens.

With two complementary channels, the BBC was clearly in a strong competitive position. As far as the companies were concerned, it was too strong. They felt caught in a pincer movement, unable to compete at the upper end of the market while being so hard pressed at the popular end. They too wanted the advantages of 'try-outs', 'repeats' and 'cost-rationalisations' that a complementary channel could provide. The pressures of assimilation that had forced the BBC to change with the arrival of commercial television were now beginning to affect ITV. The duopoly 'ought' to be balanced. There was a certain 'elementary fairness' in giving ITV a complementary channel. ITV had grown into a national institution with an international reputation. Its relationship with the BBC had matured; it no longer considered itself the brash young upstart, but an equal half of the national television system, pursuing very similar objectives to its publicly funded competitor. Its programme-makers in many areas matched and, in the case of the news, were generally felt to surpass the achievements of their BBC colleagues. Thus, ITV believed it could legitimately complain that a two channel BBC was unfair *and, more importantly, that a competitive ITV2 would make the situation even more unfair.*

On 13 May 1970, two months after the levy had been reduced and five months before the NBPI report was published, the ITA abandoned its fifteen-year-old policy on a competitive ITV2. At a meeting of the Standing Consultative Committee (which consisted of the ITA's Director-General and senior staff and the companies' managing directors), Sir Robert Fraser said that it might be assumed that an ITV2 would follow the example of BBC2 and broadcast for some 35 hours a week; that there would be a standardised network schedule with programmes being produced predominantly by the Five as in ITV1; and that advertising would be locally orginated.[31] Five months later, Fraser, the architect of independent television, retired. He was succeeded by Brian Young.

THE CAMPAIGN BEGINS

Fraser's departure from the ITA killed any possibility of a reversion to a competitive ITV2. He had been the driving force behind the Authority's philosophy about competition; the designer of the network mosaic and broken-week arrangement for competition within a single channel. He cannot have made his statement to the Standing Consultative Committee without some misgivings about abandoning the prospect of introducing real competition into independent television. The new Director-General, on the other hand, a former headmaster of Charterhouse School, was a complete outsider who knew little about the well-established industry he had been appointed to supervise. In February 1971, following the publication of the NBPI report, the new Conservative Government announced a further reduction in the levy and shortly afterwards advertising revenues showed a buoyant up-turn. But by then there was no question that the Authority, even in the light of the improved financial circumstances, might reconsider the possibility of a competitive ITV2. The subject was dead. If the Authority was going to be given responsibility for the fourth channel it would be complementary to ITV1. Throughout the 1970s this was never in doubt; the question was whether the ITA should have it, or whether there was a better use for this 'scarce national resource'.

One of the first (quasi) public indications of the new policy within ITV was an article by Howard Thomas, Managing Director of Thames Television, in his company's staff newsletter of June 1971. Under the headline 'Thames wants ITV2', he warned of the creeping threat of BBC2 to ITV's ratings. 'The inevitable result of such a reduction of audience would mean a loss of revenue and a non-viable ITV system.' The only fair division was for ITV also to have a complementary channel. In an unappealing newspaper analogy, Thomas brashly went on to spell out what he believed ITV2's programming philosophy should be:

> The way Thames sees ITV2 is that if ITV1 is like the *Daily Express*, ITV2 would function like the *Daily Telegraph*, offering a different range of programmes to a different audience and attracting new kinds of advertising. This does not mean that ITV2 would in any sense be a 'minority' service. There would need to be a full quota of entertainment, although we should want to use ITV2 as a try-out ground for programme experiments and for new concepts and new ideas.
>
> It is essential that ITV2 should be operated by the existing contractors. A completely new group of contractors could only inflate ITV costs to an impossibly high level and, in the process, debase programme standards to the lowest common denominator. ITV2 would offer a full evening-and-weekend service, using existing contractors' studios and equipment, with increased manpower. The regions would produce more networked programmes. Thames would operate a 7-day week to produce additional peak programmes.
>
> The cost? Perhaps another £20 million a year, £10 million of which would come from reducing the advertisement levy to zero ... The date? If our campaign succeeds we could begin ITV2 in autumn 1973; at worst autumn 1974.[32]

This remarkably candid article ended with an outline of a possible progress calendar for the next five years. By 1975/76 Thomas predicted ITV1 and ITV2 would be firmly established in the 'battle' against BBC1, BBC2 and commercial radio. Writing in *The Times* Chris Dunkley recognised the implicit 'milk-and-honey tomorrow' suggestion that Thames's managing director was making to the industry:

24

Mr Thomas's carrots are contained in the phrases 'increased manpower' and 'seven day week' — both promises being almost irresistible to the television unions in general and the Association of Cinematograph, Television and Allied Technicians in particular, since more than half their members are out of work. This high unemployment figure is currently playing a major part both in forming the attitudes of the ACTT — the most important of the television unions — and also the psychological battle between the union and management.[33]

Privately, the ITA and the companies began to develop detailed plans for ITV2. In July 1971 a 'strictly confidential' 15-page memorandum on ITV2 was prepared by the Programme Controllers of the five network companies and several representatives of the five medium-sized companies (Scottish, Harlech, Tyne-Tees, Southern and Anglia). The document claimed it was only illustrating certain possibilities, but for a formula not-yet-agreed it was a remarkably detailed and presumptuous plan. It started by listing the arguments in favour of the existing companies being given contracts for a second channel, but notably, it was subsequently more concerned with considering possible objections to this step and suitable replies to such attacks:

(a) An ITV monopoly position inhibits freedom of expression;
(b) Commercial incentives prohibit adventurous programming and specialised interests will continue to suffer;
(c) Central control by major companies will prevent adequate regional expression.

There will be other objections, equally predictable. It is possible to answer such opposition by giving some indication of ITV's desire to pursue more adventurous ideas, to extend its public service by offering more programmes for specialised interests and to deal, in greater depth than is possible on only one channel, with political and social issues. *But care should be taken not to discourage the instinctive drive of all broadcasters, which is to appeal to as many people as possible with every programme they make.* [34]

In a revealing comment, it also noted a crucial development within the television industry:

It would be wise to recognise that the industry has spilled into the freelance world of production talent whose creative energies cannot be absorbed by the present structure of television. *Their resistance to corporate bodies and consensus opinion is likely to be a factor in the ITV2 debate. Whether they represent a formidable opposition or not remains to be seen,* but it is reasonable to suppose that a second ITV channel would be required to show we were capable of providing opportunities for a growing number of independent programme makers, while maintaining the editorial and statutory responsibilities of the companies and the ITA.[35](author's emphasis)

Assuming an initial transmission of 35 hours a week, the document went on to give a breakdown of possible content and sources for ITV2. It showed how similar to BBC2, and keenly competitive with it, the Programme Controllers' conception of the channel was; the fact that they were already concerned that the news should pre-empt BBC2's by fifteen minutes underlined this competitive attitude:

National News: 3½ hours a week. Two 15-minute programmes from ITN to begin and end transmissions each day. (The first planned to go out at 7.15 each evening so as to get on the air before BBC2's *Newsroom.*)

US/British filmed series and feature films: 8½ hours a week, including three feature films.

The World Outside: 1½ hours a week. The best of bought-in material from foreign and domestic sources, including independent producers. Children's as well as adult material.

The Daily Scene: 2½ hours a week. The arts, films, theatre, the previous night's television. An ITV2 counter to *Late Night Line-Up.* Half an hour each day in the early evening with contributions from the regions.

Drama: 2½ hours a week. Plays, serials, some of which ITV1 rarely attempts at present.

Light entertainment: 2½ hours a week. New and sometimes experimental comedy, situation comedy and light entertainment.

Quiz game shows: Half an hour a week. Essentially experimental. Probably four pilot runs of 13 in the first year.

Specialised features and documentary series: 6 hours a week. Science, industry, the arts, medicine, social and human relations: both film and studio programmes.

Sport: 2½ hours a week, including a weekly sports magazine, live coverage of sports such as sailing, golf, skiing, show jumping which are not often covered by ITV or BBC, and also bought-in sport like boxing and golf.

Music: 2½ hours a week, including light entertainment, music shows of folk, jazz and pop as well as opera, ballet and classical music, all types of programmes rarely seen on ITV at present.

Regional Pick of the Week: Half an hour a week. A weekly showcase of the best of regional programmes.

Open Night: Three-quarters of an hour a week. An audience participation examination of television topics and programmes.

What a Week: Three-quarters of an hour a week. A personality's review of his, ours, or television's week.

Political Review: One hour a week. Discussion and interview programme about politics, domestic and international.

The Big Event: 1½ hours a week. A major arts event of the week, frequently an outside broadcast, covering ballet, opera, the theatre, and including plays adapted from the stage. From the regions as well as London.

Repeats from ITV1 and ITV2: 4 hours a week.

Living Free: Half an hour a week. Weekly film on travel, wildlife and natural history subjects.[36]

Although plans for ITV2 were already well-advanced, the ITA decided at the end of June 1971 to invite those working in independent television to express their views on the subject. A discussion paper would be prepared from the ideas sent in and this would form the starting point for a one day 'Consultation' meeting in early November (which would not be attended by the Press). On the basis of this meeting and a report by a Joint Working Party of the Standing Consultative Committee, the Authority intended to draft a submission to the Minister of Posts and Telecommunications before the end of December. In his open letter to ITV staff, Brian Young said that two assumptions should be made: (i) that ITV2 should be complementary with ITV1, and (ii) that since ITV's total audience share could not be dramatically increased, some way had to be found of financing the two services from an amount nearer to ITV's present income than to twice that income. He explained: 'The present intention is *not to have a public debate,* but rather to make sure that anyone within ITV who wants to do so has a chance to join in the collective discussion of the shape and character which a second service might have.'[37] (author's emphasis)

Some of ITV's staff were reluctant to submit ideas when it seemed that the argument over the structure of ITV2 had been largely settled. Nevertheless the Authority received over fifty written contributions. A few were made publicly; thus Peter Cadbury, Executive Chairman of Westward Television, published his response in his company's July 1971 staff news-letter. It revealed that there was some discord about ITV2 even at the most senior levels of ITV. Claiming to have the support of the chief executives of the other four smaller regionals, Cadbury expressed his unhappiness over the threat posed by ITV2 to his company's revenue. The second commercial channel, he said, could only be financed at the expense of ITV1 since there was no hidden source of new advertising revenue, and he estimated at least £20 million would be lost from ITV1. This would hit the smaller regionals hardest for they would be the first target of advertising budget cuts, and he calculated that this would mean a 10 per cent cut in Westward's income. This could be offset, he optimistically argued, if the profits from ITV2 were divided equally between all the ITV companies and not on the NARAL (Net Advertising

27

Revenue After Levy*) basis that had been suggested. He also stressed that the regionals should have a right to provide a percentage of the ITV2 programming:

> For years we in the regions have been virtually excluded from the network, not because our programmes are inferior but because the screening of a regional programme excludes a programme produced by a network company ... the satisfaction of getting our productions on a national network will give a fillip to all concerned besides injecting the freshness and competence of regional programmes into ITV2.[38]

Regional dissent was not confined to the five smaller companies. At the ITA Consultation the Programme Controllers of Scottish and Harlech, Anthony Firth and Patrick Dromgoole, both complained about the difficulty of access to the network. They were anxious that, despite comments on regional contributions made in the Programme Controllers' group document, the Big Five would make the lion's share of ITV2's programmes. These fears were to some extent allayed when both the Joint Working Party's report and subsequently the ITA's submission to the Minister supported the idea that a greater allocation of network time should be given to the regionals. Glasgow, Cardiff and Bristol, Newcastle, Southampton, Norwich and possibly Plymouth would all become centres of regular network programme production.

The lengthiest part of the seven hour ITA Consultation in November 1971 was spent considering the possibilities for the control and management of ITV2. In requesting ideas on the new channel from those working in ITV, the Authority brought into the debate viewpoints outside the 'Establishment' of independent television. The trade unions in the industry (ABS, ACTT, Equity, Electricians, Musicians, NATTKE, NUJ and Writers' Guild) had refused to accept the assumptions made in Young's letter. And the opinions of many of the individual members of the companies' staff who attended the Consultation were not necessarily in sympathy with those of senior management. At the meeting three forms of organisation were considered:

(1) The first, the companies' favoured solution, was that the jurisdiction of the existing franchises should be extended to cover ITV2 as well as ITV1. Under this arrangement no new legally constituted consortium would be created. Each company would sell advertising time in its area over two services and it would supply the second service with programmes from sources similar to that for ITV1, i.e. a mixture of its own productions, acquisitions from the network, and purchases of film and other recorded material from outside producers.

The two other proposals were:

(2) ITV2 should be supplied by a company — ITV2 Limited — owned

---

*This is the basis on which ITV companies are charged rental by the IBA for its provision of transmission services, in proportion to their income.

by all the companies, although perhaps with some participation in the ownership from either outside the ITV system or, as some wanted it, by the ITA. 'ITV2 Limited' would either sell the channel's advertising itself, or this would be done by the companies in their own areas and they would then pay an annual subscription to 'ITV2 Limited' sufficient to meet its programme budget and overheads.

(3) The ITA should run ITV2; it would decide what kind of programmes would be broadcast at given times on ITV2 and would then purchase or commission them from the programme companies (network and regional) and from outside agencies.

There were, of course, various blends and variants of all three ideas.

It is difficult to understand the latter two proposals before we have considered the background out of which they emerged. For they were mild expressions of the belief that the fourth channel should not be simply handed over to the ITV companies. This view has to be seen as part of a developing critique of both ITV in particular, and the ITV/BBC duopoly in general, that began in the 1960s and, as we shall see in the next chapter, characterised many discussions on broadcasting during the 1970s. For the moment, however, let us just consider the ITA's reaction to the three suggestions.

In drafting their submission to Christopher Chataway, the Minister of Posts and Telecommunications, the Authority decided against the idea of 'ITV2 Limited':

> Its attractions were mainly the *seeming novelty* of a fresh programme planning body (which yet could not be genuinely independent without spoiling complementary planning, as the experience of BBC1 and BBC2 has shown), and the protection that might be offered to smaller companies if revenue were being diverted to the larger areas.[39] (author's emphasis)

But such protection, the Authority believed, could be achieved by other methods and, instead, it recommended a blend of 1) and 3). The companies would run the channel in their own areas and sell the advertising. However, the Authority would have a greater influence over day-to-day planning of all programmes on *both* the ITV networks through the creation of a new body — the Programme Planning Board. The ITA would appoint to its staff two programme planners with an expertise similar to that of an ITV company Programme Controller. These two planners, together with the five Controllers from the central companies, three Controllers from the regional companies, and a chairman, would comprise the new Board. It would oversee all programme planning and scheduling for the ITV network, and thus involve the Authority in the discussion of scheduling at an earlier stage than previously.

29

Programmes for ITV2 would be supplied from three 'blocks'. Two would give planned and guaranteed access to the networks, one for the central companies and the other for the regionals. A third block, not allocated in advance, would be filled by the Programme Planning Board from equal competition between the companies and outside producers. But the concession to independent producers lacked bite. The ITA would not commit itself to specifying the relative size of each 'block', and it was not prepared to reserve a fixed quota within the third block for independent producers. There would first need to be a study of available *first class* programmes by independent producers. Earlier the submission had made the following comment; it indicates the scepticism with which they viewed the ability and value of independent producers:

> It would be *useful* also to see how valid is the proposal that there should be freer access to the medium by particular sections of the community who feel that they have some special message or viewpoint. There are dangers of *amateurishness* in production and difficulties in incorporating such programmes in a national television service without sacrificing impartiality and editorial control. Nevertheless, it would certainly be *more possible to consider* contributions of this kind in a two-channel ITV situation than it is at present.[40] (author's emphasis)

The submission was sent to the Minister in early December 1971. At the same time the Authority requested that the restrictions on broadcasting hours be abolished.

In January 1972, Chataway made a statement in the House of Commons. He agreed to lift the restrictions on hours, but on the fourth channel he had this to say:

> For many years to come, frequency channels will be available for four television networks of near-national coverage. Channels for three of those networks are being deployed and therefore only one network remains to be allocated. The Independent Television Authority recently put to me a submission, *ITV2*, published on December 8th, advocating that this network should now be allocated to a second service provided by ITV. The ITA's proposals have prompted the expression of a number of different views in Parliament and elsewhere concerning, for example, the possibility of reserving the fourth network for a specialised service or of organising a fourth general service on some different basis. I am not persuaded that the time has come to allocate the fourth network.[41]

To those who had hoped for, indeed assumed, a different conclusion, Chataway's statement was a disappointment. Why he decided to wait, and who were the people expressing different views in Parliament and elsewhere, is something we shall now examine.

Cartoon by John Kent, published in the Guardian *17 January 1972.*

Notes

1. *The Broadcasting Committee: Report* (Sykes Committee) (HMSO, 1923), Cmd 1951, p. 6.
2. Briggs, A., *The History of Broadcasting in the United Kingdom,* Volume I: *The Birth of Broadcasting* (London: Oxford University Press, 1961), p. 238.
3. Burns, T., *The BBC: Public Institution and Private World* (London: Macmillan, 1977), p. 54.
4. Williams, R., *Television: Technology and Cultural Form* (London: Fontana, 1974), p. 33.
5. Ogilvie, Sir F., 'Future of the BBC: Monopoly and its Dangers', *The Times,* 26 June 1946.
6. See Wilson, H.H., *Pressure Group: The Campaign for Commercial Television* (London: Secker and Warburg, 1961); Black, P., *The Mirror in the Corner: People's Television* (London: Hutchinson, 1972), and Sendall, B., *Independent Television in Britain,* Volume I: *Origin and Foundation 1946–62* (London: Macmillan, 1982).
7. *Broadcasting: Memorandum on the Report of the Broadcasting Committee 1949* (HMSO, 1952), Cmd 8550, para. 7.
8. *Broadcasting: Memorandum on Television Policy* (HMSO, 1953), Cmd 9005, para.17.
9. *Report of the Committee on Broadcasting 1960, Volume I, Appendix E: Memoranda submitted to the Committee* (HMSO, 1962), Cmnd 1819, p.416.
10. Sendall, op.cit., p. 63.
11. Ibid., p. 66.
12. *ITA: Annual Report and Accounts, 1957–58* (HMSO, 1958), p. 9.
13. Black, op.cit., p. 111.
14. Thomas, D., 'Commercial TV — And After', *TV: From Monopoly to Competition — and Back?* (London: Institute of Economic Affairs, 1962), p. 43.
15. Greene, H.C., *The Third Floor Front: A View of Broadcasting in the Sixties* (London: The Bodley Head, 1969), p. 132.
16. Burns, op. cit., p.54.
17. Memoranda submitted to the Committee on Broadcasting 1960, op.cit., p. 225.
18. Greene, op.cit., pp. 130–1.
19. *Report of the Committee on Broadcasting 1960* (Pilkington Report) (HMSO, 1962), Cmnd 1753, paras. 878-880.
20. Ibid., para. 906.
21. Clause 13 of the 1962 Television Bill made specific reference to 'different programme contractors' being appointed if a second ITA channel was introduced. This reference was deleted at the Committee stage on grounds of being unnecessarily detailed. Nevertheless, as the record of the House of Commons debate on the same clause shows, it was taken for granted by the Conservatives that ITV2, when it came, would be supplied by separate and additional contractors. (I am grateful to Bernard Sendall for pointing out this difference between the Television Bill and Act.)
22. Hansard, *House of Commons Debates,* 27 June 1963, col. 1810.
23. 'Tories to press for second ITV channel', *Guardian,* 21 January 1965.
24. *Broadcasting* (HMSO, 1966), Cmnd 3169, paras. 16-19.
25. National Board for Prices and Incomes, *Report No. 156, Costs and Revenues of Independent Television Companies* (HMSO, 1970), Cmnd 4524, Appendix C, p. 49.
26. *ITA: Annual Report and Accounts, 1968-69* (HMSO, 1969), p. 9.
27. Report of the NBPI, op.cit., para. 31.
28. *Second Report from the Select Committee on Nationalised Industries, Session 1971-72,* Committee B (HMSO, 1972), House of Commons paper 465, para. 646, p. 187.
29. Report of the NBPI, op.cit., para. 38.
30. Black, op.cit., p. 212.

31. Bernard Sendall (personal communication).
32. Thomas, H., 'Thames wants ITV2, says Howard Thomas', *Thames Television Newsletter*, 7 June 1971.
33. Dunkley, C., 'Power game behind the scenes of television', *The Times*, 31 July 1971.
34. 'ITV2', proposals prepared by ITCA Programme Controllers, 7 July 1971, reproduced in ACTT Television Commission, *TV4: A Report on the Allocation of the 4th Channel* (London: ACTT, 1971), Appendix 4.
35. Ibid.
36. Ibid.
37. 'ITV2', open letter from Brian Young, Director-General of the ITA, to ITV staff, 30 June 1971.
38. Cadbury, P., *Westward Television Newsletter*, July 1971, reproduced in ACTT Television Commission Report, op.cit., Appendix 3.
39. *ITV2: A Submission to the Minister of Posts and Telecommunications by the ITA* (ITA, December 1971), pp. 17-18.
40. Ibid., p. 16.
41. Hansard, *House of Commons Debates*, 19 January 1972, cols. 477-478.

2 Opposition to ITV2: The Duopoly Under Attack

The name of Lord Annan has become synonymous with a decade of public discussion about the structures and institutions of British broadcasting. From 1969 onwards demands for a major review of the industry became more insistent. One of the last acts of the Wilson Government in 1970 was to appoint Annan chairman of a committee of inquiry into broadcasting. One of the first acts of the Heath Government was to abandon the plan, but when Labour returned to power four years later Annan was re-appointed. For two-and-a-half years his Committee deliberated. When it reported in 1977, its overall recommendations were less radical than some had advocated and others had feared. Its specific proposals for the fourth network, however, were very different from what the ITA and the ITCA companies had wanted in 1971. It took a further year and a quarter for the Government to decide whether it would accept and implement the Committee's conclusions. By then, time had run out for effective legislative action – in less than a year Labour was defeated at the polls; so the fourth channel was still vacant at the end of the decade. The prolonged argument about how it should be used was to be finally settled by the Conservatives, who had opposed the idea of a committee of inquiry but were nevertheless influenced by Annan's philosophy. This chapter will consider the opposition to ITV2 and trace the origins of the Annan Committee's proposal that instead of giving the fourth channel to ITV it should be allocated to a new authority – the Open Broadcasting Authority.

PROGRAMME-MAKERS OUTSIDE THE INSTITUTIONS

In the early years of ITV the diet of programmes produced by the four central companies reflected the dominating personalities of their founding fathers. At ATV the charismatic Lew Grade was the King of Showbiz, television's equivalent of Sam Goldwyn. With the formidable resources of the Grade Theatrical Agency behind him – he had built it up from scratch with his brothers Leslie Grade and Bernard Delfont to be Britain's largest – Grade entered television with direct access to many of the biggest stars in the entertainment business. He quickly demonstrated that the same impresario skills which made him so successful as a booking agent enabled him to produce the most popular and profitable commercial television. It was he who introduced the successful variety show *Sunday Night at the London Palladium*, characteristically capitalising on his own assets, for the theatre belonged to his company and most of its stars came from his agency. Grade was not interested in making unpopular programmes; for years ATV had no film department and, unlike the other two weekday contractors, it did not produce a regular current affairs programme. In contrast, Sidney Bernstein's 'Granadaland' represented a unique mixture of cultural idealism and the practical realities of showmanship. With dreams of making Manchester England's cultural capital, Bernstein ensured that his company won itself the reputation of being the most public-spirited and adventurous of the Big Four. It was Granada that pioneered in Britain the televising of elections with its coverage of the 1958 Rochdale by-election. Its documentary series *Searchlight*, produced by the forceful New Zealander Tim Hewat (and with the young Jeremy Isaacs on its staff), introduced into British television a new kind of hard-hitting journalism that upset both public figures and the ITA, and in some cases led to programmes being banned. The company's investigative *World in Action* experienced similar problems with the Authority. But Granada also knew how to be popular; its celebrated *Coronation Street* won the audience with a soap opera of far greater authenticity than ATV's insipid *Crossroads*.

Differences in style between the companies were acceptable to the Authority, but increasingly the ITA made clear its disapproval of those who neglected whole programme areas. It was worried that the contractors would specialise: not only would this run counter to the principle, if not practice, of network competition but also, following Pilkington's criticisms and the arrival in 1963 of Charles Hill as Chairman of the Authority, the ITA was determined that the companies should become omni-competent broadcasting organisations providing a public service with a similar range to that of the BBC. At ATV the nightmare of future franchise withdrawal inspired Grade to develop his documentary and serious drama output. Bob Heller, an American documentary-maker who had left the United States during the turbulent McCarthy period, was brought in and given responsibility for ATV's factual programmes. His arrival coincided with a major upset in the BBC's current affairs department, and together these two events gave rise to an experiment in independent production that was to demonstrate with great clarity the difficulty of programme-making outside the BBC/ITV duopoly.

In 1962 the BBC's *Tonight* programme was at its zenith. Television's equivalent of a lively, irreverent evening newspaper, it was the pride of the Corporation's flowering young talent – Mrs Grace Wyndham Goldie's 'bright young men'. In a mood of typical self-confidence the *Tonight* team prepared a memorandum suggesting an amalgamation with *Panorama* and the creation of a new daily current affairs programme. It would be broadcast between seven and eight o'clock and be dominated by *Tonight*'s producers. In the event the plan was rejected, but while the prospect of a *Tonight* takeover was on the agenda it precipitated a rebellion by a number of *Panorama* presenters who feared the impact of the *Tonight* magazine style on the *Panorama* format. These included Robert Kee, Ludovic Kennedy, Malcolm Muggeridge, James Mossman and the producer Jeremy Murray-Brown. With financial support from Michael Astor and Lord Hambleden, a proprietor of W.H. Smith & Son, they left the BBC and formed Television Reporters International Ltd. It was the first major attempt by television programme-makers to work independently of the broadcasting institutions. The term 'independent', however, needs to be clearly defined. Some producers, because they were freelance, already considered themselves to be independents, but the concept has to be aligned to ownership. The greater the extent of ownership a producer has over a programme the more independent he can legitimately claim to be. People like Jack Hylton, who produced Rediffusion's light entertainment, and Michael Miles and Hughie Green, the compères for the give-away shows *Take Your Pick* and *Double Your Money*, were programme packagers. They sold formats or ideas to the ITV companies and sometimes had royalty rights on subsequent sales, but they did not own completed programmes. Television Reporters International, on the other hand, were convinced that with their impressive array of the BBC's most prominent presenters they could dominate the current affairs market and sell independently produced documentary features in Britain and worldwide.

Their formation suited Heller at ATV who made an agreement to purchase their programmes, with the aim of distributing them to the ITV network. But the agreement collapsed after the first year because Granada and Associated Rediffusion refused to take TRI's programmes. An article in *Contrast* explained: 'AR said they would not participate in the networking of current affairs programmes not made by a company directly responsible to the government', and Granada feared '. . . it would have a bad effect on their staff.'[1] Perhaps more pertinent was the fact that they resented ATV's approach; if it wanted to contribute current affairs programmes to the network it would have to match their commitment and establish its own in-house current affairs department. By buying relatively cheap, ready-made programmes from outsiders ATV, believed the other central companies, was not only benefiting financially in the short term, but in the long term was establishing a precedent that could undermine the comfortable financial security of the ITV system. The potential threat to the ITV companies' permanent workforce was clearly perceived at Elstree, where ATV's own staff resented the deal with TRI. Moreover, the ITA did not see the acquisition of outside material as an adequate answer to their criticisms of those companies that neglected certain programme areas. They were also nervous about the political content of independent television journalism. The failure to renew its ATV contract killed Television Reporters International; for the BBC had absolutely no intention of supporting the TRI 'renegades' and without a home market the company was not viable.

From our point of view, the most important thing to note about TRI's experience was the discouraging effect it had on other programme-makers who might otherwise have contemplated 'going independent'.

There was one other prestigious group of BBC producers who left the Corporation to set up their own production company. When *Tonight* came off the air in 1965 three former editors of the programme – Antony Jay, Donald Baverstock, and Alasdair Milne – formed JBM Limited. Unlike TRI, they managed to maintain a working relationship with their former employer and succeeded in selling a few programmes to the BBC. But their lifeblood was industrial training films; in particular, a large contract they had with the computer company ICL. The venture was relatively short-lived: it collapsed in 1967 when Milne, who had left the Corporation more because of loyalty to Baverstock than a burning desire to be an independent, was offered the controllership of BBC Scotland. Once again, the lesson for others was that even the most respected programme-makers found it hard to exist outside the duopoly.

At ATV, with the redistribution of the franchises looming and following Heller's failure with TRI, Lew Grade offered another former editor of *Tonight*, Peter Batty, the opportunity to produce prestige documentaries that would demonstrate to the Authority ATV's ability to make quality products. Batty expanded ATV's factual output by producing his own programmes – his *Fall and Rise of the House of Krupp* won a silver medal in Venice and other distinctions – and by encouraging Grade to commission work from freelancers like Jack Gold, Kevin Billington, John Pilger and Adrian Cowell. The switch from BBC to ATV was an educative experience: accompanying Grade on his sales visits to the United States, Batty was able to observe Grade's energetic and affable sales techniques and became acquainted with the American market. In 1968, after he had helped ATV win the new seven-day Midlands contract, he left the company to go freelance. He made two films for the BBC and then persuaded Paul Fox, Controller of BBC1, that his next film he wanted to finance himself and sell to the Corporation merely the UK rights. Fox apparently thought he was being rash but nevertheless agreed. Batty took the gamble of commuting his ATV pension and using all the money he had to make a documentary on the 25th Anniversary of the Battle of Cassino. Exploiting his ATV contacts in America, he was able to sell the US rights to the New York firm Westinghouse, who also took an option on two further films. His gamble paid off. He was to go on to make many more independently produced documentaries, but was only able to survive outside the broadcasting institutions through the returns from overseas sales, for it was always with great difficulty that he sold films to BBC or ITV. During the 1970s his success served as a model for some of those people who advocated that the fourth channel should be used to provide a regular home market for would-be independents and thereby reduce the need to have access to an overseas market. Anthony

37

Smith, for instance, has said that in proposing a National Television Foundation he had in mind a channel for people like Peter Batty.[2]

While TRI collapsed, JMB relied on the industrial training film market, and Batty sold his work overseas, Allan King Associates provides an example of a fourth development option taken by the handful of independent producers operating during the 1960s. Formed in 1962 by a group of four Canadian and two British film-makers – a producer, a director, two cameramen, a sound recordist, and an editor –AKA was set up as an independent production company with the aim of selling documentaries to the British and overseas television markets. Its connections with CBC – the Canadian Broadcasting Corporation – provided the company with a relatively secure market through which to grow. Some AKA productions, such as *Warrendale* (which won the 'Prix d'Essais' at Cannes), *A Married Couple*, and *Creative Persons*, were sold worldwide by means of Intertel, an international association of American, Canadian and German television companies to which Associated Rediffusion belonged. But sales to British television were never easy; especially because, as outsiders, AKA's producers lacked close connections with those running the BBC and ITV. When, towards the end of the 1960s, CBC began to discriminate in favour of indigenous Canadian work, AKA was forced to adapt; and within a few years, having invested in the most up-to-date production equipment, it was deriving 90% of its income from supplying crews and equipment to television and film companies throughout the world. Today it is one of the largest television and film services companies in Europe. Its path of development has been dictated by British television's refusal to encourage independent production.

The four examples considered above are obviously not intended to be in any sense exhaustive. They are merely presented as being indicative of the problems that would-be independents needed to overcome. Neither BBC nor ITV were prepared to admit that good programmes could be made outside their auspices. Yet although they shunned British independent producers, both organisations regularly bought in American television series; often exploiting to the full their quotas for foreign material (a maximum of 14% of their total outputs). The fact that a healthy British independent sector would rival the BBC and the ITV companies in the selling of British television programmes to overseas markets partly explains the broadcasting organisations' attitude towards independents. But commercial reasons alone cannot be considered sufficient explanation; there was also, as producer/director Christopher Nupen has commented, a general reluctance, especially on the part of the BBC, to cede control over the production process to independents when there seemed no pressing case for doing so:

> The absence of truly independent television producers in the United
> Kingdom, in spite of the availability of so many of the best technicians

in the world, lies in the direct commercial conflict that inevitably exists between independent producers and the ITV companies, and the self-importance of the BBC administrators in their methods of using their absolute control over two of the three networks in this country.

... the BBC has resolutely refused to relinquish even a small part of its stranglehold not only on the available outlets but on the production processes themselves and even on the world-wide distribution of the finished programmes. This is not only arrogant and unjustified but counter-productive – as has been demonstrated by the successful relationships between the television networks and independent producers in other European countries.[3]

If Britain's twin broadcasting system had created a place for the independent producer, it is likely that Channel Four would not have emerged in its present form.

THE 76 GROUP AND ANNAN'S PROLEGOMENA

The difficulty of working outside the broadcasting institutions has to be seen in conjunction with a growing number of criticisms of the duopoly made by some BBC and ITV programme-makers during the late 1960s. This mood of dissatisfaction climaxed in February 1970, when a number of leading broadcasters formed a pressure group known as the '76 Group'. Deriving their name from 1976, the year when the BBC's Charter and the ITA's Licence were due for renewal, their aim was to urge the Government to appoint a Royal Commission to review the structure, finance and organisation of broadcasting. They believed there was a general crisis in the industry and that two recent controversial events – the publication of the BBC's plans for *Broadcasting in the Seventies* and the LWT debacle – were symptomatic of this crisis. To understand their viewpoint we need to consider, in turn, the two halves of the British broadcasting duopoly.

The BBC's financial position had steadily deteriorated during the 1960s. Previously, the natural growth of radio and later of television had enabled the BBC to absorb rising costs and to finance its own capital programme. But as the market for television sets neared saturation point, the rate of growth of the licence-income was overtaken by inflation. At the same time, the BBC embarked on a major expansion with the introduction of BBC2 and 625 lines colour transmissions. By the late 1960s, the financial pressures were serious enough for the Corporation to engage McKinsey & Co, an American firm of industrial consultants. Their recommendations were never made public, but following their investigation there was a major reorganisation of the BBC intended to improve the financial accountability of the Corporation's production divisions. The heads of Television, Radio, and External Services – in future to be known as Managing Directors rather than Directors – were given financial responsibility for the operating and capital expenditure of their divisions. Total-costing was introduced in television; each programme had to be produced within the limits of a budget that included not just direct costs specific to a given programme's requirements but also an allowance for overheads (equipment, studio, resources, etc). And the forward planning system was modified to place a greater emphasis on continuous programme 'strands' that were more predictable in terms of production costs. The effect of these changes was to introduce what Tom Burns calls a 'new managerialism':

> What seems to have happened, then, is that having, between 1963 and 1973, entered a totally changed financial situation, the Director-General, with the Board of Management and the senior officials immediately subordinate to them, all backed – or prompted – by the Board of Governors, responded by carrying through a reorganisation of the administrative structure designed to give it more direct financial control, and, in consequence, more direct operational control, but in the process lost touch with, and the confidence of, sizeable sections of the staff.[4]

Additional restructuring of BBC Radio was proposed in *Broadcasting in the Seventies*. The three services, Home, Light and Third, were to be replaced by Radio 1, 2, 3 and 4. The declared aim was to provide a service adapted to perceived changes in audience needs (Radio 1, for instance, was a response to the success of the pirate pop music stations), but the plan was also to mean cheaper national radio involving stringent economies, including a reduction in the number of musicians employed and a curtailing of the expensive Third Programme. There followed a public furore. But the plan was implemented in the spring of 1970, although, in the event, there were no redundancies made in the Corporation's house orchestras. The financial resources of national radio were further stretched by the decision to speed up the development of BBC local radio; the Corporation was anxious to preserve its monopoly and believed this might be achieved by pre-empting the Conservatives' plans for commercial local radio. In the view of the 76 Group, however, the BBC were 'bleeding sorely needed finance from national radio and setting up a hopelessly underbudgeted local radio service.'[5]

In a policy paper, 'The Producer and His Relationship to Management in the BBC', the 76 Group examined the effects of the BBC's financial squeeze on the creative staff. They noted that the number of television producers in established posts was being reduced in relation to those on short-term contracts, and they argued that this was weakening the bargaining position and status of the producer:

Producers are tending to fall under the *control*, rather than *administration*, of Middle Management. Relations within Departments/Groups are becoming more authoritarian than participatory and there is declining opportunity for producers to share in the formulation of departmental philosophy and policy . . . Producers in all departments feel an increasing lack of involvement or responsibility in the maintenance and development of a total philosophy of public service broadcasting and its implementation through change and progress in the broadcasting services of the BBC.[6]

In another paper, 'The Declining Standard of BBC Television', the 76 Group argued that the Corporation's current broadcasting performance bore little relationship to its evidence to Pilkington. The BBC had asked for a second channel so that they could raise the proportion of serious programmes shown in peak hours, but in fact, believed the 76 Group, the main result had been an impoverishment of BBC1.

This process is extremely difficult to document, but everyone who has worked for BBC-TV over the last five years will have first-hand evidence of an atmosphere in which programme standards have increasingly suffered in the race for ratings.[7]

The 76 Group was equally critical of the ITV system. When the group was formed in early 1970, London Weekend Television had already begun to abandon its original, ambitious programming intentions. It had lost its audience to the BBC; the other network companies had refused to take some of its programmes; and advertisers were holding back. Shareholders had panicked and capital was beginning to drain away. Before the year was out Rupert Murdoch had acquired his interest in the company, and the LWT Board had demanded a change of programming policy and had asked Michael Peacock, the Managing Director, to leave. It was only in 1971 when John Freeman, former British ambassador to Washington, was appointed Chairman, that the company finally came to match in performance what its application had promised. As has been touched upon earlier, the ITA was strongly criticized for its handling of the LWT affair. Some newspaper editorials had urged it to cancel the contract and re-advertise. But the Authority was reluctant to make the whole workforce redundant and was sceptical that another applicant, apart from Murdoch, could be found. They adopted a wait-and-see policy. In the opinion of the 76 Group members the incident demonstrated the need to re-examine the Authority's role. An unfortunate comment by Sir Robert Fraser – 'To catch companies out on broken promises is at best childish and at worst a bore' – was picked up and considered characteristic of the ITA's acquiescent attitude to poor programming. It was felt that the Authority had available sanctions less drastic than the termination of the franchise, but that they had not been prepared to use them.

The 76 Group's inception also coincided with the general financial depression within ITV. There was concern about the detrimental effect that the levy was having on programme standards; ITV, declared the group, had always been handicapped by the subservience of programmes to profit and this was being intensified by the levy. A review of broadcasting would be able to examine the possibility of returning a proportion of the levy or changing its basis from revenues to profits; although undertakings would, it was thought, be required to ensure that this income would go into programme expenditure. In the longer term, the 76 Group argued, a reappraisal of the collection and use of advertising revenue was needed.

At their February 1970 meeting in Kensington House the 76 Group elected a committee. It included Phillip Whitehead, former BBC producer and editor of Thames Television's *This Week*; Kenith Trodd of Kestrel Productions, a documentary-drama company formed on the basis of a contract with LWT which had then been cancelled when Peacock left; Humphrey Burton, former head of music and arts at LWT, and Stuart Hood, former Controller of BBC Television. Within a month they had organised an all-party meeting with MPs at which they presented a manifesto calling for a Royal Commission to be set up as soon as possible. The manifesto was also published in an advertisement in the *Guardian* under the headline 'Crisis in Television and Radio: A Royal Commission *Now!*'[8] The names of over one hundred members of the Group who had helped pay for the advertisement were listed, but other supporters decided to remain anonymous for fear of jeopardising their prospects for future employment. Editorials in both *The Times* and the *Guardian* supported the idea of an inquiry sometime in the near future, and the Labour Party Communications Group, chaired by Hugh Jenkins, agreed to lobby the Prime Minister. John Stonehouse, Minister of Posts and Telecommunications, had already told the House of Commons in December 1969 that he was considering the possibility of an independent review of broadcasting in the light of the financial problems of the ITV companies. The activities of the 76 Group helped settle the matter. In May 1970, he announced that Lord Annan, historian and Provost of University College, London, had accepted an invitation to chair a committee of inquiry, 'to consider the future, after 31st July 1976, of broadcasting in the United Kingdom.' The Conservatives denounced the proposal as unnecessary and useless. Edward Heath had said in December that he saw no reason 'to pull up the roots of the tree once more to see if they are healthy.'[9] There was no problem in broadcasting, he believed, which could not be settled amicably and sensibly with the Corporation and the Authority by any Government. It is fair to say that the Conservatives also felt an inquiry would hamper their plans to introduce commercial radio. In June 1970

42

Heath became Prime Minister and Annan was politely informed that his services were not required by the new Government.

THE INTERREGNUM: POSSIBILITIES FOR THE FOURTH CHANNEL

Although the Annan Committee had been abandoned, it was still generally assumed within the broadcasting industry that some form of review would be required before the BBC Charter and the ITA's Licence were renewed in 1976. When he cancelled the committee of inquiry, Chataway explained that his Ministry's Television Advisory Committee would be undertaking a study of the main technical questions in broadcasting. After it had reported, he would consider whether a major inquiry was desirable. The idea that any fundamental alteration of the broadcasting ecology should take place before such a review was widely opposed. The one exception was commercial radio, for the Conservatives were committed to this and it was unrealistic to expect them to delay. (The Sound Broadcasting Act introducing Independent Local Radio came into effect in July 1972 and on that date the ITA became the Independent Broadcasting Authority.) But on the question of the fourth channel, there was no statement of Conservative policy except Bevin's seven-year-old promise. The ITA's *ITV2* submission to Chataway therefore was seen as an underhand attempt to pre-empt the conclusions of a future committee of inquiry. The opponents of *ITV2* believed that the Authority and the ITV companies were adopting 'steamroller' tactics; they had no agreed conception of an alternative to a second and complementary ITV channel, but rather a desire to prevent a hasty decision being made without consideration of all possibilities.

The first significant expression of this opposition came in a letter from Tom Rhys, Secretary of the Federation of Broadcasting Unions, replying to Brian Young's request for ideas on a second ITV channel. Rhys explained that the FBU, which represented the nine broadcasting unions, had decided, with the exception of one member, that it would be foolish to take a decision on the fourth channel at a time when an inquiry was likely to begin. 'It could seriously inhibit its work if resources were committed in such a way that the committee would find it difficult to go back to the *status quo ante*.'[10] When a committee had been set up, Rhys declared, the FBU would draw attention to a number of alternative uses of this national resource. The Federation made its views public when Rhys expressed the same opinions in a letter to *The Times*.[11] Then two members of the Federation decided on further action. The ACTT had established in 1969 a policy research commission run by Caroline Heller, and it had issued position papers on subjects ranging from LWT to television and technology. She now agreed to prepare a detailed background report on the fourth channel. At the same time, the Policy

Committee of the ABS* began to devise a scheme that was to prove to be most influential.

In October the *Sunday Times* published a long leader article headed 'ITV2: A Case Not Proven'. The paper conceded that the argument for a second ITV channel was 'a seductive case', but it begged two central questions: (i) was there any public demand for an ITV2, and (ii) what kind of programmes would it screen?

> The companies would doubtless make promises – they are making them already. But past evidence offers no reason for believing the assertion of any commercial television contractor that it will give priority to public service. . . . Any suggestion that ITV2 would resemble BBC2 should be treated with the blackest scepticism. This is not because the men promoting that idea are dishonest or even because there is necessarily a shortage of talent or idealism. It is because commercial television operates within narrow and demanding constraints, which give priority to profit.[12]

Allocation of the fourth channel, it argued, should be left to the far-ranging inquiry which would 'have' to come before 1976. It would be better, stated the paper, for the fourth channel to be left empty than made available to anyone who would cause it to resemble the present commercial network. The article concluded with an attack on the ITA for apparently acting in consort with the ITV companies. 'Instead of holding the ring between alternative strategies, it seems to have adopted a position which excludes all but one strategy.' The editorial was a remarkably forthright statement, especially coming from a newspaper owned by an organisation with an interest in Scottish Television. (Although as the article itself pointed out, there were other, conflicting interests; a quality newspaper might well be the first to suffer from a 'quality' ITV2 which drained away advertising.)

In November, pressure to delay Chataway's decision over the channel was significantly stepped up. Caroline Heller's report was published, and it concurred with the conclusions of the *Sunday Times* article that the case for ITV2 was not persuasive. Influenced by the Prices and Incomes Board's pessimistic predictions for ITV's finance, she argued that the economic basis for ITV2 was extremely weak, particularly in view of the imminent introduction of commercial radio.[13] In her view the companies were suffering from the euphoria of a temporary upswing in their financial position. The Programme Controllers group's confidential schedule had been leaked, and Heller noted that 12½ hours of ITV2's 35 hours planned output would be taken up by feature films, filmed series, and repeats. Financial pressures, she believed, would encourage an increase in this proportion. Thus, the claim that ITV2 would mean more

---

*Association of Broadcasting Staff: primarily the BBC union, as opposed to the ACTT which represents employees of ITV and the film industry.

employment and creative opportunities for ACTT members needed further examination. The introduction of a second commercial channel would be likely to mean increased instability in an already unstable high-risk industry, and it posed a distinct threat to job security and programme standards. Not all members of the ACCT, with its chronic unemployment, shared Heller's scepticism. But there was agreement that there should be a full analysis of all the alternatives before the structure of the industry was altered in any significant way.

The ACTT document helped provide political ammunition for the 'TV4 Campaign'. This was a non-party pressure group established in November 1971 following an open conference at the Polytechnic of Central London. The meeting was convened by the magazine *Time Out* and the Free Communications Group – an organisation that had been formed in 1968 to promote more active participation in staff relations in broadcasting and the Press, some of whose members also belonged to the 76 Group. At the meeting the FCG's point of view was only one among many. Over two hundred people attended the conference, including members of Mary Whitehouse's National Viewers' and Listeners' Association, the Bow Group (a research organisation independent of, but sympathetic to, the Conservative Party), the National Union of Teachers, the 76 Group and the broadcasting unions. Speakers included Professor Hilde Himmelweit, from the London School of Economics, Stephen Murphy, Secretary of the British Board of Film Censors, Labour MP John Golding, Chris Dunkley from *The Times,* Anthony Smith, former editor of BBC's *24 Hours,* and many others. Despite this diversity of opinion a consensus was achieved on the single objective of preventing the allocation of the fourth channel to the ITV companies. In a burst of activity the Campaign's Action Committee launched a national petition and commissioned a number of its members to prepare a publication – *Opportunities for the Fourth Channel* – which was submitted to Chataway a few days after the ITA's submission. Parliamentary interest in the issue was activated when five Labour politicians, including John Golding and the recently elected Phillip Whitehead, put down an Early Day Motion calling for a Commons debate on the subject. The Motion eventually attracted the signatures of about a hundred MPs. It read as follows:

> This House believes that a public inquiry into the structure of television broadcasting should be established as soon as possible; that the remaining television frequencies should not be allocated until such a public inquiry is held; and that the fourth television channel should not be allocated to the present independent television contractors.[14]

When the ITA published its submission to the Minister, the TV4 Campaign issued a statement which firmly declared their objections:

While the submission is an excellent statement of the needs of the Authority and the programme contractors — and the big five in particular — it represents an arrogant and bland ignorance of the needs of the public — the needs for access, accountability and participation on the part of the people who watch (and finance) television.

It is our view that television is for the people, not for the broadcasters, and the Authority's disregard for the viewer, who has specifically not been consulted, either directly or through his representative in Parliament, is shown blatantly in this document.[15]

Only the Authority's proposal for a Programme Planning Board was welcomed. The Board, it was believed, was a belated recognition of Pilkington's recommendation number 43 — the idea that the Authority itself should act as Programme Controller. It should be introduced immediately to oversee the output of the existing ITV service; for, argued some members of the Campaign, it would then be better placed to defend its own survival, and even expansion, to a committee of inquiry.

The TV4 Campaign's activities generated a great deal of press and broadcasting coverage, and editorials in virtually all the national newspapers responded to the ITA's submission with calls for an inquiry. In the first few weeks of the New Year, as we already know, Christopher Chataway revealed that the Government was not yet convinced by the ITA's case. There was a genuine fear in Whitehall that the immediate allocation of the fourth channel to the ITV companies would produce an undesirable party political battle in the House of Commons. This would bring television, which since the introduction of commercial television had been a bipartisan subject, into the political arena. Before an ITV2 could be introduced, the concept had to be 'sold' to Parliament and the television industry. The opposition to ITV2 had won the first round. The debate was to continue. Following Chataway's postponement, however, the TV4 Campaign, its defining objective achieved, collapsed as its various constituents began to articulate their different schemes for utilising broadcasting's empty room. Broadly speaking, they fell into six categories.

1) THE NATIONAL TELEVISION FOUNDATION

In early 1972 the ABS Policy Committee endorsed the idea of a channel that would 'publish' programmes without the creation of a full-scale institutional organisation. The proposal was the brainchild of Anthony Smith, Research Fellow of St Antony's College, Oxford. He inaugurated the scheme in an article in the *Guardian* in April 1972 and in subsequent writings he refined the idea. Smith had been a member of the *Tonight* team and editor of BBC's *24 Hours*. In 1971 he left the Corporation to become a critic and historian of broadcasting and a campaigner for organisational change. While working on a major study of the relationship between the broadcaster, the audience and the state, *The Shadow in the Cave,* he put forward the plan for a Television Foundation as a positive response to a critique of broadcasting's institutional structures.

Broadcasting, argued Smith, had become the dominant form and forum of cultural expression, but it was housed in institutions whose principal motivation was their own survival and not the enrichment of the culture they both served and helped constitute:

> Television is a serious medium, taken, on the whole, seriously by those responsible for it. But a vast and wholly accidental concentration of power is involved in broadcasting which envelops every programme and corrodes the air of broadcasting in Britain, increasingly. The two authorities are under constant pressure of every kind; they are committed to mutual competition, hour after hour, for the same audience and they are committed to keeping controversy over programmes to politically acceptable levels — and they must perforce themselves determine where those levels become unacceptable.
>
> Broadcasting has become a highly 'policed' medium, self-policed if you look at it from the standpoint of the organisations concerned, bureaucratised if you look at it from the standpoint of many of the programme-makers. The two organisations are catholic in their approach to programme material, but everything they absorb is part of a conscious public strategy, to ensure their survival in the constant political turmoils which they endure.[16]

No form of publishing, Smith conceded, whether by airwaves or on pieces of paper, could ever be totally 'open'; someone or somebody has to make choices, and there have to be some legal controls. But at present there were only two broadcasting 'publishing' houses, employing a large number of their own 'authors', and firmly imposing their own house-style on all their 'publications'. A NTF, on the other hand, with virtually no employees and without the accretions of practice and policy of the existing broadcasting organisations, would draw its 'authors' from society at large. It would provide a market for 'freelance' authors whose work was not necessarily compatible with the existing institutions. It would initiate 'a kind of right to broadcast' by encouraging anyone to bring forward programme ideas:

> It would supplement existing broadcasting by broadening the input, by allowing anyone to bring a project to it, whether an independent programme-maker with a finely worked-out plan, neatly costed, or a firm, organisation or individual with merely a well-argued complaint that some issue was failing to get across to the public. The Foundation would then play a kind of impresario role, merely by allocating

resources to some, but fitting producers, writers, technicians to others who arrived only with an idea, a grievance, a cause.[17]

It would be a mistake to see the NTF plan as primarily an access channel along the lines of the Dutch system, with its guaranteed access for qualifying interest groups, or in the style of the BBC's then recently attempted access experiment, *Open Door*. Community groups would have a role, but the Foundation would have a full range of professional creative work: factual and educational programmes as well as its own particular brands of drama and comedy. There would, however, be no regular schedules and no news bulletins at fixed times to cut up the evening. Instead there would be an emphasis on 'festive' television, programmes planned over a long period and built up with surrounding publicity, often requiring consecutive viewing, even over several evenings. In short, programmes would be chosen according to a doctrine of openness rather than balance, expression rather than neutralisation. The main aim would be to discover 'valid' audiences rather than conglomerate statistical ones. The fourth channel, believed Smith, should reflect the evolving structure of modern society; a structure increasingly compounded of interest groups rather than general mass class solidarities:

> Beneath the facade of the homogeneous mass audience the cement is cracking. In its earlier years television was heralded as a medium which brought the whole of society together into a single audience which could share common experiences through the new medium. Television now needs to set about the same or a similar task, but in a different way, by exhibiting for all to see the different elements of the whole.[18]

> The underlying virtue of television technology is that it enables a homogeneous audience which is geographically scattered to be brought together. A television channel can do something more than try to get the same message across to millions of people ... it can direct a programme at a highly specialized level, at a large audience of like-minded people... There can be programmes for busdrivers' wives, for doctors, for policemen, for teachers, for one-parent families; programmes made without compromise for one real living audience rather than at the crudely aggregated mass of overlapping audiences.[19]

The NTF's authority would be exercised by a board of individuals chosen partly by the Government — like the Governors of the BBC and the IBA — and partly by other specified institutions such as the broadcasting and entertainment unions, viewers' organisations, educational bodies and other major sources of finance. The existing broadcasting authorities should have some representation, though only with 'observer' status. The governing board would appoint a full-time director, who in turn would appoint a small staff to stimulate and receive projects from the public. With no production staff of its own, the NTF would encourage the development of private studio construction and, hoped Smith, would be able to exploit the under-used studio capacity of the ITV companies.

The method of financing the Foundation was always considered by its critics to be the major flaw in Smith's argument. Initially, in his 1972 *Guardian* article, he proposed that money should be received through direct grants from fund-holding participating organisations such as educational bodies; sponsorship by any organisation who wanted to support a particular programme subject; and from Parliament whose various Ministries could pay for programmes they believed were desirable.[20] By 1974, however, two other sources of potential finance had been identified: first, advertising, but only in 'blocks' of ten or fifteen minutes as in the German and Dutch pattern, rather than the 'spot' commercials of ITV; and second, the ITV levy, the basis of which by 1974 had been switched from revenues to profits. With a predicted annual income of £30 millions from the levy, the Treasury, Smith declared, could easily surrender a fixed annual sum of £10-12 millions without feeling the loss.[21] Criticisms of Smith's belief that the new channel, with its pluralist philosophy, should seek a plurality of revenue sources is something we will return to later in greater detail.

2) FOURTH CHANNEL FOR EDUCATION

The concept of a 'University of the Air', based on independent study in conjunction with radio listening and television viewing, was first mentioned during a campaign speech by Harold Wilson in 1963. A few years after coming to power the Labour Government set up a committee of educationalists and a few broadcasters to draw up plans for an Open University. Against a background of widespread scepticism, the OU received its charter in April 1969. The BBC had agreed to undertake the production and transmission of the new University's programmes, in return for which the Corporation received a proportion of the OU's annual grant from the Department of Education and Science. By 1973, BBC2 was transmitting 30 hours a week of OU programmes in the early mornings and evenings, and the project's critics had been generally silenced. To do its expanding job properly, argued Dr Walter Perry, the OU's Vice-Chancellor, the University needed more broadcasting hours and at more convenient times of the day; something which the BBC could only provide at the expense of the general viewer. In July 1973, therefore, Perry wrote to the Prime Minister asking for the fourth channel to be devoted to educational broadcasting, and in particular to the Open University. In support, Lord Hill, former Postmaster-General and ex-Chairman of both the ITA and the BBC, wrote a controversial article in the *Observer* recommending the idea of transferring Open University and

Schools' Broadcasting to the empty channel.[22] (The most hurtful thrust of Hill's article, however, was his contention that by their very nature the advertising-dependent ITV companies could not maintain an innovative, non-mass appeal ITV2.)

Not all educationalists agreed with Dr Perry. Some feared that an OU dominated fourth channel would become an educational ghetto, preaching to the converted, and finding it difficult to serve any role in a society in which, many believed, education ought to be a process continuing throughout life. *The Times Higher Education Supplement,* for instance, presented the case for a wider-embracing, less formal conception of educational television, along the lines of the Japanese NHK service:

> There is an overwhelming argument for giving the fourth television channel an educational and cultural focus, which could not be subverted as in the case of BBC2, *but would not be narrowly and restrictively interpreted.* The closest model is perhaps Radio 3 — although the parallel is shaky because radio is a minority medium and much cheaper into the bargain.[23] (author's emphasis)

No suggestion was put forward for how such a less academic channel would be structured or financed. Accepting the ghetto argument, some educational groups opposed any form of an *exclusively* educationally oriented channel; to reach the general viewer, what was needed was more generally educative programming on the three existing networks. Finally, there were those who questioned the implicit prioritisation of resources for education by television over other forms of education.

A separate criticism of an educational fourth channel derived from the claim that the future of education by television belonged to video-cassettes not over-the-air transmissions. Pre-recorded tapes and time-switching of broadcasts in unsocial hours (i.e. broadcasts in the dead hours of the night) would cater for the student's needs far more conveniently than an educational fourth channel.

3) LOCAL/REGIONAL TELEVISION

Recent experiments in Canada and the United States led some to suggest that with the falling cost of television equipment and the shorter range of UHF transmitters (as opposed to VHF), the available frequencies should be used to provide flexible community television services. Already universities and colleges produced more hours of programmes than either the BBC or the IBA. Community television could either be run part-time by amateurs, or full-time by non-profit making groups. According to the data collected from a sample survey of 550 people in Leicestershire, conducted by the Centre for Mass Communications Research at Leicester University in 1972, the idea of local television was popular. The respondents were offered five options and asked: 'If there was a fourth channel, which of the following do you think it should be used for?' The results were:

Local television 32.0%
Programmes like ITV 12.5%
Programmes like BBC1 . . . . 11.8%
Education and Information 23.4%
Programmes like BBC2, financed by advertisements 13.4%
Don't know, etc. 6.7%

The same survey also suggested that there was no great demand for any new service; when asked the straightforward question of whether there should be a fourth television channel, the majority (63%) were opposed to the idea. But as the Leicester team noted: 'It is, of course, notoriously difficult to ask people's opinions of things they have not experienced.'[24]

The main criticisms of the proposal for local television were that estimates of costs were over-optimistic; that production standards would be well below that which the public were accustomed to, and perhaps prepared to tolerate; and that the far less expensive local radio services were increasingly fulfilling the same community needs. Moreover, in the early 1970s it was felt that the introduction of over-the-air local television would soon be made redundant by the expected development of cable television.

Demands for the fourth channel to serve the particular needs of the Welsh language had a longer pedigree and a more insistent body of supporters than local television. The Welsh language, spoken by over half a million people (20% of the Welsh population), was, and still is, believed to be the cornerstone in the preservation of Welsh culture. The pervasive influence of English television was considered, by among others the Welsh Language Society, to be one of the chief single causes for the decline in the number of people speaking Welsh (about a 20% fall over ten years according to the 1971 Census). A coherent, comprehensive service of Welsh on a single television channel would provide substantial social and cultural support for existing and potential Welsh speakers.

The subject was not a new one. Pilkington in 1962 had recommended that the BBC provide a separate service in Wales and this had been introduced two years later. For most of its transmission time BBC Wales duplicated BBC1, but for seven hours of the week programmes were in Welsh. The ITA's original contractor for West and North Wales, WWN Television, had also been obliged to supply a similar Welsh-language service. This had proved to be a commercial disaster; in 1964 the company had been forced to merge with the larger TWW Television, the contractor for South Wales and the West of England. (WWN is the only ITV company that has failed financially.) The enlarged TWW could, however, afford to match BBC Wales' Welsh output, and this requirement was inherited by Harlech Television (HTV) when TWW lost the Welsh franchise in 1967.

The arrangements in Wales were not greeted with universal approval. Among the non-Welsh-speaking majority it' generated a surprising amount of indignation, especially in the case of those who were not in a geographically suitable position to adjust their aerials to receive the English transmissions of BBC1 and HTV. The Welsh speakers, on the other hand, asserted that a total of about fifteen hours a week of Welsh-language transmissions placed within the context of dominantly English services was wholly inadequate. In 1973 the Lord Mayor of Cardiff convened a conference of interested Welsh organisations and institutions and this conference called for special consideration for Wales when decisions were made about the fourth channel. A year later, the Government's own Committee on Broadcasting Coverage, chaired by Sir Stewart Crawford, recommended that 'whatever decision may be reached about the fourth channel in the rest of the United Kingdom, it should in Wales be allocated as soon as possible to a separate service in which Welsh-language programmes would be given priority.'[25] Responsibility for transmission and programming should rest with the BBC, the IBA and HTV, who would move their existing Welsh-language items on to the new service. The Committee also noted that a subsidy from Government for the Welsh-language service might be needed.

Requests to meet other regional television needs elsewhere in the United Kingdom were a great deal more muted. The Highland Association in Scotland were interested in some form of Gaelic broadcasting, but their main priority was a community radio service. In Northern Ireland there were some feelings that a future fourth channel should supplement the existing regional output provided by the BBC and Ulster Television. There was little demand for an English regional fourth channel as distinct from local television.

4) THE ADVERTISERS' VIEW

In November 1972 the ISBA and the IPA published, under the title *Television 76,* their views about how broadcasting resources should be allocated after 1976. As one of the main moving forces in the 1950s campaign for commercial television, the advertisers and the agencies had always opposed ITV's limitation to one channel. They had further resented the ITA's 1967 abandonment of the split-week arrangement for the North and Midlands franchise, for since then only in London did they have a choice between sellers of advertising time; although even there of course it was a restricted choice, for the two London stations did not broadcast simultaneously. The monopoly power of the ITV companies, believed the advertisers, was characterised by a general unwillingness on the part of the companies to give any signs of interest in their customers' marketing requirements. This manifested itself, they argued, in a growing number of restrictive policies and selling practices. These were becoming increasingly subtle; enabling the companies to maximise their revenues with minimum hindrance from the ITA, or as it was by then the IBA, who were unable to supervise 'off-the-rate-card' manipulation by the programme contractors. The IBA's rejection of its long-standing commitment to a competitive ITV2 was strongly condemned by the ISBA and the IPA. They asserted that it could not be in the public interest for the Government to perpetuate a system of monopoly which by 1976 would have a net annual income from the sale of advertising time in the order of £200 million.

The proposals outlined in *Television 76* were,, however, fantastically ambitious. The scheme, self-confessedly prompted by the interests of the advertisers and with little else to support it, envisaged a drastic restructuring of British broadcasting. A Broadcasting Council would be created and it would assume powers and responsibility for regulating all sectors of television and radio broadcasting, whether commercial or non-commercial. This Council would have responsibility for four separate operations:

a) *A 'Public Service Authority'*
This would be financed by licence revenue and would operate certain programme services:
— A national 'social and educational' television channel making use of the fourth channel which is as yet unallocated.
— A national 'special interest' television channel similar in character to the present BBC2.
— Non-commercial radio services as currently run by the BBC.
b) *A 'general interest' television channel*
Programmed on the lines of BBC1, but financed by the sale of advertising and operated by a publicly owned company or corporation.
c) *A second 'general interest' television channel*
Financed by the sale of advertising airtime and operated by contractors appointed by the Broadcasting Council.
d) *A commercial radio network*
Financed by the sale of advertising and operated by contractors appointed by the Broadcasting Council.[26]

Against the scheme was the entire weight of the widely held conviction, both inside and outside the broadcasting industry, that competition for advertising would inevitably lower broadcasting standards. It would result in a single-minded concentration on maximising audiences in a way that all previous British broadcasting legislation had sought to avoid. It would destroy the BBC as it was presently constituted and consign to ghetto channels all minority and special interest programmes. In reply, the advertisers and the agencies put their faith in the ability of a

53

legislative watch-dog — the Broadcasting Council — to prevent a decline in standards.

In 1972 Christopher Chataway was succeeded by Sir John Eden as Minister of Posts and Telecommunications. Within his first few months of office, Eden had revived Governmental interest in the fourth channel. A White Paper published in March 1973 announced that the Government considered a full-ranging inquiry to be undesirable at the present time. It proposed the extension of the BBC Charter and the IBA's Licence until 1981 without any substantial change, by which time the technical developments which would govern broadcasting in the last part of the century would become much clearer.[27] The White Paper also announced the appointment of the Crawford Committee and stated that separate consideration was being given to the question of the fourth channel; views as to whether, and if so how, this might be used were invited by the Minister.

In the light of these developments the ISBA and the IPA, reaffirming their belief that *Television 76* still represented their long-term ideal, presented an interim proposal, *Television 76+*, for the immediate use of the fourth channel.[28] Citing the Prices and Incomes Board's 1970 suggestion that the number of ITV contractors should be reduced, the advertisers and the agencies recommended that the fifteen existing franchise areas should be combined to make six regions. Within each region (except Ulster), there would be two 'networks' of local stations, ITV1 and ITV2, competing for the purpose of selling advertising time. With the introduction of competition, it was suggested, the rationale for the levy would be removed. Once again, the objections to competition were raised in opposition to the proposals. As we shall see in the next chapter, the downfall of the advertisers' case was their failure to convince anyone, except themselves, that the link between competitive selling and lowest common denominator programming could be broken by a supervisory authority.

5) STRUCTURAL CHANGE FIRST

Although Annan had been cancelled in 1970, there was nevertheless a major examination in the early 1970s of one half of the British broadcasting system. The all-party Select Committee on Nationalised Industries during the 1971-72 session investigated the British Transport Dock Board and the Independent Broadcasting Authority. The Committee's severe criticism of the IBA's leniency towards the industry which it had been set up to regulate strongly echoed that of a decade before made by Pilkington. There had however, noted the Committee, been an important change in the nature of public discussion about broadcasting:

There has been a shift in emphasis from considering the broadcasting media solely in terms of the programmes they produce to one in which the BBC and the Authority are seen as powerful institutions in their own right, whose style of decision-making and action profoundly affects the community. It is this view which has led to the demand for public accountability and for increased public participation and access.[29]

The Committee's thirty recommendations, although fairly drastic, were less fundamental than Pilkington's. A firmer Authority, it proposed, would result from the immediate appointment of the two programme planners envisaged in the ITV2 proposals, and steps should be taken to ensure a wider range of programmes were shown on ITV. On the question of the fourth channel, the Committee believed that no decision should be taken except as part of a general review embracing the broadcasting needs of the country.[30] The Government's 1973 White Paper was a reply to the Select Committee's report. As we have seen, the IBA's Licence was extended until 1981; no immediate changes were thought feasible, although the Minister did promise to give full consideration to the Committee's suggestions.

The Select Committee's report was used as supporting evidence by the radical elements of the broadcasting community, who believed that major structural reform had to precede discussion about the fourth channel:

If you believe ... that there are major structural weaknesses in the existing system, and it is from some such conviction that opposition to ITV2 stems, then any tinkering at the edges, whether Open University, National Television Foundation, or whatever, is diversionary. It is like building a small village in which to eke out a living at the mercy of the feudal barons, rather than laying siege to their fortresses. . .

If you want regional television you will have to confront the economics of networking on ITV and reverse the centralising trends of the BBC. If you want educational television to be more than a poor relation, you will have to alter the balance of the existing entertainment-dominated schedules.[31]

The author of this passage, Nicholas Garnham, Head of the School of Communications at the Polytechnic of Central London, was one of the leading members of a small but influential group of about fifty individuals who had been invited by the Acton Society in 1973 to form the grandly titled 'Standing Conference on Broadcasting.' Generously financed by the Joseph Rowntree Social Services Trust, SCOB undertook to do the research work on broadcasting that the Annan Committee would have done had it been established. Its membership, principally academics, excluded anyone who was an employee of a broadcasting organisation, but many did have direct experience of the industry. Nine SCOB members – Nicholas Garnham, Caroline Heller, Phillip Whitehead, Professor

James Halloran of Leicester University, Alan Sapper, General Secretary of ACTT, James Curran of the Polytechnic of Central London, John Morton, General Secretary of the Musicians' Union, Bob Hamilton, National Organiser of ACTT, and Alfred George of the Post Office Engineering Union – were also part of a Labour Party study group, chaired by Tony Benn, that in 1974 published a discussion paper, *The People and the Media*. This overlap in membership probably goes a long way towards explaining why Lord Annan has said that at times he wondered 'whether it was too fanciful to detect that the evidence of that body (SCOB), the Transport House document *The People and the Media*, and the evidence from the ACTT were drafted by the same hand.'[32]

Same hand or not, the conclusions reached by these three bodies certainly coincided. What were these conclusions? Annan scornfully sums them up:

> They argued that the time had come to reorganise the whole structure of British broadcasting and the political assumptions on which it rested. Perhaps 'argued' is the wrong word. They proceeded by assertion. Rather like the American Declaration of Independence which asserts that certain truths must be held to be self-evident, the Standing Conference roundly stated that the duopoly of BBC and IBA should be dissolved, 'the existing divided system having manifestly failed.' The licence fee should be abolished because it was *palpably* a retrogressive form of taxation, and the grant-in-aid should be merged with revenue from advertising because the present financial structure of broadcasting *clearly* had proved unworkable. The Transport House document simply announced as a known fact that 'broadcasting in Britain is controlled today by closed and autocratic institutions.'[33]

The solution? The BBC and IBA should cease to exist; in their place two new bodies would be erected. The first was an advisory and Ombudsman body; SCOB christened it the National Broadcasting Policy Council, while *The People and the Media* talked of a Communications Council. Its function would be to keep the operation and development of broadcasting (and in the Labour document, the Press and film industry as well) under continuous review, and to advise the Minister in the formation of a national communications policy. It would also be responsible for audience research, and the investigation of complaints about broadcasting. The second body, SCOB's National Broadcasting Commission and the Labour document's Public Broadcasting Commission, would be responsible for overall administration and funding of British broadcasting. Its members would comprise a mixture of Ministerial appointees (but they would not be in the majority); elected representatives of the broadcasting organisations; and selected representatives of specified bodies such as the TUC, the CBI, political parties, and viewers' and listeners' organisations. SCOB envisaged three sources of finance –

licence revenue, advertising, and direct govenmental funding – but the Labour group thought the licence fee, being a regressive tax, should be phased out. All income would be centrally pooled and used to finance two publicly owned television corporations who would produce programmes for two national channels. In the Labour document, they would also each have a regional television channel as well, while SCOB proposed a single, separate regional television service – thus leaving the available fourth channel frequencies unemployed. As for radio, there would be one national and one local radio corporation. A private enterprise element in British broadcasting was declared to be incompatible with the overall structural model proposed. In concluding, *The People and the Media* stated that within these broadcasting organisations 'internal democracy' would be established at all levels, 'which would bring benefits to the communications industry as a whole by enabling broadcasting workers to contribute directly to the management and development of their own industry.'[34]

The scale of the proposed reforms was clearly as ambitious as the suggestions contained in the advertisers' *Television 76* document. But as we shall see the Annan Committee felt the need to take them a great deal more seriously than those of the advertisers. With hindsight it is all too easy to dismiss the chances of such radical changes being accepted by any committee of inquiry or, subsequently, by any Government. But in 1974 structural reform was in the air, and as Michael Starks puts it, a Rip Van Winkle who had witnessed the start of the Annan inquiry, slept for several years and then awoken, would have found the essentially conservative outcome remarkable.[35]

As a footnote, it must be pointed out that there was not unanimity within SCOB. In its evidence to the Annan Committee the SCOB submission was divided, for it contained minority papers of dissent written by Anthony Smith and Jay Blumler of Leeds University. In essence, the difference between the two groups within SCOB was that between reformers and revolutionaries. In reply to the earlier quote from Garnham, Smith wrote in 1973 the following:

> Some of those opposed to ITV2 are currently diverting themselves towards a kind of revolutionary inertia in which good arguments against ITV2 are frittered away by useless insistence on 'solving the structural problems of British broadcasting' first. These problems are deeply rooted in our society, perhaps deeper than even Garnham's radicalism can reach.
>
> ...We still might get an inquiry at the end of the 1970s though its recommendations might still not satisfy Nicholas Garnham, who might in 1980 be writing to the *Guardian* still demanding that no one lays a hand on the fourth channel until he is completely satisfied that no major structural weaknesses remain elsewhere in the system. With

Garnham-Vision we could wait forever without achieving any change at all.[36]

6) AN INDEPENDENT ITV2 PROGRAMME CONTROLLER

Although two of the broad schemes we have so far considered – the National Television Foundation, and the arguments for major structural change – were put forward by people who had experience of working in broadcasting, they were, in general, people who by the early 1970s had left the institutions. Many programme producers who were still very much within them had a different perception of how broadcasting could and should evolve. Although sometimes sympathetic to those who wanted entirely new elements brought into British broadcasting, they believed that the particular proposals put forward were either unrealistic, undesirable, or both. Their main preoccupation was to provide creative *Lebensraum* for talent within ITV. In a letter to Sir John Eden in 1973, John Birt, producer of LWT's new current affairs programme *Weekend World*, and David Elstein, a director on *This Week*, explained:

> [The] need is for the creative forces within the present systems to be liberated from the restrictions imposed by the requirements of the institutions which presently employ them. Programmes like the Kestrel plays, *Monty Python's Flying Circus*, the dramatisation of *The Chicago Eight Trial*, or the four-hour long epic *The Sorrow and the Pity* are the exceptions and not the rule. A programme controller running the fourth channel with departmental heads (but not departments) might be able to back hunches and allow *ad hoc* production units to form in a way that is just not possible within the present institutions.[37]

Birt and Elstein were sceptical of the ITCA companies' claims for innovative programming on ITV2. Since 1971 the broadcasting hours had been extended, and the companies' income had picked up so considerably that it was now approaching record levels. What excuse, they asked, can there be for those bold new ideas not to be on the air already? But the difference between their proposals and those of many others who opposed the companies' bid for the fourth channel, was that they believed it was vital to secure the ungrudging support and co-operation of the ITV companies for any alternative scheme.

> We do not want to see wasteful duplication of television facilities. We do not want competition for audiences or advertising. We believe the carrot rather than the stick will persuade the companies to make available their spare facilities. Any attempt to coerce them will lead to such stratagems as double-pricing of studios, and loaded tariffs for OB crews. And if the reply to that is takeovers, then we have moved from the TV4 debate to the Pilkington debate and beyond.[38]

In their submission to Sir John in 1973 the two producers therefore envisaged an ITV2 which, although under the aegis of the IBA, would have a strong identity separate from ITV1. It would be a national channel run by a single, IBA-appointed, programme controller. He or she would buy and commission programmes from all sources; from the present ITV companies, as well as independent producers – who would be treated as equals of the companies. Whereas ITV1's planners agreed to apportion network time on a rigid basis, which it was felt discouraged companies from trying to replace bad network productions from other companies with better programmes of their own, the single ITV2 controller, they explained, would draw up schedules on merit alone, perhaps taking 'particular pleasure in picking up ideas that the network controllers had turned down.'[39] The IBA would then balance the two ITV channels against each other to ensure that one's interests did not predominate at the expense of the other's. The key to ITV2's distinctiveness, claimed Birt and Elstein, would be in the difference between 'balance' and 'planning': 'It is a crucial error to define complementary as *"planning* both channels" rather than *"balancing* two schedules which have been independently planned."'[40] In this way, Birt and Elstein's ITV2 Programme Controller would be a very different animal from the ITA's proposed Programme Planning Board.

The existing companies, they suggested, would sell the ITV2 advertising in their areas and retain the revenue, and the IBA would then make a (second) levy from them to pay for ITV2's budget. To protect other advertising media, they believed that the amount of advertising sold by a two-channel ITV might have to be limited, in which case the (first) levy to the Exchequer would probably be reduced. The advantage of this form of alternative ITV2 would be that the ITV companies would want to see it succeed: they would benefit from the advertising; they would want a share of its programming spending budget; they would want to use it as an outlet for their surplus ideas and as a means of employing their spare capacity. While, with his guaranteed income, the ITV2 Programme Controller would have the freedom to experiment without the financial pressure to chase the ratings. 'He would have the freedom of a BBC controller without the burden of that monolith's bureaucracy.'[41] To emphasise its separateness from ITV1, in a letter to Eden a few months after their original submission Birt and Elstein developed their conception of ITV2's institutional structure by positing an independent board of governors for the channel; all would be part-time, except for a half-time chairman. Day-to-day management would be left to a chief executive, to whom the programme controller would be responsible.

As we shall see in the next chapter, this compromise proposal between the ITV companies' claim for ITV2 and the demands for the National Television Foundation bears a remarkable resemblance to the structure of the Channel Four Television Company Ltd. It would be wrong, however, to suggest that this was the route by which Channel Four came to be. The Birt and Elstein submission to Sir John Eden was published in the trade magazine *Broadcast* and was favourably received by some, but many others criticised it for being too generous to the companies. During the debates over the next five years it did not figure prominently, for in its address to expediency it lacked the philosophical overview that kept the NTF scheme on the agenda of public discussion.

In contradiction to this, it should be pointed out that Elstein did succeed in winning the support of the Association of Directors and Producers, who presented a modified version of the 1973 Birt and Elstein proposals in their evidence to the Annan Committee (although by then far greater stress was put on the contribution that would be made by independent producers). He also went on to play a key role in the Channel Four Group, a pressure group that lobbied the Conservative Government on behalf of independent producers during 1979-80. Perhaps more important was the fact that the Birt and Elstein scheme helped some other ITV programme-makers to decide their views on the fourth channel. For instance, a few weeks after the two producers had submitted their plan to Sir John, the Controller of Features at Thames Television – Jeremy Isaacs – also sent a (confidential) submission to the Minister. His conclusions and recommendations coincided closely with those of Messrs Birt and Elstein. (This first, brief formulation by the future Chief Executive of Channel Four of what he – then – believed the structure and aims of the channel should be is reproduced as Appendix I.)

In the face of so much negative opinion the ITCA companies began to change their tune. In their submission to the Minister in 1973 they revealed that they were prepared to make concessions to win the fourth channel. Already in October 1972 Sir Hugh Greene, former Director-General of the BBC, had suggested in his Granada Guildhall Lecture that the National Television Foundation should be incorporated into the proposals for ITV2. The companies now agreed. If they were given responsibility to manage and finance the fourth channel, they would be willing to divest themselves of a significant proportion of air time and programme control to an 'Independent Production Board'. This would establish a Television Foundation that would encourage the production of all types of programming, including entertainment, but paying particular attention to the experimental. It was not made clear how much time the Independent Production Board would be offered, but it would include some peak viewing hours. There was also no statement about what the companies would guarantee to do with the rest of ITV2's time; planning and scheduling, however, would be conducted broadly under the existing arrangements for ITV1. One important aspect that was affirmed was that the companies would undertake to finance the

Independent Production Board, pledging to relate their contributions to the realistic costs of programme-making.

Sir Denis Forman, in particular, the Managing Director of Granada Television and the man who was to chair the ITCA committee which prepared the companies' evidence to the Annan Committee, had been most influential in encouraging his colleagues to see that it was in their interests to acknowledge the claims of independent, or would-be independent, programme-makers who wanted access to the medium. The ITCA proposals were intended to satisfy the needs of 'elements of our society who want access to the audience of television.'[42] But, with what they believed was the tide of public debate running in their favour, the supporters of the NTF scheme were not to be placated by this offer of a piece of the cake. Peter Fiddick, the *Guardian*'s broadcasting columnist, expressed the difficulty of conjoining the two philosophies.

That support should now come from the very bastions of the commercial system, the programme companies, must be a turn up for anybody's books. It will not, of course, be an idea that Anthony Smith himself will be likely to welcome, for like Sir Hugh's plot it represents a total watering-down of his third-force concept. The point of his NTF idea is that it should run an entire channel free from traditional pressures of scheduling and ingrained thinking about how programmes 'should' be made and when to show them. A limited number of hours within a channel that is by itself run in harness with ITV1 is by no stretching of words the same idea.[43]

The Annan Committee was to share the belief that the two proposals were mutually exclusive. At the risk of jumping the gun, it is worth noting that the Conservatives in 1979 were to disagree: coexistence might be impracticable, but integration they believed could be attempted.

The IBA also recognised the weight of opinion against its 1971 *ITV2* plan; in July 1973 it sent a supplementary submission to the Minister. It recognised five sets of objections to its proposals, and attempted to answer them.

1) *No public demand*

This the IBA thought was debatable. Demands were often not articulated for something that was still hypothetical. None of the three existing television services had been introduced primarily as a result of public demand. As for the claim that there was no public 'need', this could only be a value judgement and not an empirical question.

2) *ITV2 would mean more of the same*

Certainly ITV2 would be likely to resemble BBC2 more closely than BBC1. But, claimed the IBA, there was sufficient creative ability within the ITCA companies and amongst independent producers to ensure that ITV2 had a character of its own.

3) *There is a need for a third force*
The Authority was sceptical that a new organisation would escape the constraints that affected the existing two authorities. Broadcasting was 'privileged publishing' and therefore inevitably subject to limitations on its freedom. A new organisation that was not jointly planned to be complementary with ITV1 would necessarily compete with ITV, and BBC, for an audience. The IBA could only envisage two options: complementary or competition.

4) *The fourth channel should not be handed to the present companies*
The Authority repeated that the proposed Programme Planning Board would lead to the IBA having a greater role in the planning of the network schedules. It would ensure that there was greater national showing of programmes from the regional companies and from independent producers outside the company structure. 'In ITV2 the existing network programme providers would,' stated the IBA, 'play a *less prominent* part than they do in ITV1'[44] (author's emphasis).

5) *The Authority would not be able to fulfil its intentions*
The advertisers would not wish ITV2 to attract the same audience as already viewed ITV1; rather they would want a complementary service that provided an opportunity of reaching a new audience. Thus, the IBA maintained, there was no danger of ITV2 becoming another mass-appeal service, because commercial logic dictated otherwise. (Why the advertisers would be uninterested in reiterating their sales pitch by reaching the same audience twice was something the IBA failed to explain.)

In concluding, the IBA endorsed the ITCA suggestion that a place in ITV2 would be found for the National Television Foundation. It also suggested, in a significant move away from its earlier statements, that ITV2 might be less tied to ITV1:

It [the Authority] would now wish to allow a wider possibility than in *ITV2* for a second ITV channel to be separately financed and planned within the general pattern which was described in the previous submission . . . there are arguments for there being a single individual with responsibility for the ITV2 service, to carry out the day-to-day work of selecting material for it and to ensure it has a character of its own . . . The Authority's present view is that an arrangement could be made which would combine the benefits described in ITV2 of co-operation with the existing ITV service with the benefits of establishing for this new channel separate criteria and powers of decision.[45]

It was the first indication of an appreciation by the Authority that it would need to change its stance if it was to keep pace with an evolving public debate that was otherwise liable to run away from it.

One other submission to the Minister in 1973 that we should note came from the BBC. They made it clear that they had no aspirations to be given the fourth channel. Their concern derived from their belief that the delicate and subtle balance between public and commercial services would be upset by the allocation of a second channel to ITV:

> The present system depends on there being a rough balance of audience between the one ITV channel and the two BBC channels. Broadly speaking, 50 per cent of the audience watches the two BBC channels. It is this structure – lop-sided, sophisticated, and complex – which protects the rights of minority and majority audiences alike . . .
>
> With two channels competing against two channels, the BBC would necessarily have to intensify its competitive thrust to hold its share. In practice what this means is replacing minority programmes with popular programmes.[46]

The Corporation argued that any decision about allocation should be made as part of a general inquiry into the future of broadcasting. Substantial other claimants were emerging and their cases needed to be examined alongside that of ITV2. In February 1974, Sir Charles Curran, Director-General of the BBC, spelt out in a lecture at the Royal Institution who he believed those claimants to be: a Welsh-language service in Wales, and the Open University in the rest of the country. There was no case, Sir Charles said, somewhat tendentiously, for a fourth general television network. A Welsh-language service would not succeed, he argued, if the fourth network were used in the rest of the UK for a general service which Wales would not receive, for 'then the audience in Wales – and in this I would include even the most ardent Welsh speaker – would be very likely to turn their aerials to the English stations in order to receive that general service.'[47]

As the pile of submissions mounted on Sir John Eden's desk, the likelihood of an early decision on the fourth channel began to recede. In December 1973 the Government's emergency measures introduced in response to the miners' dispute (and which included a 10.30 p.m. shutdown of television) ushered in a period of political tension that culminated in the February 1974 General Election. Labour was unexpectedly returned to power. Within its first few weeks of office, the new Government had, in what was seen as a slightly surprising ordering of priorities, set up a Committee of Inquiry into the Future of Broadcasting. Lord Annan, whose eligibility for the job had been preserved by his non-involvement in the broadcasting debates of the previous four years, was once again chosen to be its chairman.

The OBA was born from an idea of Mr Tony Smith, who, I may say, is one of the few good academic experts on broadcasting. It was he who talked about setting up a foundation to run the fourth channel. Our Committee took that piece of dough and began to bake it. I do not think we got very far in the baking before we had to finish our report. The new fourth channel is really the same loaf, only now done to a turn. (Lord Annan, speaking in the House of Lords, July 1980)

In forming his Government Harold Wilson decided to dispense with the Ministry of Posts and Telecommunications, a post which he had created in 1969 to replace that of Postmaster-General. Instead, responsibility for broadcasting was transferred to the Home Secretary. The formation of broadcasting policy thus moved closer to the heart of Government, while conversely concern for its more mundane aspects were 'lost' on a busy Minister whose portfolio included such onerous matters as the police and the prison service. It also meant that Roy Jenkins had the job of choosing Lord Annan's companions for his two-and-a-half-year inquiry. This helped secure membership of the Annan Committee for Phillip White-head – whom Annan has described as having had a similar influence on his Committee to that of Richard Hoggart on Pilkington's[48] – for on the Home Secretary's own insistence Whitehead, one of Jenkins's loyalest supporters in the Commons, was appointed. This was done despite protestations from the Civil Service and Annan himself, who were both opposed to the idea of including any Members of Parliament, especially when the individual concerned had been a signatory to a document as controversial as *The People and the Media*. Annan explained in his 1981 Ulster Television Lecture that attempts to balance this situation with a Conservative MP failed when Sir Marcus Worsley, who had been asked to join the Committee, decided not to contest his seat in the second 1974 General Election. The other potential Conservative presence on the Committee, Sara Morrison, was also unable to provide an ear into the councils of the Opposition. For when Margaret Thatcher won her leadership fight against Edward Heath, Morrison, a Heathite, resigned her vice-chairmanship of the Conservative Party's Central Office. Annan was more successful in finding someone to counterbalance Whitehead's experience as a former broadcaster with intimate knowledge of the workings of both the BBC and an ITV company. In the face of the Home Office's declaration that an individual gainfully employed in the broadcasting industry could not possibly be a member of the Committee, Annan persuaded Jenkins to appoint Antony Jay. After the demise of JBM Ltd, Jay had formed in 1972 Video Arts Ltd, a successful production company operating at that time primarily in the industrial training film market. It was hoped that with his entrepreneurial background in broadcasting, Jay would approach matters from a different angle from that of Phillip Whitehead; although in the event, they were to agree on most of the key issues – they both, for instance, were part of the minority group on the Committee who wanted to split up the BBC.

Two other members of the Committee had some connection with broadcasting; Marghanita Laski was a novelist and a radio broadcaster, and Hilde Himmelweit, Professor of Social Psychology at LSE, had been Director of the Nuffield Television Survey between 1954 and 1958. Like Phillip Whitehead, she was also a member of SCOB. The remaining nine members consisted of two trade unionists, Tom Jackson, a former Governor of the BBC, and John Pollock; an urban affairs specialist, Dipak Nandy, who was appointed to safeguard the interests of ethnic minorities; a representative from industry, John Parkes from Unilever; a retired senior civil servant, Sir James McKay; a Welsh local government official, Dewi Lewis; the Director of the Consumers' Association, Peter Goldman; a former Labour Councillor, Hilda Lawrence; and an electronics professor from Southampton University, Geoffrey Sims. There was, however, no expert financier – a lack which Annan now agrees was to the Committee's great disadvantage. It was widely expected at the time that Anthony Smith would be included on the Committee, but apparently at the eleventh hour objections to his membership were voiced at a high political level. Nevertheless he was to be closely involved with the Committee's deliberations.

The Annan Committee began taking evidence in the Autumn of 1974. Within a year it had been saturated with over a thousand written submissions from various organisations and individuals, some of whom gave oral evidence as well. The contours of the British broadcasting landscape had changed greatly since the Pilkington Committee had attempted to map them. The report of the previous Committee of Inquiry, although its recommendations had not been implemented, had transformed the face of ITV; as the ITCA put it: 'Few would dispute that during those years ITV became more serious, more worthy and introduced many new programmes of quality.'[49] Presented in a single, well laid-out document, the crisp prose of the ITCA's evidence shone next to the BBC's smug presentation, a four-inch-high pile of wordy foolscap pamphlets packed with quotes from Shakespeare, Milton and Lord Hill. Moreover, the companies' main spokesman, Sir Denis Forman, impressed the Committee with his strong sense of public service broadcasting. The acknowledgment of ITV's performance was clearly manifest in Annan's final Report:

> In our view the [ITV] network does a good job in providing entertainment and excitement. What is more, the ITV companies now produce programmes which in prestige and intrinsic worth in a particular range are the equal of the BBC's output.[50]

At a time when the art of governance in Britain – the reconciliation of public interest with initiative, productivity and satisfaction in one's job – has fallen into some disrepute, the achievement and success of the British system of organising commercial broadcasting ought not to go unrecorded.[51]

But on the question of ITV expansion into a second channel, scepticism prevailed. The Committee found it hard to believe that an ITV2 would not be used principally as another weapon in the ratings battle. The ITCA had predicted that in a four channel situation the audience would divide ITV1: 33%, ITV2: 11%, BBC1: 24%, and BBC2: 6% of the total potential audience. Could one believe, Annan asked, that the BBC would be content with that division of the audience?

A second ITV service would confirm the duopoly and intensify competition between the BBC and ITV . . . Although ITV2 might begin by providing programmes for minorities, the result of intensified competition would be that fewer programmes for minorities would be provided both by ITV and by the BBC.[52]

We believe that to perpetuate the duopoly would be to stultify new initiatives and the formation of independent small production groups, which could bring fresh air into the system, and would help take the heat out of a number of controversies which rage today.[53]

Obviously the companies were to object. They pointed to what they saw as an inconsistency in the Report; on the one hand, 'the spur of competition between BBC and ITV' was 'an incentive to the production of good programmes',[54] while on the other hand the cut-throat fight for the audience was an anathema. No doubt the Annan Report was at times a little unclear in its analysis, but on this occasion it is obvious what it had in mind; 'the spur of competition' had produced programmes of excellence that attracted a mass audience and not a variety of minorities. It was notable that the Committee did not think that the IBA would be able to provide an effective check against popular scheduling on ITV2; in truth, there was a faction within the Committee hostile to the Authority, particularly with reference to its handling of the LWT affair, and it was a hostility that came through in the final Report.

It would be very misleading to suggest that the Committee's main preoccupation was with the fourth channel. The real question as far as it was concerned was whether the underlying concepts of British broadcasting practice should be preserved; in particular, the notion of a duality of broadcasting authorities independent of, but accountable to, Parliament. SCOB and the Labour Party's *The People and the Media* group were not alone in finding fault with the existing arrangements. Two separate strands of criticism, aimed mainly at the BBC, were voiced at that time. One was a diffuse public feeling, championed by Mary

Whitehouse's National Viewers' and Listeners' Association, that programme-makers were too permissive, and arrogant to boot. At the risk of being over-brief, one could say that the NVLA was essentially a backlash reaction to the BBC and ITV's own attempts to reflect the same restructuring of society into a plurality of groups that someone like Anthony Smith wanted the fourth channel to mirror more accurately. The NVLA supporters were incensed by the broadcasters' concessions to those who challenged traditional middle-class values and mores. The second strand was specific resentment by politicians on both sides of the House of what they believed was BBC arrogance; but what others saw as its independence. The *cause célèbre* was *Yesterday's Men*; a programme made in 1971 which had dealt mockingly with the Labour Party leadership in the aftermath of its 1970 electoral defeat.

Against this background the proposals for a Broadcasting Commission or its equivalent were taken seriously by the Annan Committee. At issue was a conflict between editorial independence and demands for greater public accountability. In the words of the NVLA: 'The sense of frustration and powerlessness which many people feel in relation to broadcasting must, in our view, be taken into account and remedied.'[55] In an important article responding to such sentiments, one member of the IBA, Mary Warnock, noted the ambiguity of the concept 'public accountability'. She argued that broadcasting authorities were *accountable* to Parliament, but *responsible* to the public – 'bearing in mind that this responsibility makes it highly desirable that its activities should be broadly intelligible and well-justified' – for the public had no power to exert sanctions against the authorities. To suggest that the public should have such powers of sanction was totally impracticable:

> In this context 'accountability' means the quite general duty to discuss every decision on equal terms with the receiving public. Accepting accountability in this sense would undoubtedly mean failing in responsibility. For the practical difficulties would be so vast that in the end no services would be provided at all.[56]

In their evidence to Annan SCOB conceded that Warnock's observations on sanctions were valid, but found her conclusions unacceptable:

> In this way, the accountability of public service is reduced before our eyes to a matter of reporting to a Parliament which will never want to interfere in the matters reported, and of a generalised responsibility to viewers and listeners vested in the ten appointed Members of the Authority.[57]

An immediate improvement in public accountability, they concluded, could be effected by the creation of machinery at central government level for the co-ordinated preparation of broadcasting policy within the context of telecommunications. Annan was not impressed:

The Standing Conference proposed that management in broadcasting – by which they meant not merely the BBC Governors and the IBA, but top management under the Director-General or under the Boards of Directors of the TV companies – should be abolished or hobbled. They went on to argue that if this was done the conflict between these two principles would somehow disappear. The argument was so transparently dishonest that it was easy to dismiss it as the politicisation of broadcasting by stealth.[58]

Two additional requisites of good broadcasting were postulated by the Annan Committee in order to combat the *dirigiste* proposals: flexibility and diversity:

By flexibility we meant the end of the BBC and IBA duopoly. We also meant that the competition which had been introduced by commercial broadcasting was good and should be extended. Indeed it was bound to be extended when new channels and transmission by satellites and by cable appeared in the not too distant future. By diversity we meant that the structure of broadcasting should resemble the pluralism of the life of the nation. We needed different types of broadcasting authorities.[59]

It was initially assumed by the rest of the Committee that Phillip Whitehead, given his earlier stands, would support the proposal for a single Broadcasting Commission. But by 1975, although he was still vociferously critical of the BBC, he was beginning to regret having signed *The People and the Media* pamphlet; he had never been totally convinced by its arguments but believed that the Labour Party would benefit from the internal discussion that such a document would generate. In December 1975, having largely finished taking evidence, the Annanites went to Churchill College, Cambridge, for a three-day private meeting where they would attempt to thrash out a skeleton plan upon which to build their final Report. Weighed down by four exhaustive discussion papers drawn up by their secretariat, their progress was productive but not rapid:

It was on the fourth paper that Phillip Whitehead made a pre-emptive strike. Instead of addressing himself to the daunting row of options before us, he produced a scheme of his own for the future structure of broadcasting. It left aside the question of a Broadcasting Council. What it did was suggest a multiplication of Authorities. The BBC and the IBA duopoly was to be broken, not once but three or four times. There was to be a separate Authority for the fourth channel, there was to be a local broadcasting Authority, there was to be a telecommunications Authority, the BBC was to be broken up into two corporations, one for television and another for radio, and local radio was to be taken from the IBA. Whitehead spoke only for ten minutes. He knew what he wanted. No-one else did. Daunted at the thought of wading through all those options in the last session of the weekend, the Committee decided to work on the Whitehead paper and see how it came out.[60]

Whitehead's plan that there should be a whole variety of institutions was an idea that had been argued by Anthony Smith, Jay Blumler and others in the minority papers submitted by the Standing Conference on Broadcasting to the Annan Committee. In a paper, 'The Accountability of British Broadcasting and its Structural Implications: A Pluralist Approach', the minority group within SCOB had suggested separate authorities should be established for the fourth channel, local radio, cable television, educational broadcasting, and technical transmission. Whitehead was clearly sympathetic to these views and was influenced by them in his speech at Cambridge.

The structural proposals contained in the Annan Committee's final Report came out remarkably like Whitehead's paper. The notion of separate authorities for the fourth channel and local radio was accepted. On the issue of carving up the BBC, however, there was major disagreement. Relying heavily on Tom Burns's analysis of BBC management, the Committee concluded that the Corporation was over-bureaucratic, and a substantial proportion of the Committee supported Whitehead's suggestion of splitting BBC Television from BBC Radio. But the majority believed harsh words and a few minor revisions were sufficient. The uncertain benefits of division were not thought to be worth the risks. In the final report, Whitehead's telecommunications authority became two bodies: the Public Enquiry Board for Broadcasting, and the Broadcasting Complaints Commission. The first was a non-executive, orbital body charged with holding seven-yearly inquiries on the performance of the authorities. It was an unhappy compromise between those on the Committee sympathetic to a policy-making Broadcasting Council, as opposed to an administrative Broadcasting Commission, and those who saw no need for such a supernumerary body, another tier of bureaucracy. The second body, the Complaints Commission, would be paid for by the broadcasting organisations, and would consider all complaints about invasion of privacy and other similar matters.

Such was the general outline of Annan's planned structure for broadcasting's future. It is, of course, the details of the authority for the fourth channel that we are most concerned with. The proposed authority was, in effect, the National Television Foundation, renamed the Open Broadcasting Authority. Smith's pluralist philosophy for the fourth channel was felt by Whitehead and the rest of the Annan Committee to be in keeping with their pluralist philosophy for the whole of broadcasting. In one important respect, however, Whitehead's OBA went further than Smith's NTF. For unlike its predecessor, whose distinctiveness would be assured by its freedom from the institutional pressures and assumptions of the BBC and ITV, the Annan Committee's fourth channel would also be free of the legal restraints imposed on the existing broadcasting authorities. As a publisher, recommended the Report, the OBA would not be required to take responsibility for the content of its programmes in the same way as the BBC and the IBA do. Its programmes would not have to be impartial, although, like a print publisher, the OBA would need to ensure that they were not obscene and did not incite crime, disorder or racial hatred. Like the other authorities, the OBA would have to see that an overall balance was achieved in its programmes over a period of time, but this would be done over a longer period and by 'new and less interventionist ways'. In short, the OBA would have the maximum freedom that Parliament was prepared to allow.

The aim of the channel would be 'to encourage productions which said something new in new ways.' Annan envisaged three programme sources: educational programmes, including those for the Open University which would be moved from BBC2 to the fourth channel; programmes made by the ITV companies, including ITN, and thus turning on its head the ITCA's 1973 proposal that it should be landlord and the NTF tenant; and, above all, from a variety of independent producers. 'We attach particular importance to this third category as a force for diversity and new ideas.' The range of programmes commissioned by the OBA from independent producers would stretch from a major theatrical production or sporting event to programmes made by a small group of people with the kind of ideas that would not be acceptable to the existing networks. No full news service was envisaged although it was thought that ITN might be able to expand its activities in some form on the channel. Annan was obviously aware that the ITV companies would not be over-excited about the concession of some programming time on the fourth channel:

> ITV who hoped to be given the whole loaf are likely to complain that their appetite for expansion is not likely to be satisfied by being thrown a crust. It is in fact a piece of rich cake that they are being offered; but we could hardly expect them to see it that way.[61]

In fact, there was an additional upset for the IBA in the OBA proposals. Because the IBA cogently argued it already had provided for transmission facilities for the fourth channel (and so ought to have ITV2), the Committee recommended that it should be given the engineering responsibility for transmission of the OBA's programmes, but without any power over their content.

The Annan Committee shared Anthony Smith's view that the fourth channel should have a variety of financial sources to match the variety of its programming. Annan estimated that between £25 and £40 million a year would be needed at 1977 prices. The Open University with its funding from the DES would have £3.5 million available for its programmes. The Arts Council, charities, the TUC, and the CBI were all suggested as other sources, but it must have always seemed unlikely that they would raise much revenue. Sponsorship by large firms seeking the same kind of publicity that support for sporting events and opera already provided was another possibility. The rest of the programmes would be funded by block advertising – longer length commercials in longer but fewer breaks – on the German model. But unlike the German model, the OBA would be competing in a market where spot advertising on ITV was already available. A majority of the Committee believed that if block advertising proved insufficient, the new channel should receive a government grant to sustain the novelty of its programmes. They were not prepared to pick up Smith's suggestion that a proportion of ITV's levy to the Exchequer should be directly appropriated by the NTF/OBA. Evidently they believed it would be too audacious to deny the companies ITV2 and at the same time require them to indirectly finance the approved alternative, the OBA. But in defence of a grant for the OBA, they pointed out that even ITV2 would cost the taxpayer money; for according to the ITCA's estimates, ITV2 would make a loss in its first three years at least, and there would therefore be a reduction in the levy paid by the ITV companies. Other Committee members rejected the proposal for a government grant. They did so for the same reasons of independence that the BBC had put forward to prevent its licence fee being replaced by direct grant income. But without a grant, they conceded, the OBA might need spot, as well as block, advertising.

Significantly, the Committee's funding arrangements for the OBA went against an earlier statement of principle in the Report:

> We recommend that, so far as possible, each Broadcasting Authority should have its own source or sources of revenue and should not have to compete with other Broadcasting Authorities for exactly the same sources of finance.[62]

It was a contradiction which was to be repeatedly emphasised by its critics when the Report was published. The fourth channel, they argued, could in the end only be financed out of advertising revenue or public funds, but each of these was already associated with one of the existing broadcasting institutions:

> The absence of additional sources of finance was the Achilles' heel of the Annan Report's thinking on pluralism. The Committee's reasoning was that intense competition reduces choice, that duopoly exhibited intense competition and that therefore new institutions would augment choice. However, neither for its LBA [the authority for local radio] nor its OBA did it propose any viable new source of funding – and the Report's reference to 'mixed' funding could not disguise this ... The OBA was open to the charge that it would have to rely on the direct

71

government grants which had been rejected as prejudicial to the independence of the BBC, or else find itself in direct competition with ITV for advertising revenue.[63]

The fact that Annan had been so determined to maintain the unity of his Committee and avoid a minority report goes a long way towards explaining the Report's failure to grapple with the inherent weakness of the OBA's financing. Annan had 'wasted a sizeable part of three years of my life'[64] on the Public Schools Commission which had been a very divided committee, and he did not want to repeat that experience. In his efforts to secure agreement there was a reluctance to face the awkward implications of what 'mixed' financing would lead to. Details of the new structure proposed by the Committee were, in fact, remarkably thin; in Annan's 500-page report, the section on the OBA occupied only seven pages.

On the timing of the OBA Annan was pessimistic. The economic climate at the time of the Report's publication was such that the Committee believed there was little possibility of any Government agreeing to authorise it in the near future. 'We therefore recommend that the fourth channel should not be allocated until the nation's economy will permit the kind of service which we have outlined. This may not be until the 1980s.'[65] Before then, however, it was thought that the fourth channel in Wales might precede the national service, for Annan supported the Crawford Committee's recommendation that a Welsh-language service should be introduced as soon as possible. The Annan Report was a little ambiguous about the status of the Welsh service – to start with it would be jointly operated by the BBC and IBA, but once the OBA had been established it would probably take over responsibility. Annan also wanted the OBA to provide some programmes adapted to the needs and interests of the people of Scotland and Northern Ireland.

The Annan Report was published in March 1977. Press reaction was lukewarm. An editorial in *The Times* called it 'a fair audit but a weak blueprint'; the Report had some pertinent comments to make on the state of British broadcasting but, the paper believed, it was doubtful whether its proposals for change would set the pattern for tomorrow. The *Guardian* said that 'At least the debate is switched on' and it was not surprisingly more enthusiastic towards the OBA. The *Sunday Times* noted that the fourth channel ranked low in national priorities and that any Government might reasonably find it hard to support the plan for the OBA. At the same time as the Report was published the Home Secretary initiated a period of public debate; all responses to the Committee's Report were to be submitted to the Home Office by 1 July 1977.

During the post-Annan debate four major sources of resistance to the proposals for the OBA could be distinguised: the ITV companies and the IBA; the ACTT and some of the other broadcasting unions; the Conservative Party; and the Home Office and the Treasury. Despite this formidable array of opposition, the Labour Government in July 1978 published a White Paper, sixteen months after the Annan Committee had reported, which endorsed the Committee's scheme for the use of the fourth channel. The reason for the OBA's victory in Cabinet can be attributed to a combination of effective lobbying by a small group of Labour MPs and, more importantly, the sympathetic hearing it received from a number of key ministers, including the Prime Minister.

Given its terms of reference the Annan Committee was a potential threat to the continued existence of ITV; the IBA and the ITCA had therefore been on the defensive in their evidence to the Committee. After March 1977, following the Report's praise for much of ITV's output and with the proposals for the OBA before them, they switched to the offensive. In their comments on the Committee's Report to the Home Secretary, they both argued that all the programming claims made for the OBA could be matched and exceeded by ITV2. Programming for minorities, suggested the ITCA, was far more likely to succeed with the fourth channel under the ITV umbrella, for 'with a two channel service, what matters in financial terms is not the size of either audience, but the combined total. If the channels are not financially competitive there is no need to achieve high ratings on both simultaneously.'[66] For the OBA to escape being a heavy burden on public funds, it would have to compete for revenue with ITV 'in a manner far more harmful to good programming than any competition between ITV and BBC.'[67] The IBA revealed, in their third formulation of the structure of ITV2 in six years, that the idea of the Programming Planning Board was now firmly dead. They talked of a separate planning group for the fourth channel, comprising representatives from the network and regional companies together with educational contributors and independent producers. This group, through a single full-time executive, would be responsible for scheduling ITV2; 40% of whose programmes would come from the Big Five, 10-15% from the regionals, 10-15% from ITN and sport, 10-15% from educational contributors, and 15% from independents.[68] Once again the Authority had shifted its position, toward an ITV2 which although still clearly complementary with ITV1 was more independent of it in programming terms than had been previously suggested.

The companies, on the other hand, maintained their 1973 view that the existing Network Planning Committee for ITV1 should be responsible for planning ITV2, while an Independent Production Board would be given a fixed portion of time to use as they saw fit. A draft programme schedule that the ITCA published as part of their response to Annan suggested six hours of independent programming out of a total 40-hour ITV2 week. It is interesting to compare this 1977 proposed ITV2 schedule with the one outlined by the ITV Programme Controllers in 1971, for apart from the presence of independent programming there were a number of significant changes. The two fifteen minute news bulletins at the beginning and end of the day had been replaced by a five minute bulletin in the early evening and a half-hour of news and comment in depth at 10.30p.m., designed to supplement ITV1's *News at Ten*. There were to be no American film series, and half an hour instead of two-and-a-half hours of comedy. There were to be less repeats of ITV1 programmes on ITV2, although three prestige programmes from ITV1 — *Weekend World, Aquarius* and *University Challenge* — would be lost to the second channel. And finally, there were to be more generally educational programmes, including a daily programme called *Indoors Outdoors* about the technology and practicabilities of everyday life, covering such diverse subjects as 'Provençal cooking, further education in the home, keeping pigeons, and how to choose and plant a rose.'(!)[69]

One point that the ITV companies were particularly angry about was Annan's proposal that the OBA should use ITV facilities and screen a large number of ITV-produced programmes. Paul Fox, by now Managing Director of Yorkshire Television, expressed this most forcefully in a letter to the *Listener*:

> In addition to the privilege of paying the Exchequer a levy of more than £60 million a year, we are now being asked to make programmes for our competitor. It is like asking the proprietor of the *Daily Telegraph* to provide a significant part of a new and worthy Fleet Street daily. We are a programme company — not a facility company for other people's programmes.
>
> Of course, we have the capacity, the ability and, indeed, the will to make more programmes. This is the basis of our case for ITV2. But to hand them over to a competitive service to be scheduled by a London-based bureaucrat who has not been involved in the making of the programmes and who will simply add it to the rest of the OBA ragbag is presuming a little too much on our goodwill.[70]

The fact that Annan did not visualise the OBA becoming operative in the near future was picked up by the ITV companies, and used to win support for ITV2 within the broadcasting industry. In their comments to the Home Secretary they wondered how long the industry would have to wait:

> In his Fleming Memorial Lecture delivered in April Lord Annan acknowleged that no fourth channel is possible without ITV, but the frustrations of the many talented people in ITV are not likely to be

assuaged by a promise of some allocation of time among the patchwork of a channel which may or may not be on the air in the 1980s; nor will the frustrations of the many workers in ITV who are looking for advancement and new opportunities in an expanding industry. The proposed OBA is jam on a tomorrow which may never come. What is to happen in the meantime? ITV2, if sanctioned now, will quickly create many new jobs as well as many new opportunities on the screen for ITV's existing programme-makers.[71]

This was a message received loud and clear by the broadcasting unions, in particular the ACTT. Although prone to exclaiming radical rhetoric, the ACTT is, in practice, a passionately conservative union with regard to maintaining and improving its members' conditions of employment; and in the case of those permanently employed these conditions tend to be, in relation to other industries, quite favourable. Despite Caroline Heller's 1971 report on the fourth channel, there had always been much support for ITV2 at the shop-floor level of the ACTT Television Branch, considering the job opportunities it was thought likely to create. (The Television Freelance, the Film Production, and the Laboratory Branches were, however, less convinced.) In June 1977, without prior consultation with the full membership, an *ad hoc* meeting of the ACTT's Executive Committee and Inter-Branch Liaison Committee formally declared its opposition to the 'de-stabilising' OBA proposals.[72] The fourth channel, it felt, should not in any circumstances compete for advertising revenue with the existing ITV channel; it would lower advertising rates and the industry would become more susceptible to cyclical fluctuations in total advertising expenditure. Standards and opportunities, believed the union, were a function of resources available. The ITV companies possessed the resources — staff, studios, expertise and revenue — to underpin the development of a new channel. 'Crucial safeguards' aimed at protecting security of employment, but with little reference to programming policy, were put forward as necessary conditions for any scheme for use of the fourth channel. An OBA without such safeguards, claimed Alan Sapper, the ACTT's General Secretary, would have to face the opposition of the total industrial strength of his union.[73] Equity, the actors' union, also threatened to boycott the new channel while its financial base remained so insecure, and in November 1978 the Federation of Broadcasting Unions expressed their criticisms of the (by then) Governmental support for the OBA. The Government's White Paper, they noted, had made no reference to industrial relations and had taken no account of the views and aspirations of broadcasting workers.[74]

The ACTT's cautious attitude towards the OBA largely represented the interests of those members of the union permanently employed by ITV. The freelance members and would-be independents had a different perception of the situation. In April 1978 at a meeting in the Churchill

75

Hotel, London, the 'Channel Four Group' was formed to lobby the Labour Government to adopt the Annan Committee's proposals for the fourth channel. Iain Bruce, a producer at Allan' King Associates, agreed to be the Group's organiser. There was a significant overlap in membership with the two previous pressure groups, the 76 Group and the TV4 Campaign. Since the early 1970s, however, the independent production sector had developed. Both the overseas and the industrial training film market had expanded, while the derestriction of broadcasting hours and the ever-growing emphasis placed on the television medium by advertisers had increased the number of production companies making advertising commercials. A survey in *Broadcast* in 1979 listed over four hundred companies, but as the magazine noted, independence in production involves a wide range of different structures, definitions, past achievements and future aspirations.[75] In addition to commercials and industrial film production companies, many animators were included. Some of the largest companies — e.g. the Robert Stigwood Organisation, Global Television, London Films, Video Arts — had financial connections with, or had broken into, the American market. A few of the independents listed were merely subsidiaries of certain ITV companies – e.g. Euston Films (Thames Television), Black Lion Films (ATV), Survival (Anglia). On the Channel Four Group's Steering Committee three organisations were represented: i) the Association of Directors and Producers, which comprised a large proportion of the freelance producers and directors who worked for the BBC and/or the ITV companies; ii) the Association of Independent Producers, a group of film-makers who had broken away from the more established British Film Producers Association; and iii) the Independent Film-makers Association, which supported the interests of non-commercial film-makers working outside the mainstream film industry, often financially assisted by the British Film Institute or the Arts Council. All three were concerned to prevent the ITV companies from dominating the programming of the fourth channel. They were not a major factor in bringing about the Labour Government's decision to support the OBA, but we should nevertheless note their existence now, in order to appreciate that the ACTT policy did not represent the opinion of all television and film industry workers. As we shall see, they were more effective during 1979, the first year of the Conservative Government.

The most significant opponent of the OBA was the Conservative Party. Julian Critchley, Chairman of the Party's Media Committee, promptly dismissed Annan's plans within its first week of publication. In the *Daily Telegraph* he called the OBA a 'dog's breakfast', and in the *Listener* he wrote the following:

No one should be surprised at the Conservative Party's support for ITV2, that is, the fourth channel being given to the existing companies

... It is wrong to deny the fourth channel to ITV. A complementary service to ITV could be swiftly introduced, would cost the Exchequer little, and then nothing, and while providing *a corner* for 'minority programmes', *would give the public more of what it wants.* ITV should be on all fours with the BBC.[76] (author's emphasis)

But although he claimed to express the mainstream policy of his Party, it was to become increasingly clear that many Conservatives, including the Shadow Home Secretary, William Whitelaw, did not share Critchley's whole-hearted support of the ITCA's intentions for the fourth channel. In Parliament and elsewhere, Whitelaw noted Annan's intentions to provide a different kind of television catering for minority interests and providing greater opportunities for independent producers. The thinking behind the OBA was, he said, original and imaginative, but he criticised the scheme on financial grounds. He had misgivings about commercial sponsorship; he believed there was a political danger in programmes being provided by organisations such as the TUC and the CBI; he doubted whether educational bodies would provide a source of funding, since the national education budget was already strained; block advertising was unattractive; and above all he did not think a major increase in public expenditure could be justified to finance the OBA at a time when public services in general were feeling the constraint of limited resources. In addition, Conservative enthusiasm to prune the number of quasi-autonomous non-governmental organisations (quangos) meant that Annan's proposal to establish a new authority was unlikely to be favourably received. The most preferable option, Whitelaw argued, was to entrust the responsibility for the fourth channel to the IBA:

I believe – and I am sure that the hon. Member for Derby North [Phillip Whitehead] recognises this – that the proposed new authority would be extremely reliant on the IBA and the ITV companies for many of the necessary transmission and technical services. It would therefore seem sensible to start the other way around, by giving the fourth channel to the IBA and ITV companies, which can immediately provide the necessary equipment and skills, but on conditions that would meet the [Annan] Committee's main purpose.[77]

The precise shape that Whitelaw believed an IBA-regulated fourth channel should take is something we shall examine later.

The advertisers and the advertising agencies anticipated that the Conservatives, as the Party declaredly representative of the interest of free enterprise, would look favourably upon their requests for a fourth channel that sold advertising space in competition with ITV. Despite very serious reservations about block advertising and minority programming, the ISBA and the IPA welcomed Annan's proposals for the OBA as an additional seller of advertising time, in preference to an ITV2 which would extend the existing contractors' monopoly. The Director of the ISBA, Gilbert Lamb, predicted that the OBA would prove to be financially viable:

We find it amazing that the Conservative Party, the champions of free enterprise and competition, should apparently favour giving the fourth channel to the ITV companies. They talk about denationalisation and that sort of thing, but here is nothing more than an extension of existing monopoly. As the people who pay, we believe we have a right to more consideration than we are given in this Report or in the Debate since its publication.

We believe the OBA proposal would be viable. We believe it should be given a chance. We believe there is sufficient advertising money available for it to start sooner rather than later, and of course it would have to start slowly and build up as did commercial radio.[78]

Thus what was seen by both opponents and many supporters of the OBA as its fundamental weakness – i.e. in order to avoid relying on government funding it would have to compete with ITV for advertising revenue – was for the advertisers its primary attraction. They recognised, however, that as it was presently conceived by Annan with minority appeal programming, it would not provide mass consumer advertisers with any real competitive alternative to ITV. But there was always the possibility, they hoped, that in practice popular programming would have to be introduced in order to attract advertising. In their comments on the Report to the Home Secretary, the IPA argued that block advertising was unacceptable; longer commercials would cost more to produce and there would be considerable fall-off in audience attention during the longer breaks.

There was some acknowledgment of the advertisers' case within the Conservative Party, but Whitelaw was above all concerned with maintaining traditional broadcasting standards; which for him meant that he was not prepared to take any risk which might lead to British broadcasting descending the slippery slope towards the bogey of competitive American commercial television. As we shall see later, he was to reject firmly the advertisers' lobby.

But it was the cold water poured on the OBA by the Home Office and the Treasury that was potentially the most effective check on a Labour Government endorsement of Annan's plans. In 1976 Merlyn Rees had replaced Roy Jenkins as Home Secretary. Rees, however, was not involved in the initial drafting of the Government's White Paper; it was undertaken by Lord Harris, who since 1974 had been the Minister of State in the Home Office responsible for broadcasting. Together with the Home Office civil servants, Harris, who was later to become the Chairman of Westward Television shortly before it lost its franchise, favoured an extension of the existing ITV network. Their objections to the OBA were similar to those voiced by the Conservatives. Two plans were drawn up by the Home Office: the first was essentially the ITCA's proposals, with the fourth channel run by the companies; the second was the revised IBA scheme which featured some form of new planning committee for the channel that would not solely represent the interests of the ITV companies.

Details of the Home Office draft were leaked and in opposition a small group of Labour MP including Phillip Whitehead and Hugh Jenkins, the former Arts Minister, began lobbying a number of senior Ministers. In January 1978 James Callaghan made it clear, just before he left for his tour of India, that 'an anti-White Paper White Paper' would be welcomed.[79] Whether Callaghan was persuaded of the need for a new Authority for the fourth channel because of the merits of the argument, or more because it would be a relatively easy concession to the left wing of the Party at a time when such concessions were few and far between, is difficult to determine. What is clear is that when Rees presented the Home Office draft to Cabinet he was challenged by a wide cross-section of the Cabinet, including Shirley Williams, Roy Hattersley, Tony Benn and William Rodgers. A high-powered Cabinet sub-committee with Callaghan in the chair was set up to re-draft the White Paper. Despite the strenuous efforts of Joel Barnett, the Chief Secretary to the Treasury, who was worried about the effect that government funding of the fourth channel would have on the Public Sector Borrowing Requirement, the OBA was pushed through. Two other new statutory bodies recommended by the Annan Committee, the authority for local radio and the Public Enquiry Board for Broadcasting, were not, however, resuscitated by the Cabinet sub-committee. The BBC and the IBA were allowed to keep local radio and the PEBB was thought to be unnecessary; although the broadcasting authorities would, in future, be required to conduct their own occasional public hearings. The Broadcasting Complaints Commission did survive. Current arguments against bureaucracy, believed Phillip Whitehead, were the main objections to the new bodies:

> Let us look at the White Paper. It is really two documents, one overlaid on the other, like successive Sumerian cities. Patient excavation shows us what the earlier document was like. The further into the White Paper you go, the more paragraphs remain almost untouched from that early, pre-OBA, draft which was the civil servants' response to the challenge of the age . . .

> There were many supporters of the Annan package in the Cabinet Committee which re-drafted the White Paper between January and June this year. On the crucial issue of the OBA they won the battle at least in the sense that at nightfall they were still in possession of the field. Some other battles were lost. In an election year the Government is sensitive to the charge that it is creating a new quangocracy.[80]

Unlike the Annan Committee, the Government wanted the OBA to be bound by the same programming obligations common to the BBC and IBA:

The concept of a broadcasting authority requires that the authority should be responsible for the service it provides, and that the service should conform with certain basic requirements, for example that due impartiality is preserved in the treatment of controversial matters, and that nothing should be broadcast which incites to crime or is offensive to public feeling.[81]

The distinction from Annan was expressed by the operative words 'due impartiality'. Only the requirement to secure a 'proper balance' in terms of the variety and range of subject matter would not apply to the OBA; for it was conceded that a bias towards educational, minority and ethnic interests was a necessary part of the OBA concept. With regard to funding the channel, the Government pledged initial financial assistance, but it did not make clear how long such subventions might need to last. Spot advertising, however, would definitely be included as a major source of revenue. On all other matters relating to the fourth channel the White Paper was at one with the Annan Committee's Report.

It would be wrong to see the 1978 White Paper as an irrelevant gesture by a dying 'lame duck' government with little over nine months left to run. The National Television Foundation had come a long way in the six years since it had first been proposed in an article in the *Guardian*. Anthony Smith had always boldly claimed it was an idea whose time had come and would simply have to be accepted. To receive governmental endorsement, albeit from an administration that was to be shortly replaced by one with a radically different philosophy, was to give it a legitimacy that would make it politically very difficult for the incoming government to ditch it entirely. As it was, the Conservatives did not in fact want to abandon it completely; we have already noted that William Whitelaw had many words of praise for Annan's broad intentions for the fourth channel.

In April 1979 a Broadcasting Bill introduced by the Labour Government became law. It was not, however, the major legislation that some Labour politicians wanted the Government to put before the House prior to the General Election. It was simply designed to allow the IBA to spend up to £28 million on the construction of a new network of UHF stations which would be available for a fourth national television service. The Government shared Annan's view that whoever had responsibility for the channel's programming, the IBA should organise the transmission of its programmes. Broadcasting's empty room was thus more than ever ready to receive an occupant. One of the first jobs for the new Government would be to settle the question of who it should be.

80

Notes

1. Cited by Jackson, M., 'Independence for producers on the fourth channel', *Television: Journal of the Royal Television Society*, Volume 18, Number 2, March/April 1980, p. 7.
2. Anthony Smith (personal communication).
3. Nupen, C., 'Inside Outside', *Edinburgh International Television Festival 1979 – Official Programme*, 1979.
4. Burns, T., *The BBC: Public Institution and Private World* (London: Macmillan, 1977), p. 256.
5. Unpublished supplementary paper to 76 Group manifesto, presented to a meeting in the House of Commons, 17 March 1970.
6. 'The Producer and His Relationship to Management', unpublished 76 Group paper, p. 10.
7. 'Declining Standards of BBC Television', unpublished 76 Group paper, p. 5.
8. *Guardian*, 17 March 1970.
9. Hansard, *House of Commons Debates*, 3 December 1969, col. 1511.
10. Rhys, T., Reply by the Federation of Broadcasting Unions to Brian Young's open letter, reproduced in ACTT Television Commission, *TV4: A Report on the Allocation of the 4th Channel* (London: ACTT, 1971), Appendix 5.
11. *The Times*, 14 October 1971.
12. *Sunday Times*, 17 October 1971.
13. ACTT Television Commission Report, pp. 18-21.
14. Motion for an Early Day No. 88, 2 December 1971, reproduced in *Opportunities for the Fourth Channel*, A memorandum presented to the Minister of Posts and Telecommunications by the TV4 Campaign, 10 December 1971.
15. 'ITA plan for second channel to be used by existing companies is called "arrogant" ', *The Times*, 9 December 1971.
16. 'The National Television Foundation – a plan for the fourth channel', Evidence to the Annan Committee on the Future of Broadcasting, December 1974, presented by Anthony Smith, reproduced in Smith, A., *The Shadow in the Cave: A study of the relationship between the broadcaster, his audience, and the state* (London: Quartet Books, 1976), Appendix II, pp. 293-4.
17. Ibid., p. 296.
18. Smith A., 'The Open Broadcasting Authority and the Fourth Channel Debate', *Educational Broadcasting International*, December 1977, p. 163.
19. Ibid., p. 162.
20. *Guardian*, 21 April 1972.
21. Smith, *The Shadow in the Cave*, p. 291
22. *Observer*, 29 July 1973.
23. 'Fourth channel for education', *Times Higher Education Supplement*, 27 July 1973.
24. Halloran, J.D., et al., 'Research Findings on Broadcasting', *Report of the Committee on the Future of Broadcasting: Appendices E-I, Research Papers Commissioned by the Committee* (HMSO, 1977), Cmnd 6753-I, pp. 69-73.
25. *Report of the Committee on Broadcasting Coverage* (Crawford Report) (HMSO, 1974), Cmnd 5774, para. 75.
26. *Television 76: The ISBA/IPA View* (London: ISBA/IPA, 1972), pp. 6-7.
27. *Second Report from the Select Committee on Nationalised Industries, Session 1971-72. Observations by the Minister of Posts and Telecommunications and the Independent Broadcasting Authority* (HMSO, 1973), Cmnd 5244.
28. *Television 76 + : The ISBA/IPA Proposals for the Allocation of the Fourth Channel in 1976* (London: ISPA/IPA, 1973).
29. *Second Report from the Select Committee on Nationalised Industries, Session 1971-72*, Committee B (HMSO, 1972), House of Commons paper 465, para. 145.

30. Ibid., para. 171.27.
31. *Guardian*, 17 August 1973.
32. Annan, Lord, *The Politics of a Broadcasting Enquiry*, The 1981 Ulster Television Lecture delivered at the Queen's University, Belfast, 29 May 1981 (Ulster Television, 1981), p. 9.
33. Ibid
34. *The People and the Media* (London: Labour Party, 1974), p. 15.
35. Starks, M., 'Government Review of Broadcasting 1974-81: Outcome and Expectations', *Political Quarterly*, Volume 52 Number 4, October-December 1981, pp. 467-481.
36. *Guardian*, 18 August 1973.
37. Unpublished letter from John Birt and David Elstein to Sir John Eden, the Minister of Posts and Telecommunications, 25 September 1973.
38. Elstein, D., 'Can a dual-channel ITV work without a clash of interests?', *Adweek*, 8 June 1973.
39. Birt, J., & Elstein, D., 'The Fourth Television Channel', A submission to the Minister of Posts and Telecommunications, May 1973, p. 5.
40. Ibid., p. 12.
41. Ibid., p. 11.
42. *The Fourth Channel: Proposals by the Independent Television Companies*, 27 July 1973.
43. *Guardian*, 13 August 1973.
44. *ITV2: Further submission from the IBA to the Minister of Posts and Telecommunications*, July 1973, p. 4.
45. Ibid., p. 7.
46. 'The Fourth Television Channel: The BBC's Memorandum', *BBC Record 87* (London: BBC, August 1973), pp. 3-4.
47. Curran, Sir C., *The Fourth Television Network: A Question of Priorities*, a lecture given by the Director-General of the BBC at the Royal Institution, 1 February 1974 (London: BBC, 1974), p. 17.
48. Annan, Ulster Television Lecture, p. 17.
49. Independent Television Companies Association, *ITV Evidence to the Annan Committee*, March 1975, p. 13.
50. *Report of the Committee on the Future of Broadcasting* (Annan Report), (HMSO, 1977), Cmnd 6753, para. 11.7.
51. Ibid., para. 13.46.
52. Ibid., para. 11.27.
53. Ibid., para. 15.32.
54. Ibid., para. 4.3.
55. Cited in Annan *Report*, para. 4.10.
56. Warnock M., 'Accountability or Responsibility – or Both?', *Independent Broadcasting*, Number 2, November 1974, p. 3.
57. Standing Conference on Broadcasting, *Evidence to the Committee on the Future of Broadcasting* (London, January 1976), pp. 44-55.
58. Annan, Ulster Television Lecture, p. 12.
59. Ibid.
60. Ibid., p. 13.
61. Annan *Report*, para. 15.32.
62. Ibid., para. 7.6.
63. Starks, op.cit., p. 480.
64. Annan, Ulster Television Lecture, p. 11.
65. Annan *Report*, para. 15.30.
66. Independent Television Companies Association, *The Annan Report: An ITV view*, June 1977, p. 22.
67. Ibid., p. 20.

82

68. 'The Annan Report: The Authority's Comments', *Independent Broadcasting,* Number 12, July 1977, p. 17.
69. ITCA response to Annan, op.cit., p. 22.
70. Fox, P., 'The misbegotten fourth child', *Listener,* 17 August 1978, p. 207.
71. ITCA response to Annan, op.cit., p. 23.
72. See *The fourth television channel,* A paper produced by ACTT members in consultation with the Channel Four Group, 10 May 1979.
73. Sapper, A., speaking on LWT's *Look Here,* broadcast 4 February 1979, cited in *ADP Newsletter,* Issue 13, March 1979.
74. *Film and Television Technician,* December 1978, p. 1.
75. *Broadcast,* 1 October 1979.
76. Critchley, J., 'Good prose, bad thinking', *Listener,* 31 March 1977, pp. 397-8.
77. Hansard, *House of Commons Debates,* 31 March 1977, col. 1037.
78. Lamb, G., speaking at *The Annan Debate: A Conference for Practitioners,* edited transcript of proceedings (London: British Academy of Film and Television Arts, June 1977), p. 2.
79. *Scotsman,* 26 July 1978.
80. Whitehead, P., 'Television's Long March to Pluralism', *Television: Journal of the Royal Television Society,* Volume 17, Number 5, September/October 1978, p. 11.
81. *Broadcasting* (HMSO, 1978), Cmnd 7294, para. 16.

3 Compromise: The Channel Four Television Company Ltd

The British electorate voted on 3 May 1979. Twelve days later in the Queen's Speech Mrs Thatcher's incoming Government briefly stated its intentions for the fourth channel:

> Proposals will be brought before you for the future of broadcasting. A Bill will be introduced to extend the life of the Independent Broadcasting Authority, which will be given responsibility – subject to strict safeguards – for the fourth television channel. [1]

The OBA was dead. There was to be no new regulatory authority. The major questions, however, remained unresolved; for what was primarily at issue was the structure of the channel's editorial controlling body. Between May 1979 and the publication of the Broadcasting Bill in February 1980, the Home Office sought to determine the content of the 'strict safeguards'. Throughout those crucial nine months the interested parties which had been battling it out over the previous decade impressed upon the Government their views of what an IBA-regulated fourth channel could and should look like. Remarkably, when the legislation finally appeared it received a guarded welcome from all except the advertisers and the Welsh. 'A typically British approach to this new problem' was the conclusion of the 1952 White Paper which had spelt out the arrangements for ITV; perhaps the same could be said of the arrangements for the fourth channel? The Broadcasting Act received Royal Assent in November 1980; insistent Welsh protests had brought about one major change to the Bill during its passage through Parliament – the Welsh were after all to be given a separate service. In December 1980 the Channel Four Television Company Ltd was incorporated as a private company with its own Board of Directors, and on New Year's Day 1981 it became operational.

CAMBRIDGE PHILOSOPHY

The gap between the IBA's intentions for the fourth channel and those of the ITV companies grew significantly wider during 1979. As we have already noted, the Authority in its response to the Annan Committee had substantially revised its earlier plans. Increasingly, the IBA was persuaded that to allow the Big Five to dominate ITV2 was both undesirable and politically unacceptable. Ten years of Annan-style criticism of the original ITV2 proposals had had its effect. Moreover, by the late 1970s the Authority was a somewhat different animal from what it had been at the beginning of the decade, and certainly from what it had been in the early years of ITV. The introduction of independent local radio had diversified the Authority's charge and had been a turning point in distancing the IBA from the companies. Another factor was changes in personnel; for instance, in 1977 Bernard Sendall, one of the few remaining senior executives who had been on the Authority's staff since its inception, was succeeded as Director of Television by Colin Shaw. Former Chief Secretary of the BBC, Shaw had written and edited the BBC's evidence to the Annan Committee, including the last set of papers dealing with the fourth channel in which the BBC announced its conversion to the OBA in a slightly modified form. It was a scheme for 'open' television that married elements of Anthony Smith's NTF plan with the Corporation's long-standing desire to see a separate channel on which it could place some of the programmes it made for special minority interests, such as Welsh-language and Open University programmes. At the IBA, Shaw was to be the person principally responsible for drafting the Authority's final proposals for the fourth channel; a compromise between the IBA's earlier statements and the ideals of the OBA.

Following the Queen's Speech, there was a mixture of great relief at the IBA's headquarters in Brompton Road together with a determination to demonstrate that the Authority was now very much the senior partner in its relationship with the companies; its views about the channel and not the companies' would prevail. Anticipating the Authority's proposals, Peter Fiddick explained the situation:

It is already clear that the IBA's existing position, as represented by the scheme it proposed to Annan and the Labour Government, has become outdated in some areas and was always too vague to be classed as a blueprint in others. The thinking on how independent producers might be integrated into the fourth channel has already been acknowledged by the IBA's Director of Television, Colin Shaw, as one area in which the old ideas no longer fit the bill. More generally, although the Authority came to recognise the need to separate somewhat the decision-making mechanisms of the two channels it would be supervising, quite how to do this has remained one of those discomforting problems whose natural place is a pending tray. [2]

In June 1979, Colin Shaw confirmed that the companies would have a substantial share of the fourth channel's programming. But it would be intolerable, he said, if the Big Five were seen to be in total control. He added: 'It is reasonable that he who pays the piper should have the right to call at least half the tune, so we have to find a way to let them have their proper share of control of the fourth channel, without letting them take over.'[3] Shaw went on to reveal he was sceptical about the ability of independent producers to keep the screens alight for many hours with a regular provision of programmes. He distinguished between the (relatively few) independent production companies, whose instincts were often as resolutely commercial as that of any ITV company, and the (more numerous) individual producers, who tended to be primarily interested in the major programmes – the striking play or the significant documentary. 'No television service,' he believed, 'could live exclusively on a diet of that kind.'[4]

Throughout the 1979-80 planning period the ITV companies were in a weak position to object to the Authority's plans for the channel. Franchise renewals were pending; for following the extension of the IBA's Licence to the end of 1981, the Authority had prolonged the contracts of all fifteen companies to the same date. At the beginning of 1980 the IBA invited applications from anyone who wished to bid for the new contracts starting in January 1982. The hands of the incumbent contractors were thus partially tied by their obvious reluctance to upset the Authority in any way. As we shall see later, their one concerted attempt to persuade the IBA to structure ITV2 along lines they believed were preferable received short shrift.

The freelance 'and independent producers, on the other hand, were free to throw their full energies into lobbying the IBA, the Home Office and Conservative politicians. Their first success came in the same month as the Conservatives' victory at the polls. In a well co-ordinated action the Channel Four Group overturned the ACTT's policy on the fourth channel during the union's 1979 annual conference. The leading instigators were David Elstein, who had been chosen as the ADP's representative on the Channel Four Group's Steering Committee, and Iain Bruce, the Group's organiser. In the light of the Queen's Speech, three motions supporting the idea of the OBA were dropped and replaced on the morning of the conference by an emergency motion. After stressing the need to safeguard existing jobs, the motion read as follows:

> Conference urges the creation of a new organisation under the IBA, which would operate the fourth channel and would draw the majority of its programmes from a variety of British independent production sources other than the existing ITCA companies.
>
> It shall be one of the IBA's duties to see that the new channel is funded in a manner that does not jeopardise the existing structure of ITV. It shall also be the IBA's duty in the public interest to ensure that the new channel is neither controlled nor dominated by the present ITCA companies.[5]

On moving the motion, Elstein challenged the assumption that an ITV2 dominated by the companies would mean many more jobs. He noted that the ITV companies themselves had estimated a figure of only a thousand new jobs, of which less than half would qualify for ACTT membership:

The smallness of that figure is not surprising. The whole point of the ITV companies' clamour for the fourth channel has been to maximize the return on the capital invested in their studio hardware – not by increasing jobs, but by raising productivity and introducing new technology.

Commonsense dictates that by looking outside the existing contractors for most of channel four's programmes far more new jobs are bound to be created, either in existing facilities companies, or in new production houses set up to ACTT standards to meet the new demand for programmes.[6]

But what was at stake, Elstein claimed, was not just jobs but the question of free expression in society. Supporting the motion, Iain Bruce complained about the manner in which the union's existing policy had been decided without the prior consultation of the full membership. The Television Branch objected. Existing policy, argued the Branch's secretary, Dennis Sippings, had developed out of the ACTT's evidence to Annan and the Select Committee on Nationalised Industries. Basing the fourth channel on the expertise of the ITV companies, he believed, was the best way to provide a viable channel with stable employment for ACTT members. It had long been apparent that there was a fundamental clash of interests between ITV's permanent staff on the one hand, and the union's freelance television members and the Film Production Branch on the other. This was amply borne out by the heated Conference debate on the subject. The film-processing laboratories, a marginal constituency without an obvious preference in either direction, were placed in a key position to influence the union's overall policy. The Channel Four Group strove hard to convince them that an ITV2 dominated by the companies would increase the proportion of television programmes recorded on video tape as opposed to film. It was less likely to benefit the laboratories, therefore, than a channel largely supplied by independent producers who generally worked with the cheaper, less capital-intensive medium of film. When it came to the vote, Alan Sapper, the union's General Secretary, made a direct plea not to support the motion. 'It would be highly dangerous,' he argued, 'for the Television Branch to be driven into a corner with a policy that they believe very deeply seriously affects their employment prospects.'[7] But the delegates rejected the leadership's request to maintain the *status quo*. The emergency motion was carried by 111 votes to 55.

During the summer of 1979 freelance and independent producers collectively, and individually, attempted to establish their credibility as potential major suppliers of programmes for the fourth channel. In June, the British Academy of Film and Television Arts arranged, in conjunction with the ADP, a showing of extracts from nineteen independent productions, financed wholly from outside the BBC, ITV, or publicly funded bodies such as the Arts Council. The presentation was an attempt to answer the question 'Who are the independents?' – something that many politicians, civil servants and IBA staff were asking at that time. It was attended by a large number of journalists, but the 'real' audience were the few Home Office and IBA officials who were also present. The productions shown covered a wide range of programming, from comedy and adult education to current affairs and animation. Programme budgets varied from as little as £2,000 for a seven-minute film, to £2 million for a series of ten one-hour programmes. Many of the producers prefaced their screenings with explanations of the problems of financing and distribution they had faced. A press statement issued afterwards explained in some detail:

Time after time, the audience heard how the BBC and ITV refused even to look at independent productions, or (if they deigned to purchase them) offered insultingly low percentages of production costs to buy the UK transmission rights – 10–13% on average, with a maximum of 25%.

Christopher Nupen, for instance, described how he had mortgaged his house to make *Itzhak Perlman: Virtuoso Violinist* – one of the finest music films ever produced. The only reliable market for his programmes is Germany: ironically his latest film was ZDF's official entry to BAFTA's International Television Festival – and won the top award.

Nick Downie's *Front Line Rhodesia* contained extraordinary war footage; it was his third film, and each had won prizes. Yet, because of the cartel operated by ITV and BBC for buying independent productions, Downie has still not covered the costs of his programmes, and has pawned most of his equipment to finance his next war report.

Other superior documentaries had been turned down by British television. One producer told of the cassette of his film which had been sitting at the BBC for seven months, still unviewed. Another told of how his film had been ignored until it had won a string of prizes, and was then thought worthy of the front cover of the *Radio Times*. Other producers found that cinema release in support of a feature film was the only means of recouping costs.

Of course, the large independent production houses thrive, but not on sales to UK television. Hence, Video Arts is making its major series on the political theories of Milton Friedman not for British screens, but for America's Public Broadcasting Service.

Alan Parker (now Britain's most successful cinema director) had to invest his own savings as a commercial director in his own script, and make *No Hard Feelings* at his own expense, before the BBC was persuaded of his talents, bought the film at a knock down price, and transmitted it. Peter Webb, whose *Butch Minds the Baby* was also shown at BAFTA, has had to follow the same course.[8]

The statement concluded that a fourth channel which only offered a token 15% of air time to independent producers would waste the opportunity to broaden the base of British television; to make a comprehensive range of outstanding programmes; and to encourage a significant flow of additional export earnings.

The entrepreneurial aspects of independent production were repeatedly emphasised to the Conservative Party during 1979. For instance, when an ADP delegation consisting of David Elstein, Christopher Nupen, Peter Graham Scott (who conceived *Mogul* and *The Onedin Line*) and Mark Shivas (who originated *The Six Wives of Henry VIII* and *Glittering Prizes*) met the Conservatives' backbench Media Committee, they stressed that compared to the ITV companies the small independent producers had a far greater incentive to maximise overseas sales. With their advertising monopoly at home, the ITV companies generally left the handling of overseas exploitation to agents, whereas the independent producers could not afford to rely on other people selling their programmes and would travel abroad themselves, making the contacts and creating a market for their work. One of the reasons that American programmes were so successful worldwide, they suggested, was because in the United States independent producers who supplied the networks with a major proportion of their output vigorously competed with each other to sell their programmes abroad. The same could happen in Britain if the fourth channel was used to provide a reliable domestic market for the presently virtually non-existent, but potentially prosperous, independent production sector. There was, moreover, reason to act fairly quickly, for the new hardware technologies of cable, video, and possibly satellite, would soon require a supporting software industry. If Britain initially lacked an independent production sector capable of meeting this demand, other countries might achieve a domination of the field that would be hard for British producers to break into subsequently. On a slightly different tack, it was argued that an ITV2 run by the ITV companies would probably perpetuate what was widely seen as the 'grossly inefficient' industrial practices in ITV; overmanning, resistance to new technology, and artificially high wage rates. It was put to the Conservatives that a fourth channel supplied largely by independent producers would diversify television production in Britain and perhaps, at the same time, break the union's grip on the industry and alleviate the existing hidebound industrial relations. It was a persuasive line of argument to certain elements in the Conservative Party, and helps explain the support that the independent producers received from free marketeers such as Sir Keith Joseph's Conservative policy group.

As the summer months passed, conference time approached. In late August 1979 the television industry gathered in Edinburgh for the annual International Television Festival, and a few weeks later the Royal Television Society held its biennial convention at King's College, Cambridge. Both occasions were marked by important policy statements. In Edinburgh, Jeremy Isaacs delivered his influential MacTaggart Memorial Lecture in which he spoke in some detail about how he believed the fourth channel should be organised. One of ITV's most progressive and respected senior executives, Isaacs had quit as Director of Programmes at Thames Television in 1978, after a clash of temperament with the then recently appointed managing director of the company, Bryan Cowgill. At the time of his Edinburgh lecture he was working as an independent/freelance producer making a film for Scottish Television, *A Sense of Freedom*, about the life of the notorious Jimmy Boyle. Isaacs was already tipped as a strong contender for the job – assuming it would exist – of controller of the fourth channel, and the content of his forward-looking but sensible speech did not harm his prospects.

Addressing himself to the future of broadcasting in the 1980s, Isaacs made a strong plea for raising the BBC's licence fee. Maintaining the BBC's well-being, he argued, ought to be a higher priority than activating the fourth channel; for it was the Corporation who set the standard of television in Britain. He was not, however, short of praise for the quality of ITV's programmes; the most important characteristic of ITV, he contended, was not that it had been set up to make a profit, but that it was set up in the image of the BBC and given public responsibilities similar to those set out in the BBC's Charter. But it was unrealistic to expect that ITV could continue providing a public service unless its advertising monopoly remained intact, 'however much this sticks in the craw of those who believe in a free market.'[9] Turning to the fourth channel, which he asserted should be and would be called 'ITV2', Isaacs declared that it would have be supplied with programmes without any diminution of quality on ITV1. The IBA, he noted, had rightly seen that it was a positive advantage to be planning the second channel at the same time as considering applications for the new franchises; applicants would be required to make clear their intentions for both the new and old channels. On the organisation of ITV2, Isaacs envisaged a structure fairly similar to what he had suggested in his unpublished submission to Sir John Eden in 1973. He advocated a degree of separateness from ITV1:

> If the channel is to have a different flavour it needs a different chef, perhaps a new unit, on the analogy of ITN, funded by the companies, answerable to a board on which they and the IBA are represented, but at a little distance from both, such a unit to plan not just the independent sector's contribution, but, in conjunction with the Controllers' Group, the whole of ITV2.[10]

90

It was important that day-to-day control of the channel should rest with an individual not a committee, and restrictive obligations and rigid quotas should be avoided at all costs. The budget for ITV2 would be provided by the ITV companies, who would collect and keep the advertising in their areas for both channels. 'The budget would be used to commission programmes from the ITV companies, who would thus have an opportunity to earn some of it back, and from independent producers.'[11] But Isaacs shared Colin Shaw's scepticism about the ability of independent producers to produce very substantial hours of programmes for the channel:

> Independent producers do not represent a great new untapped source of energy and ideas. Many of them are gainfully employed at this time in BBC and ITV. Their problem outside will be to assemble behind their projects, when they have backing for them, the people and the facilities that will make them happen. And that is easier said than done . . . .
> Better by far, for all concerned, that the independent production sector begins modestly, supplying only what it knows it can supply with people and facilities it knows are there, than blow itself up to unrealistic dimensions.[12]

Isaacs agreed that independent producers had so far received a raw deal, but the point was that neither the BBC nor ITV needed their programmes since both broadcasting systems produced sufficient themselves to keep their schedules full. When they did buy in, they did so at the lowest possible price in a tight buyer's market. Others who worked within the system, selling ideas and packages of talent, were not independents in the true sense; if they went over budget it was not at their own expense. 'From now on independent producers ought to receive a fair price for their programmes, but they will have to walk on their own feet, not travel in the company car.'[13]

Isaacs had a clear conception of what he thought ITV2's programming philosophy should be. The channel would aim at a variety of audiences and at a 10% share of the total television audience. He wanted the channel to cater for substantial minorities presently neglected, but the programmes should not become ghetto slots:

> I hope, in the eighties, to see more black Britons on our screens in programmes of particular appeal to them *and aimed at us*; more programmes made by women for women *which men will watch*; more programmes for the young, for the age group that watches television least partly because so little television speaks to them.[14]

He talked of actuality programmes that would embrace a complete spectrum of political attitude and opinion. He felt that a clutch of programmes should be designed to hit some broadly educational target;

but the emphasis would be away from formal education, and the Open University with its close links to the BBC should remain with the Corporation. Above all, the channel would 'somehow be different':

> We want a fourth channel that will neither simply compete with ITV1 nor merely be complementary to it. We want a fourth channel that everyone will watch some of the time and no-one will watch all of the time.[15]

The 1979 MacTaggart Lecture stands as an important statement of policy by the future Chief Executive of Channel Four. As we shall see later, it accurately predicted the structure and philosophy of the channel in all but three matters: the name; the size of the independents' contribution; and the composition of the channel's Board. With its broad appeal to all sections of the industry, Isaacs's plan was only moderately satisfying to many would-be independents. 'A fine radical speech advocating more of the *status quo*,' quipped one BBC executive.[16] It seemed to some that Isaacs's approach was most accurately summarised when, in reply to someone who queried how the channel could be that different if the majority of its programmes were drawn from the ITV companies, he said that what we are likely to see are programmes that are different, but not all that different. And there was a notable contrast at Edinburgh between the pitch of Isaacs's lecture and another one given by John Birt, by then Controller of Features and Current Affairs at LWT. Birt, who was also considered a likely candidate for Channel Four's top job, had shifted, since 1973, towards the ideals of the OBA. He argued for pluralistic broadcasting. The fourth channel should be seen 'as an opportunity for us to listen to the raw, unfiltered, immoderate and sometimes angry views of those excluded.'[17] Others disagreed. They maintained that such an unregulated future belonged, if it belonged anywhere, to the new technologies, to the multiplicity of outlets provided by optic-fibre cables carrying a thousand channels at a time. While television was limited to four channels, there would always be certain restraints. It was a prognosis Birt himself seemed partly to concede. In the meantime, the more radical interpretations of the OBA's programming philosophy were as defunct as Annan's proposed OBA structure. 'Those who argue still for an OBA,' said Jeremy Isaacs, 'as if that is what the Government really intends should be brought about, are wasting their energy and our time.'[18]

At Cambridge, some of the wilder speculation ended when William Whitelaw made clear, in general terms, what the Government did intend to bring about. The Home Secretary chose the RTS convention in September 1979 as the occasion to make his first public statement on broadcasting since his return to office. In retrospect, it is clear that his speech was, to all intents and purposes, the Government's 'White Paper' for the Broadcasting Bill that was to be introduced early in the New

Year. Whitelaw began by reiterating his endorsement of the Annan Committee's broad intentions, together with his objections to their specific organisational proposals:

What the Annan Committee had to say about the prospect which a fourth television channel could afford for innovation – to give new opportunities to creative people in British television, to find new ways of finding minority and specialist audiences and to add different and greater satisfactions to those now available to the viewer – all of this has commanded a remarkably wide measure of agreement and support.

[However], I am convinced that not only would the creation of an Open Broadcasting Authority directly dependent on the Government for funds be potentially dangerous; it is also unnecessary to achieve what we want. The experience and ability of the IBA, if used to the full, the money, equipment and skills of the ITV companies, and the talents of independent producers, can be harnessed to provide a different and worthwhile service on the fourth channel.[19]

He then went on to spell out the nature of the, until then, enigmatic 'strict safeguards' mentioned in the Queen's Speech:

It can be summarised as follows. The IBA will be expected to develop a distinctive service on the fourth channel, subject to similar general statutory provisions as now exist on programme content – for example, the avoidance of offence against good taste and decency and the like – in a creative way which is designed to give new opportunities to creative people in British television and to add different and greater satisfactions to those now available to the viewer. It will be expected to extend the range of programmes available to the public, to find ways of serving minority and specialised audiences and to give due place to innovation. It will be expected not to allow rivalry for ratings between the two channels for which it has statutory responsibility, nor to allow scheduling designed to obtain for each of those services the largest possible audience over the week. It will be expected to make arrangements for *the largest practicable proportion of programmes on the fourth channel to be supplied by organisations other than the companies contracted to provide programmes on ITV1.* It will be expected to increase the number of programmes shown which are originated by the regional ITV companies and ITN and, in consequence, to ensure that those companies which have networking rights on ITV1 have much less time on the fourth channel. It will be expected to provide an allotment of time for educational programmes, both structured and informal, on the fourth channel, and for Welsh-language programmes on the fourth channel in Wales. It will be expected to ensure that *the arrangements for planning and scheduling of the fourth channel service are not dominated by the programme companies contracted to provide programmes on* ITV1, *especially the network companies*, that the budget for the fourth channel is adequate to achieve the sort of service I have described and that a fair payment is made to all contributors on the channel.[20] (author's emphasis)

Whitelaw confirmed that he was not prepared to introduce competitive sale of advertising between the two channels. The ITV companies would keep their monopoly and pay the fourth channel's budget; the size of which, he asserted, would not necessarily be governed by the revenue earned from advertisements shown on the fourth channel. Competition for revenue, he believed, would inevitably result in a move towards single-minded concentration on maximising the audience for programmes, with adverse consequences for both commercial channels and, eventually, the BBC as well. He noted, however, that the IBA had invited the advertisers and the agencies to inform the Authority of particular selling practices which they would find objectionable in a two-channel situation. And he was willing to consider whether some safeguards should be added to the provisions regulating the sale of advertising time.

The most unexpected aspect of Whitelaw's speech was the disclosure of a volte-face in Government policy on the subject of Welsh-language broadcasting. In its election manifesto the Conservative Party had committed itself to a single Welsh-language service on which both the BBC and HTV Welsh programmes would be transmitted.[21] During the summer of 1979 a number of critics, including HTV, pointed out that a single Welsh-language service would be unattractive to advertisers and would require some form of financial assistance from Government. In his Cambridge speech, the Home Secretary had second thoughts and offered the Welsh a continuation of the existing mixed system; there would be more Welsh-language programmes, but spread over at least two channels.

We are now convinced that the fastest, most efficient and *most economical* way of doing this is to concentrate on one of the IBA's two channels all the programmes produced by the ITV1 programme companies and independent producers which are made in the Welsh language and to concentrate on one of the BBC's two channels the BBC's Welsh-language broadcasts.[22] (author's emphasis)

It was a change of policy that was to provoke a surge of Welsh nationalism. The more immediate reaction to the Home Secretary's speech, however, concerned his plans for the fourth channel in the rest of the United Kingdom.

The speech was received by the industry with a certain enthusiasm. The IBA, in particular, were well pleased; the ball was now clearly in their court and they would shortly prepare and submit their detailed proposals to the Home Secretary before the legislation was drafted. Speaking at Cambridge, Colin Shaw explained the need for ITV2 to be distanced from the Authority as well as the ITV companies. 'The IBA must not appear to be the judge of ITV1 and the co-inspirator of ITV2 – the new channel must be at one remove from the IBA, and with an independent budget.'[23] The possibility of the channel being run by a department within the Authority was thus firmly ruled out. Shaw also affirmed the need for a single controller of the channel rather than a committee. 'This is, I realise,' he admitted, 'a recipe for megalomania on a scale unparalleled since Diaghilev or Randolph Hearst. Unlike those megalomaniacs, however, this controller will be accountable in this world rather than the next.'

The two contenders for the IBA's favours – the companies and the potential independent producers – also welcomed Whitelaw's speech. To quote from Peter Fiddick's column:

> The barons of the ITV companies clapped not just, it seemed, out of politeness. And less institutional spirits, those who might hope to become the independent programme-makers of the four-channel tomorrow, found in his words, maybe not a manifesto, but at least a text capable of being hammered into one. [24]

At the invitation of the Authority, the ITCA in October 1979 prepared a confidential memorandum setting out their views on the fourth channel in the light of the Home Secretary's statement at Cambridge. The document reveals how differently the IBA and the companies were to interpret Whitelaw's general comments. First, regarding the structure of ITV2, the ITV companies advocated that overall responsibility for the channel should be vested in a form of a Trust, following the model of the *Observer* Trust. The trust would be jointly owned by the IBA and the ITV companies. In turn, the trust would appoint a board of governors, who would oversee the running of the organisation. There would be an independent chairman and deputy chairman; one governor with special responsibility for education; two governors with special responsibility for independent production; two governors from the central ITV1 companies; and three from the regional ITV1 companies. Thus, half of the Board's membership would be representatives of the ITCA companies. Day-to-day management of the organisation would be undertaken by a chief executive, a programme controller and a director of finance; all three appointed by the board of governors. Second, regarding the scheduling of ITV2's programmes, the ITV companies rejected the suggestion that the schedules for the two channels should be planned in isolation from each other. 'Experience in the various intricacies of scheduling,' declared the memorandum, 'indicates that this would not prove practicable.'[25] It was essential that ITV1, the major channel, should be scheduled first and the second channel designed to fit in with its requirements. 'The viability of the whole system could be jeopardised if the scheduling of ITV1 were to become conditioned by the needs of ITV2 at the expense of maintaining audience sizes on the majority channel.'[26] In order to ensure close co-operation, ITV2 would, therefore, have two representatives at meetings of the ITV1 Programme Controllers Group and, reciprocally, a member of the ITV1 Programme Controllers' Secretariat would attend ITV2's programme planning meetings as an observer. Third, regarding the contributions from independent producers, the ITCA memorandum noted that the IBA's current thinking was against fixed quotas, but the companies nevertheless assumed the independent production contribution would amount to no more than 10–15% of ITV2's total output. The companies' strong opposition to 'seed money' for independent producers revealed their measured commitment to encouraging work of this kind:

> The independent producer should bear all development costs up to the point of presenting a proposal. ITV2 should never become involved in prospective or retrospective finance for development before a proposal is put and accepted. If, once it is accepted, a project is abandoned before production starts, then the write-off should be charged against ITV2, but experience has shown that heavy development costs over a lengthy period can be made into a livelihood.[27]

The companies prepared a much-criticised draft ITV2 schedule which was similar to the one they had published in their 1977 response to the Annan Committee, although with more comedy and extra quiz shows it was slightly more popularly oriented. Estimated audience ratings for peak-time programmes ranged from 3 to 15% of the total television audience. 'One consequence of this schedule,' said the memorandum, 'is that the financial viability of the new channel is far from assured . . . the companies find naive in the extreme the belief that since the new channel is to be funded from advertising revenue it will inevitably be financially secure.'[28] It was imperative, therefore, that the advertising airtime on ITV2 should be sold regionally by the companies' existing sales forces in order to maximise revenue; a view that the IBA was not to disagree with.

Just as the companies, understandably, construed the Home Secretary's remarks in a way that departed as little as possible from their earlier proposals for the fourth channel, so the independent producers' lobby pressed the IBA to take note of those comments in the Cambridge statement that implied the channel should be independent of ITV1. In October 1979, the same month as the companies submitted their memorandum to the Authority, almost four hundred individuals and organisations from both within and outside the television industry signed an 'Open Letter to the Home Secretary'. In a move reminiscent of the 76 Group's tactics, the letter, together with a list of the signatories, was published by the Channel Four Group in a half-page advertisement in the *Guardian*. The letter referred to Whitelaw's Cambridge address:

> We, the undersigned, wholeheartedly endorse the spirit of your

address. It remains for the Independent Broadcasting Authority, to whom responsibility has been given, to follow the Government's challenge, which will demand a radically different approach to broadcasting in this country.

. . . We believe that in order to protect the independence of the new channel the following principles must be incorporated into the legislation of the channel:

A management board answerable to the Independent Broadcasting Authority.

A Programme Controller, who, once appointed, should have no connection whatsoever with the BBC or ITV. He or she should be free *to schedule independently of the ITV companies in consultation with the IBA.*

A progressive build-up of hours for TV4 with *a majority of the channel's programmes to come from sources wholly independent of the BBC and ITV.*

Guaranteed finance for the channel which should be both independent and adequate to fund programme needs so that no organisation has a lien on programme time.

The Fourth Television Channel must accord with the Government's stated view that it should 'extend and enhance' the range and quality of British television.[29] (author's emphasis)

The Open Letter was an impressive display of unity by a large number of independent, freelance, and BBC/ITV staff producers, directors, writers, technicians, actors and journalists, as well as politicians, trade unionists and academics. There was no doubt, however, that the Channel Four Group was an umbrella organisation under which a great variety of differently shaped independents and would-be independents sheltered. It became increasingly clear that although they all shared a desire to maximise the independents' contributions to the fourth channel, there were differences of emphasis between them about how the channel should operate in practice. One of the more obvious distinctions was that between the commercially minded, entrepreneurial independent producer, already established and with connections to overseas markets, and the non-profit-making, and nowadays grant-aided, independent film-maker, represented principally by the IFA. At a meeting at Brompton Road in late September 1979, 150 'independent producers' met with the IBA in order to tell the Authority what they wanted from the fourth channel. The size of the meeting surprised the Authority; Lady Plowden, the IBA's Chairman, admitted that they had under-estimated the likely response from independent producers. It was on this occasion that the Independent Film-makers Association first formally presented their case for special arrangements to be made within the fourth channel's structure for 'innovative and experimental work.'[30] They proposed that at least

97

10% of the channel's budget should be formally allocated to a legally distinct 'Foundation', which would support programmes 'from that area of independent production that is demonstrably the most promising source of new practices and perspectives.'[31]

> The inevitable pressure of ratings, consensus wisdom and scarce finance make inevitable the need for special arrangements to stimulate audio-visual 'research and development'. Without special measures, innovative work for the Fourth Channel will be still-born. As it will not fit conventional production patterns, its financial needs will be neglected. As it will not service a definable 'minority interest', it will be squeezed out of the schedules. As it will be controversial, it will tend to be avoided for safer pursuits.[32]

The IFA had in mind, of course, the type of work produced by their members, notably the small film workshops supported by the British Film Institute and the Arts Council – e.g. the London Film-makers Co-op, founded in 1966, the 'home' of avant-garde film-making throughout the 1970s; Cinema Action, founded in 1968; the Berwick Street Collective, founded in 1971, consistent experimenters in documentaries such as *Nightcleaners*; and Amber Films, founded in 1968, operating in Newcastle and a pioneer of regionally based workshop production. The IFA's Foundation was a far cry from the Television Foundation proposed by the ITV companies in 1973, which would have featured the work of *leading and established* practitioners in the field of film and television programme-making.[33] Moreover, programmes initiated by the companies' Foundation would have had to meet the IBA's existing technical standards, something that the IFA proposal was firmly opposed to. The IFA members worked with less expensive, lower quality video and film equipment than that used on British television. The IBA's strenuous efforts to maintain high-grade image quality on its television services would have to be relaxed, argued the IFA, if the fourth channel was to meet the Home Secretary's comments about 'a due place for innovation'. The question of technical standards was one that was to be repeatedly raised once Channel Four began to commission programmes. The proposal for a separate Foundation was not to be taken up by the IBA, although a final decision would be the prerogative of the Channel Four Board. The Authority believed that responsibility for encouraging IFA-type work could be incorporated into the channel's executive structure without the creation of, what it saw as, a costly additional level of decision-making.

BROMPTON ROAD DETAILS

The blueprint for the Channel Four Television Company was published by the IBA in November 1979. Headed *The Fourth Channel: The*

Authority's Proposals, the document aimed to present 'the broad outcome of the consideration which it [the IBA] has given during the past six months to the way in which the Fourth Channel could best be run.'[34] The IBA noted that its proposals could only be provisional, since final decisions rested with Parliament. But when the Broadcasting Bill appeared three months later its content was consistent with the IBA's document, although less detailed. The Bill was permissive in respect of the fourth channel, not mandatory – it left the IBA to put the flesh, and even the bones, on the Government's intentions. The Authority's proposals were the fourth formal statement of its plans for the fourth channel in eight years. The contrast with the 1971 *ITV2* submission is striking. What follows is an edited version of the proposals:

STRUCTURE

Delegation and control
The Authority must distance from itself the running of the Fourth Channel, following the principles that govern its relationship to the present single ITV service, but developing arrangements to meet the new situation.

The Fourth Channel Company
The Authority would intend to establish a company, with its own board, which would be responsible for the running of the Fourth Channel. The responsibilities placed upon the company for the operation of the Fourth Channel would require it to:

– commission and acquire programmes, and plan programme schedules
– appoint and employ staff
– operate within established budgets

The Board of Directors would have overall responsibility for the company.

Board membership and composition
The precise composition of the board of the company awaits further discussion. A possible model, however, is a board of twelve to fourteen people, of whom the eleven non-executive members would be chosen by the Authority after consultation. There would be an independent chairman and deputy chairman. The other members would broadly represent those who are likely to provide programmes for the service, but they would not be direct delegates. *Four members would come from the ITV companies,* which, as well as providing some of the programmes for the Fourth Channel, will be providing virtually all its budget; *five more members would be able to speak on behalf of other potential suppliers of programmes,* having the trust of independent producers, for example, or

99

a special concern for the educational role of the channel. The Authority would not itself be represented on the board. One of the board's first tasks would be to appoint its senior staff. We would expect one at least, and more probably two or three, to be made executive members of the board.

Relationship with the Authority
The company would have a considerable degree of independence – but it would be subject to the ultimate control of the Authority. The Authority would, it is envisaged, exercise control through:

– appointing, after consultation, the non-executive members of the board
– approving the appointment of the executive members
– approving the Fourth Channel programme schedules
– ensuring that the planning and scheduling of Fourth Channel programmes and ITV1 programmes are co-ordinated
– establishing the annual budget

Relationship with the programme providers
The company will not make programmes itself, but will commission and acquire them from others. It seems likely that it will have contractual relationships with programme providers, based on programmes or series of programmes, and varied in the light of the creative, technical and financial circumstances.

PROGRAMMES

The Fourth Channel is to have its own distinctive character. One important element in this is that it will be 'complementary' to the service which is at present provided by ITV. This means not only that it will provide as far as possible a choice at any one time between two programmes appealing to different interests: it means also that both the Fourth Channel and the present ITV service will be able to schedule programmes with less concern than is possible on only a single channel about potential loss of a majority of the audience. The consequence will be that programmes, while still intended to appeal to as many viewers as their individual terms of reference allow, can address themselves to particular interests or concerns and adopt new approaches far more freely than at present. Our wish is that the Fourth Channel will take particular advantage of this freedom, and that enterprise and experiments will flourish. *It must provide opportunities for talents which have previously not been fully used, for needs to be served which have not yet been fully defined, and for the evolution of ideas which, for whatever reason – personal, structural, institutional – have yet to be revealed.*

But it would be quite wrong on at least two counts to deny to the new channel programmes likely to draw very large audiences. First, it would be fatal if the broad public, the sum of countless special interests, were to feel that it was somehow not for them. Even if, by its nature, the Fourth Channel will be a service visited from time to time rather than watched constantly, as BBC1 and ITV1 have tended to be by significant parts of their audiences, it must remain in the public's mind accessible. Secondly, there is a need to present the work of independent producers within a popular context rather than simply as a fringe activity.

We would not intend therefore to make the Fourth Channel wholly a 'minority' service; nor would we want the present blend of the first independent channel to change in the direction of an unrestrained search for popularity. Rather, we would see the present 'mix' on ITV's single channel continuing, while *the Fourth Channel roughly reversed that 'mix', with about two-thirds of its programmes addressing sections of the audience who want something particular or who want something different.* In the remaining one-third there would be programmes intended to appeal to larger audiences, though often in a style different from that of some popular programmes now seen.

Controls
The Home Secretary has made clear that the general statutory provisions for programme content will be the same for both channels. We believe it is possible, however, that the availability of a wider choice of programmes *will allow controlled encouragement to be given to the presentation of a wider range of opinions and assumptions.*

The provision of programmes
The overriding concern of the programme controller will be with the quality of programmes; and therefore *there should be no quotas, or rights to contribute, for anyone.* However, with that prime qualification, *a possible pattern at the start would be that between 15 and 35% of the output would come from independent producers, with between 25 and 40% coming from the major ITV contractors, a further 10–20% from the regional contractors, up to 15% from ITN, and 5–14% from foreign sources.*

News, religion, education
The Authority does not intend at this stage to prescribe particular categories of programme. There are, however, three exceptions to this general intention. The first concerns news. Through ITN, the Fourth Channel will be expected to make regular provision for bulletins or summaries, although not necessarily following existing models, and for programmes providing background information on matters of public interest.

The Authority does not believe that the Fourth Channel should adopt the Sunday evening 'closed period' but it will expect the schedule to contain at least an hour a week of programmes recognisably religious in aim.

The Authority expects [educational programmes] to constitute about 15% of the channel's output. The Authority hopes that the Fourth Channel, in turning to service fresh educational needs, will use to the full some new and exciting opportunities. We attach a special importance to reaching individuals and not only audiences: and this requires connections to be made between broadcasts and the means which exist outside broadcasting to follow up the interests created by programmes – popular and specialist journals, home study, local clubs and societies, volunteer service, classes in a variety of institutions and so on.

Networking and opt-outs
With the exception of the provision made fór Welsh-language pro-grammes*, the network, at the outset, will be a national one. When the service has been established, the providers of programmes may wish to seek an opportunity for occasional opt-out programmes, but these would have to have the agreement of the programme controller.

Scheduling
In scheduling, as in the production of programmes, an important fact is that programmes on the Fourth Channel are to complement those on the existing Independent Television Channel. One aspect of complementarity is a matter of mechanics: the arrangement of a number of common junctions between the channels on any average evening. It would, however, simply inhibit the new channel's choice of programmes if it were never free to schedule programmes and events which call for longer spaces than are customarily found on the present channel.

The Authority will clearly have a key role in ensuring that the schedules of the two channels for which it is responsible are so arranged as to give viewers the best possible choice.

It is not possible to say, at this stage, for how many hours a week the Fourth Channel will initially be on the air. Our hope would certainly be that, at the outset or very soon after, programmes would be shown for 45–50 hours a week.

FINANCE

The combined advertising revenue of the two channels is not expected during the early years to show an increase of more than 10%; and on some predictions it could well be less.

Although the Fourth Channel is not to be solely dependent on the revenue it earns, it and the existing ITV channel will be wholly dependent

---

*The IBA's provisions for Welsh-language broadcasting have been omitted, since they alone were not to survive the passage of the Broadcasting Bill.

on the revenue that they earn between them. The Authority is confident that there will in time be sufficient revenue to support two services of high quality, but we must be on our guard against over-confident planning. *Money is bound to be tight; programmes will not all be able to have the budgets that are sought for them; the profits received by the ITV companies (of which some five-sixths pass to the Government in levy and tax) will be diminished for the first year or two at least.*

The Fourth Channel's budget

The annual budget for the Fourth Channel would be determined by the Authority, after consultation with the channel's board. Initially, our forecasts suggest that it could be of the order of £60–80 million, in 1979 terms. The sum would be raised from the ITV programme contractors, as a Fourth Channel subscription; the total sum would be divided between them in roughly the same proportion as their IBA rental. *We would not wish to see the Fourth Channel as a permanent pensioner of ITV1: we should hope to see the Fourth Channel in due course adding between a fifth and a quarter, in real terms, to the total advertising revenue now earned by the programme contractors.*

SALE OF ADVERTISING

It has always been clear that a channel of the kind suggested over the last eight years by the Authority and envisaged by Government is not compatible with the competitive selling of advertising. The addition of a second channel carrying advertising should itself bring benefits to advertisers: the availability of much more time, and the chance of appealing to more specialised audiences, should relieve some of the tensions that have arisen between those who sell and buy advertising time on television. The Authority recognises, however, that some advertisers had hoped to have competitive selling of time, and that they will be disappointed that the needs of good broadcasting rule this out.

The advertisers' expressed concern is that the programme contractors' position should not permit the imposition of arbitrary conditions governing the sale of advertising time.

It would be possible to have a separate sales force or selling organisation selling time on the Fourth Channel on the ITV companies' behalf. Such an arrangement would, in the view of the representative bodies of advertisers and agencies, help relieve some of their members' frustrations at having only one point of contact for the purchase of television time. The contrary view is that advertisers' problems stem mainly from the necessary limitation on the amount of television time available, and that a separate sales force would produce only the appearance rather than the reality of competition; furthermore such an arrangement, including provision for regional as well as national selling, would lead to higher costs and lower revenue for the system as a whole, and would diminish the resources available for the Fourth Channel.

The Authority has formed the opinion that, on balance, it is preferable for time on the Fourth Channel to be sold by the ITV companies in their own regions. At the same time it will wish to discuss possible safeguards; for example, *that there should be no conditions relating the sale of ITV air time to the sale of the Fourth Channel air time; that there should be no linked discount between the two channels; and that separate rate cards should be published for the two channels.*

The Authority will also propose the establishment of an Advertising Liaison Committee in which representatives at the most senior level from the ITV companies, from the ISBA, and from the IPA, would be invited to take part. The aim would be to improve liaison on advertising matters of common concern, but not, of course, to take up the untenable position of seeking to control pricing or to act in any sense as an appeal court on matters which are the legitimate prerogative of a seller or buyer of television time.

FUTURE PLANNING

To attempt to meet *the target date in the autumn of 1982 for the start of the service,* the Authority needs to proceed with the provisional planning of the service with all practicable speed. On the engineering side authorisation was given to the Authority under the IBA Act 1979 to proceed with the provision of the new transmitters. The intention is that, by the time the service comes on the air, some 30 main stations and 80 relay stations should be built, providing *coverage of some 80% of the UK as a whole.*

The Authority plans to set up the Fourth Channel company as soon as legislation is passed which will enable it to do so. With the proposed start of the service now less than three years ahead, planning must continue to take place before the company can be established and its board appointed. For that reason the Authority is likely to establish special consultative arrangements during the early part of 1980 to ensure that, when the Bill is passed, the Fourth Channel can go ahead with all possible speed.[35] (author's emphasis throughout)

The Home Secretary's Cambridge speech had been sufficiently ambivalent for both the ITV companies and the independent producers' lobby to interpret it in a manner favourable to their interests. The IBA's proposals were too detailed to allow such tailoring, and consequently they faced a far less cordial reception from both parties. 'ITV2 by the back door,' said the independents. 'Milk and water, trying to please everybody,' said one ITV managing director.[36] Once again, it was the would-be independents who were the more vocal in expressing their opinions, although not necessarily the more effective. In early December 1979, the Channel Four Group organised a Commons conference on the subject and simultaneously published their reply to the IBA's proposals. Their criticism centred on the construction of the fourth channel's Board and the distribution of programme supply – both of which they believed would be dominated by the ITV companies. Although the IBA had said that the Board members would not be acting as direct delegates, and although the four ITV members of the Board would be in a minority, the Channel Four Group felt that their presence would give the ITV companies a large measure of control over acquisition and scheduling. It was not just the numbers involved that they objected to, but also the principle of a representative Board. It would lead to division, in-fighting, and encourage a tendency towards package-offerings and carve-ups. On the subject of programme suppliers, the Channel Four Group argued that the IBA's suggestion of between 50 and 75% of the channel's programmes to come from ITV (majors, regionals, and ITN) and a maximum of 35% to come from independent producers went 'totally against the letter of the Home Secretary's statement.'[37] The IBA's reference to no fixed quotas and a criterion of quality was not good enough for the Channel Four Group. They stated that the Fourth Channel should 'discriminate in favour of independent production.' Even if in the first few years the independent producers were not able to provide much more than 35%, as the channel's broadcasting hours expanded, the programme controller should set a minimum target of 51% of the channel's output to be independently produced. The independents feared that if their contribution started small it would stay small. The ITV companies' surplus capacity of the early 1970s had been greatly reduced by the derestriction of broadcasting hours and an increase in regional programming. They would therefore need to gear themselves up to supply extra programmes for the new channel, and once they had expanded their facilities and entered into new staffing arrangements, they would be very reluctant to cut back their production to make way for independents. The independents' attitude to the IBA's proposals, and the Authority's reply to their criticism, was neatly summed up in the Letters page of the *Listener* in an exchange between Colin Shaw and Michael Darlow, a freelance director and producer. Darlow wrote:

The IBA's problems *vis-à-vis* outsiders are largely a matter of trust, or rather distrust .... Over the years the Authority has put forward successive plans for ITV2, and each has been rejected. Yet the IBA's latest proposals still actually talk of 'a channel of the kind suggested over the last eight years by the Authority.' Previously they suggested that 15% of programmes should come from independent producers. Since Mr Whitelaw spoke of 'the largest practical proportion' coming

105

from independents they have altered their wording to read 15–35% – something or nothing! In other ways, too, their proposals look as if they have borrowed Mr Whitelaw's words but have not changed their own ideas.[38]

To which Shaw replied:

It is true, at least in its early years, the fourth channel will depend heavily on the [ITV] programme companies for its programmes. The choice of those programmes, as well as their placing, will be in the hands of the fourth channel. If it appears that a company is seeking to 'dump' material on the fourth channel, then the Controller would be able to refuse it. The Board would surely back him in his refusal. In any case, the Authority's power to approve the schedule (as well as its nomination of the Board's members) would provide a firm safeguard against that kind of action. It is my belief that the Controller will also, in time, be able to turn to the independent production sector to redress the balance.[39]

Two other areas that concerned the Channel Four Group were scheduling and finance. They noted that nowhere in his speech did the Home Secretary refer to complementary scheduling, yet the IBA was proposing that the fourth channel's programmes should be 'chained to those of ITV through complementary scheduling and programme "junctions" between the two channels.'[40] Unfair, retorted the IBA: 'a number of common junctions' did not mean that the fourth channel would be subordinate to ITV1. Writing in the *Listener* in January 1980, Colin Shaw explained:

It [the fourth channel] would not be treated in scheduling matters as a junior partner in the Authority's services, free to act only in reaction to the plans of the first independent television channel. The requirement to avoid competition between the channels – itself a consequence of the Home Secretary's decision against competitive advertising – does not, in the IBA's view, call for a relationship of that kind. Each schedule would be the responsibility of a distinct planning team. As now, the first channel would be planned by the programme controllers of the network companies, while the Fourth Channel would be planned by its programme controller and his staff, appointed by the Fourth Channel company. And, finally, the two schedules would be put to the Authority for its approval.[41]

The Channel Four Group contended that there was a similar marked contrast between the Home Secretary's remarks about the financing of the channel and the IBA's. Whitelaw had stated that he expected the IBA to ensure that the budget for the channel would be adequate to achieve the sort of service he had described. The Authority's financial pessimism, however, had led them to talk about programmes not all being able to have the budgets sought for them. 'Channel Four,' declared the Channel Four Group, 'should not be open until the IBA can fulfil Mr Whitelaw's requirements.'[42] If the channel could not provide 100% finance in the majority of cases, many small independent producers, whose projects would probably not attract additional (multi-national) financial backing, would be excluded. And even in those large-scale, big budget productions where co-production would be possible, the Channel Four Group were anxious that 'financial motivations not those of quality, foreign and not British culture, will be the primary factors in programme selection.'[43]

The ITV companies were also concerned about being tied too rigidly to the Autumn 1982 deadline. 'No starting date should be adhered to regardless of the state of the industry's economy,' said Sir Denis Forman in February 1980. Speaking at a press conference on the publication of the Broadcasting Bill, Sir Denis, the Chairman of the ITCA's Service Two Policy Working Party, explained the companies' attitude to the IBA proposals:

> The companies welcome the Bill without reservation: any reservations we may have are confined to the way in which the Bill may be interpreted . . . The Companies will not get Service 2 in the form that they originally wanted it. This is now clear, and we have to accept the IBA's right to interpret the present climate of opinion in devising what seems to them the best form of control and operation for the new service.[44]

Although Sir Denis did not explicitly state how the IBA's proposals departed from the companies' position, if we consider them in conjunction with ITCA's October 1979 memorandum to the Authority, the differences are evident. As far as the IBA were concerned, and they in conjunction with the Home Office were now the people who mattered, the fourth channel company would not be jointly owned with the ITV companies, but would be a subsidiary solely of the Authority; the ITV companies would only have four representatives out of eleven non-executive Board members, not five out of ten; the fourth channel's schedule would not be jointly scheduled with ITV1's and the companies' draft schedule would certainly not be binding on the channel's programme controller; the independent producers might contribute as much as 35% of the channel's programmes and not the assumed 10–15%; and as for 'seed money', the IBA said nothing. It would be a matter of policy for the fourth channel's board to decide.

One other point, with perhaps psychological significance, was the name of the channel. The companies were convinced that no matter what the official designation, it would be called 'ITV2' by the public. The Channel Four Group wanted it to be known as 'TV4' as a mark of its independence from all other channels, and the IBA appeared to concur;

in their proposals they talked of the 'Fourth Channel'. In the Broadcasting Bill it was initially and feebly referred to as 'Service 2', but this was changed at the Bill's Committee stage to the 'Fourth Channel Service'. The Authority settled the matter when, following the enactment of the Broadcasting Bill, they established the 'Channel Four Television Company'. It seems unlikely that with its distinctive '4' logo, the public will now insist on calling it anything else. Thus, in name as well as form, Channel Four is neither ITV2 nor the OBA.

LEGISLATION: A THREAT OF MARTYRDOM

A reading of the statutory programming obligations for the fourth channel laid down in the Broadcasting Act reveals the full extent to which the delicate and subjective matter of interpretation was to be left to the IBA. As Merlyn Rees commented during the Bill's second reading, some of the clauses had the ring of an idealistic newspaper editorial; they read well but were surely too vague to ask anyone to put into practice – the lawyers at any rate would certainly have a marvellous time!

3 (1) As regards the programmes (other than advertisements) broadcast in the Fourth Channel Service it shall be the duty of the Authority:
(a) to ensure that the programmes contain a *suitable* proportion of matter calculated to appeal to tastes and interests not generally catered for by ITV;
(b) without prejudice to so much of main section 2 (2) (a) as relates to the dissemination of education, to ensure that a *suitable* proportion of the programmes are of an educational nature;
(c) to encourage *innovation and experiment* in the form and content of programmes;
and generally to give the Fourth Channel Service a *distinctive* character of its own.[45] (author's emphasis)

And regarding the provision of programmes, it would be the duty of the IBA to:

4 (1) (b) to secure that, so far as is consistent with their duties in relation to the Fourth Channel Service under section 3 and main section 2 (2), a *substantial* proportion of the programmes broadcast in the Fourth Channel Service are supplied other than by persons of either the following descriptions, namely a TV programme contractor and a body corporate under the control of a TV programme contractor.[46] (author's emphasis)

Speaking during the second reading debate, William Whitelaw responded to some of the financial worries that had been raised by both the companies and the Channel Four Group. In a move away from his

108

Cambridge remark that 'the budget for the fourth channel will not necessarily be governed by the revenue earned from advertisements shown on that channel,' he now stated that the channel must be financially viable and self-supporting:

> There are, of course, risks with any new venture, and it may take a while to establish financial viability for the new service, but financial viability must be achieved and, if it is not, we shall be entitled to reconsider the future of the service.[47]

Whitelaw was not prepared to set any time limits, his only answer to the question of how long would he allow the fourth channel to prove itself being 'as soon as possible'.

The Government was concerned about the effect that subsidising of the fourth channel by the ITV companies would have on the ITV levy. The IBA's proposals had estimated that a second commercial channel would generate a revenue increase of 10% for the ITV system as a whole. This suggested that the fourth channel would earn an income of some £45 million in 1979 figures; given that ITV's 1978 revenue was £410 million and allowing for inflation. But the IBA had also mentioned an annual budget for the channel of £60–80 million (also in 1979 terms), which implied an annual deficit of £15–35 million to be made good by the ITV companies, and would mean a *pro rata* reduction in their profit levels. With the ITV levy on profits set at 66.7%, and the balance subject to a further 52% of Corporation Tax, this 'making good' by the companies would lead to a £13–29 million fall in the Exchequer's annual appropriation. At a time of severe public spending cuts, this was obviously politically contentious. The Government reacted by producing its own set of estimates. In concluding the Bill's second reading, Leon Brittan, Minister of State at the Home Office, explained that the Government reckoned that by 1984, once the fourth channel had settled down, its revenue would be up to £80 million and there would be no continuing effect on the levy. However, there would be a significant effect while the channel was incurring its initial start-up costs. Brittan estimated the reduction in the levy would be in the order of £18 million for 1981-82; £40 million for 1982-83; and £15 million for 1983-84.[48] There was a fundamental difference, he stated, between the Government's proposals in which there was a reasonable prospect of the channel being financially self-supporting in a comparatively short span of time, and the OBA proposals which would have entailed a continuous call for direct Government assistance.

Brittan's jibe at the OBA was made in the light of strong hankerings by many Labour MPs for the implementation of their 1978 White Paper proposals. The Government had introduced 'a compromising hybrid Bill', said Dr Shirley Summerskill, creating a service which would be 'schizophrenically torn between the desire to produce high-quality, original programmes and the need to attract advertising revenue with mass audiences.'[49] The Government was putting total faith and almost blind confidence in the IBA, a faith and confidence, said Dr Summerskill, certainly lacking among independent film producers. Only the establishment of a third television broadcasting authority, the OBA, would ensure a commitment to quality, diversity, experiment and innovation. Some Labour MPs, notably Austin Mitchell, a former broadcaster, were less enthusiastic about giving the OBA the kiss of life. As Mitchell conceded, the OBA, torn between its aversion to competing for advertising revenue and its reluctance to rely solely on Government subvention, would have been even more dichotomised than the proposed fourth channel company. The Bill was basically right in the outline it proposed, but it needed to be strengthened, for its safeguards were too vague. Phillip Whitehead, criticising the Home Secretary's 'bland phrases about financial viability', wanted to know what would be the new service's first criterion: programme quality or financial self-sufficiency?

Despite Labour fears that the Bill was too permissive, its passage through Parliament was not dominated by a great desire on the part of the independent producers' lobby or the ITV companies to amend it in any significant way. Channel Four Group sympathisers such as Phillip Whitehead and Dr Shirley Summerskill did attempt to bring about some changes of emphasis at the Committee stage; for instance, by proposing to substitute for descriptions like 'a suitable proportion' of matter calculated to appeal to tastes and interests not catered for by ITV, the phrase 'a substantial proportion'. These amendments were nearly all unsuccessful and except for the change in the name of the new service the Bill emerged from Committee virtually untouched.

Although the two main actors in the principal plot were essentially content with the proposed legislation, the leading protagonists from two sub-plots – the supporters of Welsh-language broadcasting, and the advertisers – were definitely not satisfied.

Welsh-language broadcasting was the issue that dominated the Bill's passage through Parliament and, for a while, the front pages of the national newspapers as well. Whitelaw's announcement in Cambridge of the Government's decision to renege on its electoral manifesto promise to concentrate Welsh-language broadcasting on to one television channel was a gift for a minority party like Plaid Cymru. Support for the Party had diminished since its zenith in the mid-1970s, when it had been capturing 10% of the Welsh vote, and just over a year before the Broadcasting Bill's introduction the Welsh had roundly rejected even a limited form of devolution in a national referendum. The Bill's affront to Welsh sensibilities revived the Party's fortunes. It encouraged a surge of applications to join the Party and provoked a campaign of civil disobedience in which more than 2,000 Welsh viewers refused to renew their licences, while the extreme militant campaigners raided transmitters and blanked out programmes. The most effective and notorious measure of Welsh protest, however, was not undertaken by the Welsh collectively, but by a single Welshman. In April 1980, sixty-eight year old Gwynfor Evans, President of Plaid Cymru, declared that unless the Government changed its mind about the way the fourth channel was to be introduced in Wales he would, in the first week of October 1980, begin starving himself to death. His threat was serious and, as the *Observer* argued, the Government would have to take him seriously or else face the prospect of violence following his death:

> In the shadows in Wales are figures who would turn to violence – Wales has gone a small but significant way down the road to terrorism in the past year. Attacks on TV transmitters and English-owned cottages, incendiary devices left here and there, the smell of violence at this month's National Eisteddfod; the threat of a 'fast to death' by Gwynfor Evans, Welsh nationalism's peaceful patriarch and mentor – all these are warning signs ... Is it politic to let the allocation of a TV channel be used as a rallying point for romantics and bigots when it could be a gesture of goodwill instead?[50]

In September 1980 the Government backed down. An amendment introduced while the Bill was in the House of Lords changed the arrangements for Welsh-language broadcasting. Not only would all Welsh-language broadcasting be concentrated on a single channel, but a new and unique authority, the Welsh Fourth Channel Authority or Sianel Pedwar Cymru (S4C) would be established. Programmes for the channel would be supplied by the BBC, HTV (assuming it retained its franchise), and independent producers. The BBC would provide its share (which S4C now estimate is likely to be about 10 hours) free of charge; the Government promising that the next time the licence fee was fixed, an allowance would be made to ensure that there was enough money to finance the Welsh-language programmes. HTV's and the independent producers' shares (likely to be 7½-8 hours and 4-4¼ hours respectively) would have to be paid for by the Welsh Authority, who would receive an annual budget from the same source as the Channel Four Television Company – i.e. a subscription paid by all the ITV contractors on a basis roughly proportional to their NARAL levels. The size of S4C's budget would be settled through negotiations with the IBA, but the revised legislation made it clear that in the event of a default of agreement the sum would be determined by the Home Secretary. Advertising time on the Welsh Channel would be sold and retained by the IBA's Welsh contractor, HTV, although no advertising would be allowed to appear alongside, let alone within, BBC productions on the channel. Unlike Channel Four S4C would not be expected to be financially self-sufficient. An adjustment in the levy allowing the ITV companies to keep a larger free slice of their profits before being subject to the levy would, hoped the

Government, ensure that the Exchequer, not the companies, would pay for the Welsh service. The Lords' amendment did not stipulate that S4C should broadcast Welsh language programmes exclusively. It merely stated that 'the programmes broadcast on the fourth channel in Wales between the hours of 6.30 p.m. and 10.00 p.m. [should] consist mainly of programmes in Welsh.'[51] The Government also made it clear that the Welsh arrangements had only experimental status; they would be reviewed after their first three years of operation.

The Government's climb-down was not without its critics. Economically, the revised arrangements were likely to be far more expensive than those originally proposed in the Bill. Could the high cost be justified for so small an audience? Several Conservative backbenchers accused the Government of giving into blackmail by the Welsh nationalists. 'It cannot make economic sense,' said one Conservative MP, Delwyn Williams. He estimated that the single Welsh Channel would cost £138 million over five years for a peak viewing audience of only 75,000.[52] Culturally, the proposed output of 22 hours a week was very ambitious. 'Can something like half a million Welsh speakers,' asked the BBC's Welsh political correspondent, Patrick Hannan, 'provide enough talent to produce even three hours a day of television without the performers being reduced to broadcasting to one another?'[53] Despite the problems associated with the Welsh channel's long-term viability, it seemed to the Government that Realpolitik dictated the necessity of setting up the channel and perhaps letting the Welsh see it fail, rather than flatly denying it and allowing it to act as a lightning conductor for Welsh protest. At Brompton Road, the IBA were not upset about losing responsibility for the fourth channel in Wales. As one senior IBA executive has put it: 'An increase in Welsh-language broadcasting is likely to attract more kicks than ha'pence, so why not let others receive the kicks?'[54]

Throughout the Bill's passage through Parliament the advertisers and the agencies lobbied to change the arrangements for selling advertising on the fourth channel. In the event, however, no major amendment to the proposals was even tabled, let alone considered. As William Whitelaw had mentioned in Cambridge, the IBA had invited the ISBA and the IPA to inform them of sales practices on the fourth channel that they would find objectionable. The two associations took this as an opportunity to present their criticisms of the ITV companies' existing practices. In a list that was not intended to be exhaustive, the IPA produced under the following headings 14 examples of restrictive or coercive practices: collaborative fixing of rates; ITCA Cancellation Committee; 'package' selling; deliberate underselling of airtime; LWT's 'Gold Star' rate; double standards on 'special' programming; 'pre-empt' rate cards; further refinements in 'allocation' policy; Thames's allocation 'policy'; Thames's 'carry-through' rate; 'incentive share' deals; confirmation of bookings; lack of consultation or consideration; lack of serious effort to provide off-peak programming.[55] This is not the place to examine these practices in detail; the above list is merely intended to give an indication of the range of the advertisers' complaints.

The ITV companies, of course, challenged these allegations. They cited the conclusions of a 1979 detailed study by Professor Harry Henry on the economics of television advertising which stated that, regardless of the advertisers' complaints about restrictive practices, the general level of advertising rates on ITV had been trending downwards not upwards since 1961. He estimated that the costs of the average commercial-home-minute at constant prices had fallen by 15% between 1961–78.[56] However, this is a misleading figure, for the number of commercial-home-minutes had greatly increased since 1961, after the derestriction of broadcasting hours in 1972. Since the extra hours gained were all at the off-peak times, which commanded a low price, they would obviously drag the price of the average commercial-home-minute downwards. In fact, as Henry's own figures showed, the rate for peak airtime had increased by over 15% in real terms since 1974.

Producing a convincing alternative to the Government's and the IBA's proposals for selling airtime on the fourth channel was a considerably harder task than criticising the ITV companies' existing practices. The advertisers' and agencies' case was not helped by their failure to agree upon a joint policy. The ISBA insisted on pursuing a more ambitious and, in effect, politically unrealistic line than the IPA. Under the ISBA plan the ITV companies would have absolutely no involvement in the finances of the fourth channel. *The ISBA Alternative Proposal* envisaged a number of sales agencies selling the air time on the new channel and providing it with its annual budget. The shareholders of these agencies would have no representation on the fourth channel board, no voice in the application of their funds, and no connection with the programme-making process. In this way, the ISBA argued, competition for the sale of advertising time could be introduced into television without the risk of adversely affecting programme standards. Many organisations, believed the ISBA, would be 'eager to take up the potentially lucrative task' of running these agencies. The ITCA, however, was extremely sceptical. In February 1980, Donald Harker, on the behalf of the ITCA, wrote an open letter to the ISBA's Director, Kenneth Miles, criticising his society's proposals. The fourth channel, stressed Harker, would not be able to pay its way in the early years at least and had no prospects of high profitability if it was to fulfil the programming function that had been assigned to it. One could not, therefore, count on any enthusiastic response to the opportunity to invest, especially, argued Harker, when it was appreciated that the potential investors would be committed, under the ISBA plan, to provide the initial and substantial funds for commissioning programmes well in advance of the service going on the air. 'On these terms,' said Harker, 'the new channel looks more like a philanthropic adventure than a recognisable commercial enterprise.'[57] The only way the ISBA proposal would be attractive to investors was if the new service was designed to be immediately profitable, something that could only be done if it sought high ratings by presenting programmes of mass appeal. Such a policy would undermine the channel's agreed and stated *raison d'être*.

Pragmatically, the IPA recognised the need to involve the ITV companies in the selling of the fourth channel's advertising. They advocated that rather than rely on the company's existing sales forces, a separate organisation should be formed to sell the channel's air time on behalf of all the ITV companies, both on a network basis and by region, in a way similar to that in which *TV Times* sold its advertising space. Such a sales force could single-mindedly advance the benefits of advertising on the fourth channel, and concentrate on encouraging new advertisers into the television medium. The income earned by the organisation would be shared by the ITV contractors roughly in the same proportion to their NARAL levels, and the fourth channel budget would be provided by the companies in the way already spelt out by the IBA. It would be possible under this scheme for those advertisers requiring network air time to buy this from a single source. It would also, believed the IPA, be more effective than requiring separate rate cards to be published for both channels by the fifteen companies, and for air time to be sold by extra staff in each of them.

The IPA plan was, as we have already seen, seriously considered by the IBA in its 1979 proposals. They were not convinced that a separate sales force would be more cost-effective; for it would lack the regional flexibility of the ITV companies' sales forces. Besides, for many it seemed a pointless compromise. Either the ITV companies monopoly should be broken or kept intact. Were there any real advantages in a separate selling company that was not welcomed by the companies, but would nevertheless act on their behalf? One possible benefit was that it might reduce the likelihood of 'linkage' in the conditions of air time sale on ITV and Channel Four. But to admit this would be to admit a scepticism about the IBA's ability to prevent the companies from practising 'linkage' if they were allowed to sell its air time. It was a scepticism that the Government apparently did not believe was justified.

At the Bill's Committee stage the ISBA, remarkably, seemed the more confident of the two advertising societies that it would bring about an amendment to the Bill. In March 1980 Kenneth Miles revealed his optimism:

We are discussing with a number of the members of the Committee possible changes in the Bill. I would like to emphasise that there is still a long way to go and still a lot of reason to believe that many members of the Committee are not entirely happy with the Bill as it now stands.[58]

The ISBA had the advantage of one of its leading members, John Watson, a Conservative MP, being a member of the Standing Committee that examined the Bill. He favoured competitive selling on the new channel. More notable, however, was the fact that the other member of the Committee with a professional connection with the advertising industry, Conservative MP Geoffrey Johnson Smith, a non-executive director of David Williams and Ketchum Advertising Agency, did not support the case for competitive selling. And, when the time came to consider the clauses relating to the sale of air time, the Committee's eighteen other members shared Johnson Smith's dismissal of the ISBA plan. Watson, realising the situation, did not even table an amendment on the subject. He did, however, succeed in winning support for one amendment; a change in the clauses dealing with the contents of the IBA's annual report. In future, any complaint received by the Authority about the conduct of the ITV companies in connection with the sale of advertising time, together with the action taken by the Authority in relation to these complaints, would have to be listed in the IBA's annual report. The advertisers hoped that this amendment might give some teeth to the IBA's proposed Advertising Liaison Committee. It was a minor victory for an otherwise most unsuccessful campaign to persuade a Conservative Government and Party of the supposed merits of denying the ITV companies control of Channel Four's advertising sales – a campaign whose failure stands in sharp contrast to the success of the independent producers' lobby in realising their aim of preventing the ITV companies from controlling Channel Four's programming.

ESTABLISHING THE COMPANY

In its 1979 proposals the IBA had said that it would be establishing 'special consultative arrangements' for the fourth channel during early 1980. This was a reference to the Authority's intention to appoint eleven consultants to undertake the initial planning of the channel, in anticipation of the Broadcasting Bill's enactment. Upon incorporation of the Channel Four Company in December 1980, these consultants were to become the company's directors. The delicate job of choosing the consultants was the sole responsibility of the IBA. In February 1980, Sir Brian Young wrote to a number of organisations who had an interest in the channel, inviting them to suggest a list of individuals whom they believed should sit on the Board of Channel Four. He explained that the Board would, unlike the IBA (or the Board of Governors of the BBC), be drawn, with the exception of the Chairman and the Deputy Chairman, from 'men and women with experience directly relevant to the subsidiary's function of preparing and assembling a television programmes service'[59] – i.e. they would be broadly representative of the channel's future suppliers.

In their reply, the Channel Four Group reiterated their belief that any form of a representative board would lead to a conflict of interests. In fact, they delayed writing to Sir Brian to see if there was any amendment to the Broadcasting Bill at the Committee stage regarding the composition of the Channel Four Board. Of the 22 names they eventually put forward, two – Anthony Smith and Sara Morrison – were to be accepted by the IBA. Smith, following the publication of the Annan Committee Report, had continued to campaign both individually and through the Channel Four Group for an independent fourth channel. In 1979 he had been appointed Director of the British Film Institute. Morrison, an executive director of the General Electric Company, Chairperson of the National Council for Voluntary Organisations and a former member of the Annan Committee, had maintained a close interest in the politics of broadcasting. As two of the three board members who would look after the interests of the independent producers, they were to be joined by an experienced programme-maker, Roger Graef. An American-born free-lance director, who had worked for Allan King Associates during the 1960s and has since made many successful films for the BBC, he is best known in recent times as the director of the BBC's controversial documentary series on the Thames Valley Police Force.

In the face of ITCA disgruntlement, the IBA were adamant that the companies should only have four 'representatives' on the Board, not five out of ten. The companies' discontent was exacerbated when the Authority revealed it was not prepared to allow all four of these 'representatives' to be managing directors of ITV companies. This, the IBA felt, would give the companies too unified and solid a block at the heart of the channel's board. Instead, it proposed that there should be two managing directors and two senior programme-makers; it was hoped that the latter would, despite obvious loyalties to the companies, have a somewhat different set of priorities from those of the former. In the stormy exchanges that followed, some ITV managing directors went so far as to contemplate a boycott of the channel by the companies. But, in the event, the two sides compromised; the Channel Four Board would include three managing directors – Brian Tesler of LWT, William Brown of Scottish, and David McCall of Anglia – and one company programme-maker – Joy Whitby, Head of Children's Programmes at Yorkshire. Thus the Big Five were to have only one of their managing directors on the channel's board.

There were two other 'representative' consultants: an educationalist, Anne Sofer, a member of the Inner London Education Authority, and, since the consultants were appointed before the Lords' amendment creating the Welsh Fourth Channel Authority, a Welshman, Dr Glyn

Tegai Hughes, the Warden of Gregynog Hall, University of Wales. The nine consultants – Smith, Morrison, Graef, Tesler, Brown, McCall, Whitby, Sofer and Tegai Hughes – were all appointed in July 1980. One month before this, at the beginning of June 1980, Edmund Dell and Sir Richard Attenborough had taken up their appointments as Chairman and Deputy-Chairman respectively. In keeping with the IBA's 1979 proposals, Dell, a former Labour Secretary of State for Trade and Chairman and Chief Executive of the Guinness Peat Group, had no experience of the television industry. Sir Richard, on the other hand, with his distinguished career in the film industry and as Chairman of Capital Radio, could not really be described as an outsider.

One of the consultants' first tasks was the selection of the future Chief Executive. It was obviously the key appointment; the character and the ability of the individual chosen would largely determine the character and content of the channel. The post was advertised in July 1980. Of the 29 candidates, the name of Jeremy Isaacs stood out. A strong-minded, talented Scot, Isaacs had an impressive track record: beginning with Granada in 1958; then producer of Rediffusion's *This Week* and BBC's *Panorama* during the 1960s; and moving on to Controller of Features and then Director of Programmes at Thames during the 1970s, where he was responsible for successes such as the epic *World at War* series. The strength of his application lay in his proven ability to champion quality and independence both in his own work and in that of the producers who worked for him. His departure from Thames in 1978, which he described as 'something between resignation and the sack',[60] was itself a statement of his determination to stand up to, and voice disapproval of, IBA intervention. Following a ban by the Authority of a Thames documentary, *The Amnesty Report*, which alleged brutality by the Royal Ulster Constabulary in Northern Ireland, Isaacs had, in the public interest, handed the embargoed film to the BBC, who had been prepared to show it on their *Nationwide* programme. This collaboration with the opposition was the final straw in an already strained relationship that Isaacs had with Thames's competitively-minded Managing Director, Bryan Cowgill. Finally, as the prospective boss of a channel that would draw a substantial proportion of its programmes from independent producers, Isaacs had the advantage of having worked, since he had left Thames, as a freelance and independent producer. After the Jimmy Boyle film for Scottish Television, he had made *Ireland: A Television History* for the BBC.

In his letter of application Isaacs spelled out what he believed Channel Four's programming philosophy should be:

My priorities for the new channel are these:
– To encourage innovation across the whole range of programmes
– To find audiences for the channel and for all its programmes

117

- To make programmes of special appeal to particular audiences
- To develop the channel's educational potential to the full
- To provide platforms for the widest possible range of opinion in utterance, discussion, and debate
- To maintain as flexible a schedule as practicable to enable a quick response to changing needs
- To make an opening in the channel for criticism of its own output
- To accord a high priority to the arts
- If funds allow, to make or help make films of feature length for television here, for the cinema abroad.[61]

Isaacs also had some clear ideas about how he would run the channel. He wanted to appoint a small staff of 'commissioning editors', to whom the ITV companies and independent producers would address their programme ideas. Each commissioning editor would be responsible for commissioning programmes in certain subject areas, although it was obviously too early to specify what these categories would be.

Isaacs was not the only contender for the top job. His two serious rivals were Paul Bonner, Head of BBC Science and Features, and John Birt from LWT. In contrast to Isaacs, who was essentially an ITV programme-maker, Bonner's career had kept him solely within the Corporation. Editor of BBC's Community Programme Unit during the mid-1970s, he had been in charge of the access series, *Open Door*, while as Head of Science and Features his responsibilities included *Horizon* and *Tomorrow's World*. The Channel Four consultants were clearly not short of choice. Their final decision was announced at the end of September 1980. Isaacs was to be appointed Chief Executive, to run for five years from 1 January 1981, while Bonner, whom the consultants had found most impressive during interviews, was offered a position specially created for him, that of Channel Controller; essentially, deputy to the Chief Executive with regard to programming. It was a move that surprised many observers for its lack of formality; the Controller's job had not been advertised, and no one was aware that the consultants intended to make such an appointment.

Speaking to the Press on the day of his appointment, Isaacs made it clear that he was firmly opposed to either the ITV companies or the independent producers providing a fixed quota of the channel's programmes. No one, he said, would have programmes accepted 'as of right and willy-nilly'.[62] The channel would be run on an offers basis, with people bringing in their ideas for acceptance or rejection. He challenged the companies to extend and improve upon the service they already provided. He challenged the independents to demonstrate the quality of their work. And he challenged innovators and newcomers to the screen 'to speak to television audiences in a language they will understand.' When asked to define the broad spectrum to which the channel would appeal, he said that it would serve a full range of opinion in a circle from extreme left to extreme right. 'But there must be a selection,' he added; 'there will not be room for everybody and there will not be room for loonies.'

A few weeks after Isaacs's appointment, the Broadcasting Bill received Royal Assent, and the Channel Four Television Company Ltd was officially incorporated as a wholly owned subsidiary of the IBA. After twenty years gestation the occupant of the empty room had at last been born. It would now have slightly under two years to prepare itself before moving in. The long wait had generated great expectations. As one senior ITV executive put it:

Viewers are led to expect a channel that appeals to individuals and minorities but excludes none; that offers more of everything that is good on television, only different, in greater depth, at better times, preferably produced by people who have not produced it before. There will, we are told, be room for ITN, access, come-back, minority programmes, popular entertainment, popular education. There is even a *statutory* obligation to be different.[63]

The question was whether some people would have to be disappointed.

Notes

1. Hansard, *House of Commons Debates*, 15 May 1979, col. 51.
2. Fiddick, P., 'The Four Channel Future', *Edinburgh International Television Festival 1979 – Official Programme*, p. 34.
3. Shaw, C., speaking to the Broadcasting Press Guild, *Daily Mail*, 7 June 1979.
4. Shaw, C., address to the Broadcasting Press Guild, *Independent Broadcasting*, Number 21, August 1979, pp. 8–10.
5. *Film and Television Technician*, June 1979, p. 12.
6. Elstein, D., unpublished speech to the ACTT 1979 Conference.
7. *Film and Television Technician*, June 1979, p. 12.
8. 'Who are the independents?', press statement issued by the organisers of a British Academy for Film and Television Arts presentation, 28 June 1979.
9. Isaacs, J., 'The 1979 MacTaggart Lecture', *Edinburgh International Television Festival 1980 – Official Programme*, p. 60.
10. Ibid., p. 63.
11. Ibid.
12. Ibid., p. 64.
13. Ibid.
14. Ibid.
15. Ibid.
16. Karpf, A., 'Battle for TV4', *Observer*, 2 September 1979.
17. Birt, J., 'Freedom and the broadcaster', *Listener*, 13 September 1979, pp. 336–8.
18. Isaacs, op.cit., p. 59.
19. Whitelaw, W., speech by the Home Secretary at the RTS Convention – 'Television in

a Free Society' – King's College, Cambridge, 14 September 1979, Home Office news release, p. 3.

20. Ibid., p. 7.
21. *Conservative Manifesto for Wales*, Conservative Party 1979.
22. Whitelaw, op.cit., p. 6.
23. 'New communications order: Channel Four and more', *Television: Journal of the Royal Television Society*, Volume 17, Number 12, December 1979, p. 25.
24. Fiddick, P., 'Tossed by cross-channel currents', *Guardian*, 8 January 1980.
25. 'ITV2: The Fourth Channel', A confidential memorandum from the ITV companies to the IBA, October 1979, p. 2.
26. Ibid.
27. Ibid., Appendix D.
28. Ibid., p. 3.
29. 'An Open Letter to the Home Secretary', *Guardian*, 10 October 1979.
30. *Channel Four and Innovation – The Foundation*, Independent Film-makers Association, February 1980, p. 1.
31. Ibid., p. 2.
32. Ibid.
33. *The Fourth Channel: Proposals by the Independent Television Companies*, 27 July 1973.
34. *The Fourth Channel: The Authority's Proposals*, IBA statement, 12 November 1979, p. 1.
35. Ibid., pp. 1–18.
36. *Guardian*, 12 February 1980.
37. *The Fourth Television Channel: A Reply to Proposals by the IBA*, Channel Four Group, 3 December 1979.
38. *Listener*, 7 February 1980.
39. *Listener*, 14 February 1980.
40. Reply to IBA Proposals by Channel Four Group, op.cit.
41. Shaw, C., 'ITV2: Some swine, some rush', *Listener*, 31 January 1980, p. 140.
42. Reply to IBA Proposals by Channel Four Group, op.cit.
43. Ibid.
44. *Television Today*, 14 February 1980.
45. *Broadcasting Act 1980*, Eliz. 2, Ch. 64, 1980.
46. Ibid.
47. Hansard, *House of Commons Debates*, 18 February 1980, col. 52.
48. Ibid., col. 156.
49. Ibid., col, 149.
50. 'Breaking faith with Wales', *Observer*, 17 August 1980.
51. *Lords Amendments to the Broadcasting Bill*, Bill 272, 6 November 1980, Amendment No. 5 (2), p. 2.
52. Hansard, *House of Commons Debates*, 10 November 1980, col. 53.
53. Hannan, P., 'Government may be off the hook, broadcasters are now on it', *Listener*, 2 October 1980, p. 429.
54. Personal communication.
55. 'An examination of airtime selling practices', unpublished IPA paper, 9 October 1979.
56. Henry, H., 'The commercial implications of a second (and complementary) independent television channel', *Admap monograph*, 1979.
57. Harker, D., open letter from the ITCA Future of Broadcasting Policy Committee to the Director of the ISBA, 1 February 1980.
58. *Campaign*, 11 April 1980, p. 13.
59. Letter to the Channel Four Group from Sir Brian Young, Director-General of the IBA, 29 February 1980.
60. Tinker, J., *The Television Barons* (London: Quartet Books, 1980), p. 139.

61. Isaacs, J., letter of application for the position of Chief Executive, Channel Four Television Company Ltd.
62. *The Times*, 1 October 1980.
63. Pagnamenta, P., 'Will we see a "peaky-looking infant in 1982?" ', *Listener*, 9 October 1980, p. 468.

4 Putting the Show on the Road

At the end of 1980 Channel Four consisted of a Board of Directors, two senior executives-designate, and some temporary office space at the IBA's headquarters in Brompton Road. Now, at the end of 1982, installed in its stylish 'high-tec' premises in Charlotte Street, it is broadcasting sixty hours of television programmes a week to nearly ninety per cent of the British population.

Jeremy Isaacs's first job was to appoint his staff. His second was to start commissioning programmes. The offers from the few established, and the many more budding, independent producers flooded in. Fearing blank screens and impressed by the quality of many of their programme ideas, Channel Four gave a large number of independents the go-ahead. The ITV companies, a little shell-shocked by the announcement in December 1980 of the IBA's decision on the award of the new franchise contracts, were slower in coming forward. Even when they did start making offers, initial failure by the companies to agree on terms of trade with the channel delayed any firm decisions being made. By the beginning of 1982 Channel Four had made over two hundred commissions, virtually all with independent producers. This imbalance was rectified over the next few months, but the independents' early start, the quality of their offers, and their ability to price themselves competitively vis-à-vis the companies, helped them secure a much greater share of the channel's first year's output — about 50% of newly originated material — than almost anyone, including Isaacs, had originally predicted. Channel Four has thus comfortably fulfilled its obligation to draw a substantial proportion of its programmes from producers other than the ITV contractors. Whether the content and form of its programmes fulfil its other celebrated obligation, to be distinctive and innovative, is something its audience can now begin to decide.

MOBILISATION

While the Broadcasting Bill completed its journey through the legislative system, many aspirant independent producers metamorphosed from being propagandists into entrepreneurs. The Channel Four Group lost its steam as its members drifted away in search of inspiration for programme ideas to offer the soon-to-be-appointed Channel Four Controller. In May 1980, the IBA held a consultation on production facilities for the fourth channel. Colin Shaw, who chaired the meeting, explained that apart from its transmission facilities — its own machinery for playing out and its own presentation studio — Channel Four would be free from the production facilities train which the existing networks carried. The question the Authority wanted to ask was whether the independent sector had the facilities available to become substantial suppliers to the new channel. Peter Wayne, speaking on behalf of the Association of Television Facility Companies, informed them that the equipment existed and was ready to be used; at present it was employed by the makers of advertising commercials, industrial films, programmes for overseas markets, etc.:

> There are 64 broadcast-quality videotape machines within our Association, and we know that there is probably more than half that number outside our Association; nine tele-cine machines; 29 cameras capable of working at 16 different locations simultaneously; eight computer editing facilities; four picture manipulators; a standards converter; and two tape/film transfer systems. We have fairly massive capacity. We suspect that within the independent sector there are as many videotape machines as there are in the BBC.[1]

Another independent producer, Michael Darlow, commented that much of the BBC's and the ITV companies' equipment was becoming increasingly dated. 'On the whole, one can find better stuff around Wardour Street, and we would rather use it; it works quicker, it works better and it produces more the sort of pictures we want.'[2] There were also plenty of studios available, said Mike Luckwell, Managing Director of the Moving Picture Company, a production company with its own film and video facilities. He estimated that there were forty studios in the London area alone. In short, the independents believed they had the facilities to provide a highly professional product. The main worry that they expressed concerned financing. Assuming something like fifty hours transmission a week, it was easy enough to calculate that with a £70-80 million annual budget Channel Four would have an average of slightly under £30,000 an hour. Was this enough? In the face of a certain degree of scepticism on the part of the independents, Shaw asserted that it was. The BBC, he pointed out, had recently claimed that its costs were in the order of £19,000 an hour:

> You can qualify that by saying that the BBC does a lot of programming during the day, that it does an awful lot of cheap programmes which bring the average price down, and that, if you are going to be in the business of broadcasting from 5 to 11 at night, a fair proportion of what you do will be at the more expensive end of the bracket. But we do not feel, from the calculations we have done, that £70 million is an altogether unpromising starting point.[3]

In the summer of 1980, following an open meeting in the London Hyde Park Hotel, the Independent Programme Producers Association was formed. It aimed to become the main trade association representing the interests of independent producers, and acting as a counterweight to the ITCA in dealings with Channel Four and the IBA. IPPA declared that it would endeavour to ensure that Channel Four:

a) discriminates positively in favour of independent productions;
b) agrees prices with independent producers which fairly reflect the real costs of productions and wherever possible pays the entire cost of production;
c) recognises that a genuine independent production cannot be one financed in whole or in part by any ITV contractor, its parent, associated or subsidiary companies.[4]

An *ad hoc* interim council was set up to organise the association until elections could take place. These were held in January 1981, by which time the IPPA had over two hundred paid-up members. The formally constituted IPPA Council was unsurprisingly dominated by directors of the few already well-established independent production companies; such as Graham Benson from the Robert Stigwood Organisation, Mark Shelmerdine of London Films, Mike Luckwell from Moving Pictures, and Iain Bruce of AKA. The managing director of Video Arts Television, Michael Peacock, formerly of the BBC and LWT, was elected to be the first chairman of the association.

As IPPA developed it concentrated its activities in four main areas. First, it began negotiations with Channel Four over terms of trade for independent producers. These were largely concluded by the beginning of 1982. Second it undertook to co-ordinate labour relations with the broadcasting unions, in particular the ACTT. Originally IPPA intended to appoint its own industrial relations officer, but strong union opposition to a fragmentation of employers' organisations in the film and television industry led to the formation of a Joint Industrial Relations Service with the British Film Producers Association. As the film employers' association, the BFPA had long been criticised for being out of touch and ineffectual, having failed to adapt to the demise of the British feature film industry. In early 1981, however, a change in personnel within the organisation allied to a re-examination of policy and organisational questions that was to lead to the BFPA becoming the British Film and Television Producers Association, produced a situation in which close co-operation in certain areas with the newly formed IPPA was possible. The BFPA already had national agreements with the ACTT governing the production of feature films and television film series and covering the production of shorts and documentary material. During 1980 the 'shorts and documentaries' agreement, which had not been significantly altered since the heyday of British cinema, was substantially renegotiated to cover independent production for Channel Four, and was retitled the 'Specialised Producers' Agreement'. Virtually all production by the independent sector for Channel Four is now governed either by this new agreement or by the existing BFTPA agreement on feature film and television film series. (One exception to this rule is the 'Workshop Declaration' governing the production of material by film workshops; see below, p.150) Waging and staffing levels for production by the ITCA companies for Channel Four are governed by the existing ITCA agreements with the ACTT.

The third area of IPPA's activity was the provision of opportunities for quasi-training and education by organising seminars with titles like 'How to be an independent producer and live to tell the tale', as well as supplying more specialised advice on, for instance, copyright and other legal matters. And fourthly, it aimed to become a general information clearing house between Channel Four and the independent sector.

There was no question of IPPA becoming a closed shop. This was something that Jeremy Isaacs emphasised in January 1981, when he made his first public address to independent producers since his appointment as Chief Executive. Speaking for two-and-a-half hours to a packed audience in the Royal Institution, he said that although Channel Four recognised and supported the possibility of IPPA becoming the negotiating body for independents, no one would be excluded because he or she was not a member of IPPA. Aiming to clarify some of the uncertainty about the procedure for the commissioning of independent work, Isaacs made a number of separate points. First, he stressed caution. 'Do not leave steady jobs, mortgage the house and send the family out to work unless you've had your programme commissioned,' he said.[5] To those who were still on the staff of the BBC and ITV companies and were contemplating 'going independent', his message was think twice before leaving the security of a safe position. Unless you are marvellous, he warned, you are probably better off where you are. On the subject of financing, he confirmed that the average budget for Channel Four programmes would be a little under £30,000 an hour. But this was an average figure; a small proportion of programmes would be allowed as much as five times that amount and a larger proportion would have a great deal less. Nobody would make a great fortune out of the channel. Profit margins for the independent producer would vary according to the scale of a given programme's budget; the higher the budget, the lower the percentage profit margin would be. Isaacs went on to say that Channel Four would aim to finance the entire cost of the majority of its commissions. However, in some cases where it could not afford the whole costs, independents might be asked to find additional funds from other sources, but, he stated, co-production would not be permitted to weaken the original concept of the programme. In answer to a question about the sources of additional finance, he said he was not worried about the integrity of co-production money, so long as the integrity of the programme idea remained intact.[6] With regard to the size of the independents' contribution to Channel Four, Isaacs talked of a minimum

125

of ten hours a week; a minimum figure that some independent producers mistakenly feared would become a norm. Finally, Isaacs outlined the timetable for commissioning. Serious consideration would begin in April 1981, but firm commitments would only be given then for high-budget ideas and major drama and documentary projects that needed early finalisation if they were to be available for broadcasting during the channel's first few weeks on the air. The bulk of the commissions would start being made after August 1981. If, however, the channel's commissioning staff believed there was a need to see a pilot version of a programme idea before then, a development fund would be available to finance such work. Channel Four's commitment to supporting seeding or pump-priming as an integral part of the overall commissioning process was something that was to become clearly manifest over the following year.

The formation of IPPA was not the only sign that the independent sector was organising itself to meet the opportunities created by the arrival of Channel Four. While IPPA aimed to represent the interests of mainstream independent producers, other organisations sought to promote the concerns of more specific sections of the independent sector. During the summer of 1979 a small group of women media professionals came together to discuss how the fourth channel could be used to improve the position of women in broadcasting. Following a series of public meetings, the Women's Fourth Channel Lobby, later more ambitiously renamed the Women's Broadcasting and Film Lobby, was established to campaign for:

1) Significant improvement in employment and training opportunities for women at all levels and in all types of work;
2) The appointment at the highest level within the Fourth Channel of a woman responsible for a positive programme to remedy the effects of past discrimination;
3) Equal representation of men and women in the governing and administration of the Fourth Channel;
4) A reassessment of the way in which women are portrayed on television.[7]

The ACTT's *Patterns of Discrimination* report had drawn attention to the fact that only a very small proportion of women were employed in the broadcasting industry in either technical or decision-making grades. The key to improving this situation lay in the provision of training and re-training schemes for women. The WBFL demanded that both Channel Four and the applicants for the new ITV franchises should be required to provide such schemes. While the Broadcasting Bill was at its Committee stage, the WBFL successfully lobbied to have a clause on training by the ITV contractors included, although in the event when the clause was formally drafted it made no actual reference to sexual discrimination. In a meeting with Lady Plowden, Chairman (*sic*) of the IBA, the WBFL pointed out that over half of the ITCA companies had no women on their boards of management, and that the remaining seven only had a token one or two at the most. They proposed that the IBA should ensure that the Channel Four Board had a minimum of three women; one of whom would be responsible for monitoring training and advising on the employment of women. They were semi-successful; three women — Sara Morrison, Joy Whitby and Anne Sofer — were appointed, but none had specially defined responsibilities for women's interests.

It would be a mistake to attribute Channel Four's positive attitude on women's issues solely to the activities of the WBFL. The channel's programming philosophy, to cater for substantial groups presently neglected, meant that it was well-disposed towards improving the position of that majority of 'minority' groups — the 51% of the population who are women. The WBFL was the most forceful expression within the broadcasting industry of a general social climate, a climate characterised by the fact that the feminist movement had, to a certain extent, come of age. It was a climate that Jeremy Isaacs recognised and welcomed. In an interview in December 1980, a few weeks after his appointment as Chief Executive, he talked to the editor of the *Guardian's* Women's page, Liz Forgan, about women and Channel Four:

> One of the things women say is that there are too few opportunities for them to make a complete range of programmes and that if they did get a chance to make certain kinds of programmes — say current affairs — we would get an interestingly different view of the world. I intend to give them the opportunity to demonstrate that. We have got *Panorama* and *World in Action* on our screens already. I don't see why my weekly current affairs programme shouldn't be produced by women. I would like to get women to make such a programme which depends for its success on its ability to interest viewers, not to promote a cause, but which had the added bonus that it comes from people who are standing at a different angle to the universe from the male sex. It may therefore come up with a different set of attitudes, a different mix, a different set of priorities.[8]

Isaacs's intentions clearly impressed Forgan and she in turn impressed Isaacs. Afterwards, he offered her the opportunity to put the idea of a current affairs programme run by women into practice by inviting her to join Channel Four's staff as senior commissioning editor for actuality (i.e. news and current affairs). She accepted.

Two other organisations pressing for recognition by Channel Four were the Fourth Channel Development Education Group and the Independent Film-makers Association. The former had been set up in the summer of 1979 following the Government's decision to cut overseas aid and effectively terminate the budget for 'development education'. The members of the FCDEG, a consortium of thirty-three voluntary and educational organisations, development agencies, minority race groups and churches, were linked by a common desire to use the fourth channel as a means of heightening public awareness of world development issues. Optimistically, the Group campaigned for 5% of Channel Four's total transmission time to be allocated to 'development education', with a proportion of that time perhaps being taken up by the Group's own programme output. Essentially a form of adult education, the Group's aims were to receive a sympathetic hearing from Channel Four's senior commissioning editor for education, Naomi McIntosh.

The IFA's proposal for a separately funded 'experimental' Foundation within the fourth channel is something considered briefly in the previous chapter. The IBA's unwillingness to incorporate the idea into its plans for the channel did not quash the proposal, for, if it wished, the Channel Four Board had itself the power to establish such a body. The IFA, whose members would not be joining the commercially oriented IPPA, reiterated its conviction that innovative work from the grant-aided sector of the independent market needed special protection to ensure a presence on the channel. In April 1981, Jeremy Isaacs wrote to the IFA informing them that after 'very careful consideration' the idea had been turned down. The Channel Four Board shared the IBA's view that a Foundation was not necessary; it would risk replicating the bureaucratic structure of the channel itself in the funding of film-makers and, as a matter of principle, the Board was not prepared to renounce its right to dispense its own funds. Moreover, it could not afford to set aside anything like so large a sum — 10% of the channel's total budget — for IFA-type work as the proposal had suggested. Isaacs went on, however, to say that he believed there was a role for such material on Channel Four:

> The Board was quite clear, however, that the work of the film-makers you represent, although having no exclusive claim on us, was fully deserving our support. Instead of the Foundation, therefore, we propose the following:
> 1) to appoint a commissioning editor knowledgeable in, and sympathetic to, work being done by independent film-makers;
> 2) to provide funds to regional workshops on a bursary basis after publicly inviting applications for such bursaries;
> 3) to fund provision of additional facilities in at least two centres, one out of London, at which experimental programme-makers can learn to use video equipment;
> 4) to commission, on its merits, the work of the best independent film-makers.[9]

A sum in the region of £250,000 had been earmarked by Channel Four to provide for 2) and 3), and more would, of course, be spent under 4). The commissioning editor, Isaacs hoped, would soon be appointed.

In the closing months of 1980, as the eager independent sector busily prepared itself, the ITV companies, anticipating the awarding of the new franchise contracts, were concerned with matters more pressing than the opportunities created by Channel Four. The IBA announced its final decision in December 1980. Two companies received the chop: Southern and Westward were to be replaced by TVS and TSW respectively. The contracts for East and West Midlands (ATV, but to be renamed Central), Yorkshire (Yorkshire Television), and North-East England (Tyne Tees) were only offered to their incumbents subject to strict conditions relating to changes in their future structure and ownership. And in other regions the IBA placed additional emphasis on the further development of regional programming. The Authority also awarded, for the first time, a contract for a nationwide breakfast time television service to TV-AM, one of eight groups who applied.

In their franchise applications, the companies had outlined their programme plans for the fourth channel.[10] LWT said it would be 'disappointed' if it did not supply at least 130 hours of programming annually and Yorkshire declared it would be 'necessary' for it to provide more than 100 hours. With regard to the independent sector, Granada boasted of having 'pressed the case that independent producers should have a proper place in the scheme of things by right'. On the other hand, LWT thought that it was an 'odd notion that new ideas in programming and the ability to realise them are the prerogative of independent producers'. The companies' programme ideas tended to be large-scale and aimed to impress. Thames proposed *The History of the Twentieth Century* and *The Renaissance,* while Granada wanted to present *The End of Empire, Fifty Years of Television,* and *The History of Western Music.* Addressing itself to Channel Four's goal of appealing to specific and neglected audiences, LWT suggested *The Gender Agency* for women and a series on *Black History.* Above all, the companies were concerned that Channel Four, despite the fact that it had been set up at a distance from both the companies and the Authority, should support and not weaken the financial basis of the two-channel IBA system; as Granada put it, 'the health of the service as a whole will rate above the demands made by Channel Four should they be excessive'. When Jeremy Isaacs went on record as saying that the new channel was going to be very much about entertainment and that it would earn its keep, he was talking directly to those in the companies who feared Channel Four would become a financial burden.

Upon awarding the new contracts, the IBA informed the companies that they would be expected to start paying their subscription to Channel Four from January 1982, the same month that the new contracts would come into operation. Until then, the Authority itself would finance the channel from its own reserves, although eventually this would have to be paid back by the companies. It was also emphasised that the companies' one and only compensation for having to pay the subscription would be to sell and retain the new channel's advertising time. They would have no other special privileges. The programmes they sold to Channel Four would have to be commissioned in exactly the same way as those made by independent producers; it would be up to Jeremy Isaacs and his staff to accept any offers they made, and in turn, they would then have to decide whether they were prepared to make the programmes for the amount Channel Four was prepared to pay.

From the beginning, Isaacs was aware that with their high overhead costs, the ITV companies would find it difficult to produce programmes within his budgets. Speaking to the Broadcasting Press Guild in January 1981, he explained that although the companies had an interest in Channel Four being watched, they were unlikely to have a great financial interest in supplying programmes:

> I said a couple of years ago that I thought they could earn back from Channel Four [by selling programmes to it] the money they pay out to fund us in subscription, but actually they cannot. They could only do that if they were able to sell to us at so substantial a margin of profit that they could get back everything they spend on making their programmes. It is extremely unlikely that that will be the case. I doubt that I can buy at full price and at over the odds — certainly not at the upper limit of the programme cost range.
>
> Nevertheless, the ITV companies have two major interests in the channel. They really do have a desire to show what they can do on it, and certainly their programme-makers do. And, more importantly if you like, they have a very considerable interest in ensuring that the channel is watched because, and this is their hope of getting their subscription back, they sell the advertising the channel carries.
>
> ... Obviously the volume and quality of work put forward by the ITV companies will to some extent determine how much the independent sector contributes in the end.[11]

As always, it is important to differentiate between the ITV companies; the five network companies were not in quite the same position as the ten regionals. The Big Five had never had any need to calculate the cost of their programmes on an individual basis. The programmes they made for the network were not sold, but exchanged free of charge to the other network companies. Each of the five contributed roughly the same number of programmes and, it was assumed, had roughly similar overheads. Programmes sold by the network companies to overseas buyers were priced at the going international market rate and not tied to the cost of their production; such programmes had already 'paid for themselves' by having appeared on ITV and thus having contributed to the overall output of a service financed by the sale of advertising. Any additional exploitation through overseas sales was simply an added bonus. Producing programmes for Channel Four was a very different matter. These would be programmes that would not have a prior showing on ITV, and Channel Four would not be exchanging other programmes in return. The network companies would therefore want to charge Channel Four at least the cost of production and, if possible, include a profit margin as well. Calculating costs for individual programmes, as opposed to overall programme output, came as something of a revelation to the Big Five. As one ITV executive has said: 'It was a shock to discover that some of those cheap programmes we thought cost £30,000 turned out to cost £90,000, while conversely others were in fact less expensive than we thought.'[12] The regionals, on the other hand, already knew the costs of their individual programmes. As junior partners in the ITV system, they paid a fee to the network companies to transmit the network programmes in their franchise regions, and the relatively few programmes they supplied in return were actually sold to the network at a price related to the cost of production.

The term 'cost of production' is, of course, ambiguous; it is a figure that will vary enormously depending on whether or not indirect overhead costs (permanent staff salaries, studios, equipment, ancillary resources) are taken into account. When the regionals supplied programmes to the network they were required to give detailed direct cost breakdowns for each programme, and a fixed indirect cost charge was then added. So, for instance, if the direct cost of a programme was £35,000, an additional indirect cost allowance was likely to be £7,000. Both the network and the regional companies wanted to charge Channel Four a similar indirect cost allowance for the programmes they supplied to the new channel. They were to be unsuccessful. Channel Four argued that a) it only just had sufficient funds to pay the direct costs of production, and b) even if it could have afforded to pay toward indirect costs as well, it saw no reason why it should; such overhead costs would have to be borne by the ITV companies even if they were not making additional programmes for Channel Four. As Justin Dukes, its Managing Director, has explained, Channel Four felt obliged only to try to meet the companies' marginal costs of producing extra programmes specifically for Channel Four:

Channel Four's task is not to improve nor is it to worsen the net corporate profitability of the ITCA contractors by virtue of purchasing programmes. So I am talking about reimbursing to them the net marginal cost of the manufacturing of a programme, which is not total cost. Even then, I cannot afford to pay that sometimes — in which case we and they have to look at the benefits from further exploitation, the benefits from positive cash flow (because we have money to pay for programmes ahead of manufacture), and all other devices with a view to bridging the gap. But it's a gap between what we can pay and the net marginal cost —no way am I interested, nor is there a case for, my paying their total costs, which are horrendous, but they are nothing to do with me.[13]

The ITV companies protested. Some of them claimed that (despite all that had been said during the 1970s) they had no surplus capacity to make programmes for Channel Four. To produce additional programmes for the new channel would therefore require them to expand their studios, staff and other overhead costs. Channel Four was sceptical; they believed that in many cases spare capacity could be created if the ITV companies used their resources more efficiently. The extravagant industrial practices of the ITV companies, especially the Big Five, had been the subject of criticism over the years. The companies would have to improve their working structure if they were to operate competitively with the leaner independent producers, who could afford to work with Channel Four's average £30,000 per hour budget. Protracted negotiations between the ITV companies and Channel Four followed. Initially the companies wanted to agree upon a single terms of trade contract which they would all abide by in their dealings with the channel. But in February 1982, while discussions were still under way, Thames Television reached its own deal with Channel Four to provide eighty hours of programmes for the first year at a price which one ITV executive put at 50% below the rate the companies were collectively pressing for.[14] Thames, who had lost an hour-and-a-quarter to LWT on Friday evenings in the new franchise allocation, did have a serious over-staffing problem, and were faced with a choice between making redundancies or securing a deal with Channel Four, even if it meant supplying programmes at below total cost. It was a move that effectively undermined the ITV companies' collective negotiations and opened the way for a free-for-all approach in which separate deals were concluded with the different companies. Those companies who had argued that they did not have surplus capacity (unlike Thames) were, nevertheless, prepared to make programmes for the channel, for the first year at least, at a rate below that needed to cover their full costs. As Jeremy Isaacs explained above, the companies' financial interest in ensuring that the channel was watched, together with the simple desire of their programme-makers to demonstrate their abilities, was sufficient reason for them to compromise. A Channel Four without their programmes would fail, however productive the independent sector turned out to be, in which case the companies would have no chance of recovering their subscription through the sale of the channel's advertising. Thus LWT, which had soaked up whatever spare capacity it had when it had gained an hour-and-a-quarter on its franchise, was willing to reduce its production for the ITV network in order to create the surplus capacity needed to make programmes at the

132

margin for Channel Four. This was possible because LWT had a healthy stockpile of programmes and the company's Managing Director, Brian Tesler, was prepared to take the calculated risk of depleting his reserves for one year while the new channel was being launched. One of the uncertainties that hangs over Channel Four is the nature of the agreement that will have to be reached between Channel Four and the companies regarding the supply of programmes for its second year. The companies are attempting to streamline their operations, while Channel Four hopes in future to be able to increase its average programme budget in real terms.

COMMISSIONING THE PROGRAMMES

Channel Four's broad programming philosophy began to be realised during 1981 as specific programme commitments were made following the staggered appointment of its fourteen commissioning editors and two film purchasers. In keeping with the channel's goal of being different, the names of some of the people chosen, as well as the job titles, were new to television. Isaacs wanted a mixture of critical newcomers without television production experience who might be expected to question professional practices and assumptions, together with some established broadcasters knowledgeable about the television industry. On the point of the novel titles, Paul Bonner has elaborated:

If we are to do something different then it is quite important that the old compartmentalised structures that grew up in the BBC and were replicated, to a certain extent, in the ITV companies should have a chance to be modified by practice. This will create flexible and, hopefully, creative overlapping, blurring the edges of strict programme classifications.[15]

When he named the first three senior members of his commissioning team in January 1981, Isaacs was criticised by members of his own Board for neither consulting them over the appointments nor advertising the posts. Once again, people complained that, as with the position of channel controller, they would have liked to have had the opportunity to apply for the jobs. To choose the rest of the commissioning editors Isaacs went to the other extreme by putting, as he himself describes it, 'a cheerfully idiotic' advertisement in the newspapers that produced nearly 6,000 replies. These were read, interviews conducted, and by the beginning of July the full editorial team, save one or two late-comers, was assembled.

On the management and financial side, the Board advertised for a financial controller. A large number of applications were received. None was accepted. Justin Dukes, the Joint Managing Director of the Financial Times, then arrived on the scene as a kind of volunteer. He

133

explained he did not wish to be financial controller but rather managing director — a post which had not been advertised or even envisaged by the Board. He was interviewed and appointed to the job he himself had designated. He was also given a seat on the Board alongside Jeremy Isaacs. (A financial controller, David Scott, was in fact subsequently appointed to work under Dukes.)

The full organisation of the company is an eight-legged structure which aims, in Dukes's words, at 'accurately representing and facilitating the "flow process" through which the programmes travel from commissioning to being transmitted and marketed to the maximum potential audience.'[16] (It is a structure that is diagramatically presented below in Appendix 3.) The first stage in the 'flow' is the Commissioning Department. All fourteen commissioning editors are members of the Programme Committee, which is chaired by Isaacs with Bonner as his deputy. The committee identifies those ideas, from the many submitted, that Channel Four believe should be realised as programmes. The next stage is the Acquisition Department, headed by Colin Leventhal, former BBC Head of Copyright. Leventhal's acquisition team negotiate terms between the channel and the programme supplier whose idea has been accepted by the Commissioning Department. These terms include legal contractual arrangements as well as detailed pre-production budgeting. The Programme Finance Committee, which Isaacs also chairs but this time with Dukes as deputy, then gives final approval to the commissioning of a programme once terms have been agreed. The Finance Department, run by David Scott, allocates finance to the supplier at various stages of production and monitors expenditure. Completed programmes are passed to Pam Masters's Presentation Department which is responsible for Channel Four's continuity and on-air promotion. The last stage in the 'flow process' is the Transmission Department, headed by Chief Engineer Ellis Griffiths, which organises the technical transmission of the channel's service via the company's control rooms and play-out suite at their Charlotte Street headquarters.

Channel Four's three other departments are Marketing, Business Development, and Administration and Industrial Relations. Sue Stoessl, Head of Marketing, is in charge of off-air promotion of the channel to the public and, more controversially, to the advertisers and agencies. The latter is controversial because, as marketing correspondent Torin Douglas has explained, the ITV companies believe that they should have sole responsibility for all dealings between the channel and its advertisers.

It is not generally known just how firmly Channel Four has been 'warned off' trying to market the station to advertisers and agencies, not merely by the ITV contractors but by the Independent Broadcasting Authority itself . . . The IBA's line is that the airtime on Channel Four is the contractors' airtime and is to be sold as they see fit . . . If they decide that Channel Four should be projected as a cross between *Close Encounters of the Third Kind* and *Sunday Night at the London Palladium*, there is nothing Channel Four executives can do about it.[17]

The Business Development Department of the channel supervises the subsequent exploitation of programmes, including overseas sales and spin-offs such as books, video cassettes and other goods. Finally, supporting all seven departments is Frank McGettigan's Administration and Industrial Relations Department.

Despite the obvious importance of all eight departments, our prime concern has to be with the first, the commissioning team who determine the content of the channel's output. With their open brief to find distinctive and worthwhile new programmes, the task of the commissioning editors has been, and continues to be, both daunting and exhilarating. As a generality distinctiveness is without meaning; it is only in particulars attached to individual projects that it becomes more easily recognised.

ACTUALITY

The question of who would supply Channel Four with its news service was a virtual *fait accompli* settled before the Channel Four consultants, let alone Jeremy Isaacs and his senior commissioning editor for actuality, Liz Forgan, were appointed. ITN, although not actually referred to in the Broadcasting Act, had been mentioned in connection with the Fourth Channel by William Whitelaw in his Cambridge speech, by the IBA in their 1979 proposals for the channel, and by the Authority again in a statement on programme policy which they presented to the Channel Four Board upon its incorporation. ITN's presentation of news, together with that of its BBC counterpart, was, however, a controversial subject; something that had come under fire from various quarters during the 1970s. Critical evaluation of the practices of journalists has a long history. As early as 1922 Walter Lippmann had complained that the sensationalism of news priorities encouraged the journalist to concentrate on reporting discrete and dramatic events rather than explaining underlying and developing causes. 'News,' he wrote, 'does not tell you how the seed is germinating in the ground, it only tells you when the first sprout breaks through the soil.'[18] It was this 'bias against understanding' that was taken up in 1975 by John Birt of LWT and Peter Jay, the presenter of *Weekend World*, in a series of articles in *The Times*. Film-making imperatives, they argued, restricted television journalism to the level of the particular rather than explaining the general, to showing things happening rather than dealing with unfilmable ideas. This aggravated the already existing tendency within print journalism to concentrate on the 'whats' to the neglect of the 'whys'. The dismantling of broadcasting's doggedly defended distinction between news and current affairs, and an extension in the length of the news to a daily one hour programme containing brief headlines and a detailed analytical treatment of a few main stories, would, they posited, be one step towards improving the situation.

Others believed the problems of television journalism were more deep-rooted than a failure to provide sufficient contextualisation and explanation. News, it was argued, cannot be some kind of objectively established entity. Journalists have to choose out of countless millions of daily events those they believe will interest their audience and should thus be presented as the day's 'news events'. The criteria, or news values, that journalists use to make their decisions are not absolutes, but are defined by professional, technological and organisational factors. In the words of the Glasgow Media Group: 'News is a cultural artefact: it's a sequence of socially manufactured messages, which carry many of the culturally dominant assumptions of our society.'[19] The Glasgow Group went further; they declared they could actually measure the way in which news 'favours' certain individuals and institutions by giving them more time and status. It was a contentious claim that inevitably provoked a heated debate in which many broadcasters vehemently defended themselves against the accusation that they were not impartial. In fact, it seems questionable that any attempt to *measure* bias can ever be successful; for the concept of bias is itself not an objectively establishable entity. Such difficulties do not, however, detract from the point about selection. As the Annan Report put it: 'News may be dictated by events, but who can doubt it is journalists who decide which events to take note of and how these events should be presented to the public?'[20] To say that television news chooses only one of several different ways in which to perceive the world is not to suggest that television journalists are conspirators acting to deceive. But the problem of presenting only one perspective is that the audience remains ignorant of alternatives.

Against this background Channel Four planned its actuality programming. A small minority of the Board questioned the need for a regular daily news service that would lie like a fixed log across the weekly schedules, restricting flexibility. But the majority believed a daily news programme was essential; although it would have to be 'distinctively different' from those on the other three channels if it was to be justified. Despite the Home Secretary's and the IBA's earlier pronouncements, alternative sources to ITN were seriously considered. But could a separate news organisation be set up, given Channel Four's limited resources and November 1982 deadline? Writing in *Broadcast* in November 1981, Christopher Griffin-Beale, shortly to be appointed Channel Four's Press Officer, explained the channel's dilemma:

Could ITN really be expected to deliver something 'distinctively different' from its existing output: there is scarcely a precedent for such corporate schizophrenia among any television news organisation, and BBC2 has never established any such overall distinct news identity in 17 years. But on the other hand could it be practical or economic for any other organisation to attempt to rival the news gathering resources — professional, logistical and technical — which ITN already fields?[21]

One of the strongest possibilities Liz Forgan explored was an offer from LWT to provide the analysis part of the news, but this would have led to an impracticable splitting of the sources for news intake and analysis. ITN's willingness to establish a separate team involving additional staff to work exclusively for Channel Four's new programmes helped Isaacs and Forgan eventually to accept a deal with ITN. The decision was announced at the end of 1981, and shortly afterwards former *Sunday Times* journalist Derrik Mercer was appointed editor of the new team.

Financially it was a bargain. News is a highly expensive form of programming, but Channel Four is paying ITN less than its £30,000 per hour average. The form of the programme owes much more to the Birt/Jay criticisms than those of the Glasgow Media Group. Running every weekday evening from 7.00-8.00 p.m. Channel Four's news is twice as long as any other news programme on British television. It will aim to explain the issues behind the headlines. 'We do not want more incident or event,' said Isaacs, 'we want more background and perspective.'[22] It will also attempt to broaden the traditional agenda of news by tackling subjects previously confined to the inside pages of quality newspapers; e.g. business and industry, science and technology, and the arts. And, by regularly including broadcasts from foreign news services, Channel Four's news will, in one respect, seek to show that there is more than one perspective from which to report world events. Finally, the inclusion of a nightly five minutes editorial over which ITN has no editorial control is a clear sign that Channel Four is determined to ensure that their news is different.

The decision to commission ITN to provide the news was not without its critics. Whatever ITN said about the establishment of a new and distinct team, some doubted that it would be possible for any such team not to be imbued with the same institutional philosophy as ITN. It was partly in response to such worries that Channel Four decided that at the end of the week ITN's news would be limited to half an hour. It would be followed by a half-hour review programme which would give various groups the opportunity to comment on the week's news coverage from their own standpoints, and to contribute their account of the week's events; for instance, industrial workers might challenge the way a dispute had been presented. But *Friday Alternative* will not be an access programme as familiarly understood; i.e. licensed polemic with an implicit disclaimer from the channel that is broadcasting it. A new company, Diverse Productions, headed by ex-BBC producer David

Graham and video artist Peter Donebauer, has been commissioned by Channel Four to provide high quality professional support to those groups who will, from week to week, be involved in the programme. As Graham explained:

> We have the scope to reach a diverse range of people and opinions, but we will be putting our professional skills at their disposal to help them come over as persuasively as possible — and we will be doing this at peak time. The core of the programme will be a series of contributing groups who will have a constant relationship with us: for instance, trade union groups, blacks, perhaps even small shopkeepers, as well as *ad hoc* groups that emerge around particular topical events.[23]

Half an hour of alternative viewpoints is unlikely to change the face of television news, but as a step towards meeting the criticism of those who complain that conventional news authoritatively presents a particular view as the whole and only incontrovertible truth of the matter, *Friday Alternative* is an interesting experiment. It is worth noting that a working party of consultant advisers to Diverse Productions includes a leading member of the Glasgow Media Group, Greg Philo. In a policy paper to the Board of Channel Four, Liz Forgan has summed up the philosophy behind the new programme:

> I would like to unsettle viewers sufficiently to disturb their notion that they know what is going on because they saw one television programme. The *Friday Alternative* is designed to make that comfortable certainty quiver. This may prove such an uncomfortable feeling that viewers will turn away in droves to seek security elsewhere. If we can persuade them to stay and understand the process I think we shall have rendered a real service to democracy.[24]

A handful of current affairs programmes will complement Channel Four's weekday hour-long news, and give actuality programming a very high profile on the channel. The suggestion that Isaacs made in his *Guardian* interview with Liz Forgan — i.e. that Channel Four should have a current affairs 'flagship' in which women make all the editorial decisions — has been realised. The half-hour programme is, like *Friday Alternative,* an attempt by Channel Four to introduce new points of view into actuality programming. It will not be tackling purely women's subjects, nor will it want to address a solely female audience. Liz Forgan has described it as a journalistic experiment rather than a form of positive discrimination. 'Given that roughly half the world is female,' she explained, 'and given that the vast majority of the editorial decisions in newspaper, radio and television are taken by men, there seems to us a glimmer of a chance that we, the media, may not always be getting the story right.'[25] Broadside, a production company formed by some of the core members of the Women's Broadcasting and Film Lobby, shares responsibility for the programme with another production company, Gambles and Milne, formed by two women producers previously at Thames and Granada.

In April 1982, Channel Four announced that an independent company run by David Elstein, formerly of Thames and leading activist in the Channel Four Group, together with Anne Lapping, previously labour correspondent of the *Economist,* had been commissioned to produce a weekly politics programme. It will centre on Westminster and Whitehall, but will also cover local government, grassroots political activities, and Europolitics. 'We want to provide a breathing-space,' Elstein said, 'for those involved in politics to talk in a relaxed way at the end of a week about their ideas and work.'[26] *Report to the Nation* is a monthly 'social audit' programme of nationalised industries that Channel Four commissioned from Video Arts Television. Devised by Michael Peacock, and produced by Paul Ellis, former editor of BBC2's *The Money Programme,* it aims to offer the public, as shareholders and customers of nationalised industries, the opportunity to hear the managers of those industries account for their performances and be cross-examined by informed experts. In addition to these new series, Channel Four has obtained two programmes from ITV companies — *What the Papers Say* from Granada and *Face the Press* from Tyne Tees — which it will be showing closer to peak viewing times than the ITV network was ever prepared to do.

FICTION

In his letter of application for the job of Chief Executive, Isaacs mentioned his desire to make or help make films of feature length. It was a desire strongly shared by David Rose, Channel Four's senior commissioning editor for 'fiction' — the channel's house term for drama. With his 25 years at the BBC, Rose has more television experience than almost any other member of the commissioning team. His achievements include responsibility for originating *Z Cars* and *Softly Softly,* and as Head of English Regions Drama in Birmingham during the 1970s he produced *Second City Firsts.* Weary of traditional forms of television drama, Rose wanted Channel Four to avoid, if possible, studio-based work. He was reluctant to duplicate what the rest of the industry already did so well and so prolifically:

> We have got to ask what is television drama and what is film on television. The present television companies have huge capital investments in studios, and they have been reluctant to emphasise the film element. But we have got to grow up now, we have been at it long enough. With electronically recorded drama in studios we know the constraints, the emphasis on text and character relationship. With film the visual is stronger.[27]

Channel Four, agreed Rose and Isaacs, would make its first priority the commissioning of twenty original films to fill a weekly prestige *Film on Four* slot. Written by British authors, they will be feature films for a British audience; in Isaacs's words: 'the sort of films which a healthy British cinema would be supplying if there were one.'[28] As such, they will act as one of the most important stimuli to the British feature film industry for decades. They are expensive, costing anything up to £500,000 each; one of the few types of programme on Channel Four which are denied very little in resources. With Channel Four contributing around £300,000 per film, international co-production deals have been arranged in many cases. By the end of September 1981, the first five films, all 90 minutes long and all produced by independent companies, had been commissioned; *Remembrance* by Colin Gregg, *Angel* by Neil Jordan, *The Disappearance of Harry* by Joseph Despins, *Courtesans* by Ruth Jhabvala, and *Hero* by Barney Platts-Mills. Over the next six months, Channel Four committed itself to a further fifteen scripts.

The second main strand of Channel Four's fiction output is a bi-weekly serial or, as the Press have insisted on calling it, a soap opera. Written by Phil Redmond (who wrote the inspired children's serial *Grange Hill*), *Brookside* is set on a new Merseyside housing estate twenty-five years on from *Coronation Street* — in other words it will be very much of the 1980s. Channel Four hopes that, like its Granada predecessor, *Brookside* will be popular; pulling in an audience which will stay to see what else the channel has to offer. Shot on location by Mersey Television Company using light-weight electronic cameras, the early commission of the serial provided a clear indication of Channel Four's commitment to independent production, for it was precisely this kind of long-running, high budget programme that many commentators assumed would be the preserve of the ITV companies.

Other sources of fictional output envisaged by Rose and his script associate, Walter Donohue, include: recording stimulating work from fringe theatre and, but to a lesser extent, established companies (e.g. the RSC's epic *Nicholas Nickleby* production); exploring the economical, imaginative and non-naturalistic use of video in studios and on location; expanding the possibilities of the 'short' film; and buying, or inexpensively co-producing, overseas drama series from countries such as Poland, Brazil and Ireland — all countries whose work is rarely, if at all, seen on British television. But not all of these sources will be available to the channel in its first year. Summarising their policy for fiction, Rose and Donohue have written:

> Our overall aim is the provision of entertaining work which boldly examines the complexities and realities of contemporary society; film and video programmes which are not just honourably crafted but ones whose veins are vibrant with blood, feeling, imagination and ideas.[29]

Channel Four is also preparing to show repeats of the best ITV drama series, something the ITV companies have been very keen to include as part of their package deal with Channel Four in order to offset the low price they are receiving for the new programmes they are making for the channel.

ACQUIRED FILMS

A quarter of Channel Four's sixty-hour week will be feature films bought from Britain, America, Europe and Asia. In preference to expensive Hollywood blockbusters and the major film distributors, the emphasis will be on 'art house' films, many never seen on British television before. Film seasons of the work of directors such as Kurosawa, Satyajit Ray, Godard, Buñuel, Fassbinder, De Antonio and Wiseman have all been provisionally planned. Buying at today's prices for tomorrow, Channel Four's two film purchasers, Derek Hill and Leslie Halliwell (also ITV's film purchaser) have stockpiled a large and varied collection which will keep the channel supplied for its first two to three years. But in generally avoiding the major distributors, Channel Four have been concerned not to exploit the position of worldwide independent film suppliers. Hill, a former critic, who in recent years has been responsible for programming two London cinema clubs — the ICA and the Essential — publicly expressed his views within weeks of being appointed Channel Four's buyer. In an open letter to his new boss, he told Jeremy Isaacs that he wanted the channel's absolute priority to be the need of the supplier:

> Traditional buying practice, which has inexorably resulted in furtive competition, must be abandoned at once, and our prices geared according to need ... If we attend to the most desperately needy independent film suppliers first, whether film-makers, agents or distributors, we can ensure their survival as future sources of supply ... So far we have committed about £2½ million on some 400 hours of film, working on the usual television assumption that the independents offer films of such cheap market value that they can subsidise other programmes. But Parliament has instructed Channel Four to support the independents, not to milk them, and we can easily pay much, much more.[30]

Such frankness was unlikely to be appreciated by other television film buyers. In the United States, Hill's radical statement made the front page of Hollywood's *Variety* newspaper.

Isaacs was not sympathetic to his film buyer's public outburst. In a private reply, he told Hill that his open letter did more justice to his heart than his head. Isaacs pointed out that Parliament had instructed Channel Four to encourage television production by independent British

141

producers. In contrast, the independent suppliers Hill referred to were, to a great extent, foreign film-makers of the kind whose work Hill had consistently sought to exhibit during his time at the Essential and the ICA. Hill was wrong, Isaacs believed, to suggest that Channel Four with its tight budget could afford to pay above the market price for any material, let alone work from overseas:

> We do not want to screw anybody, but must buy film at the market price. Only by doing so, can we possibly sustain the channel's principal objectives which are of course to provide a distinctive television service and also to foster independent production — not distribution and exhibition — in this country, not abroad.[31]

Foreign language films on Channel Four will be subtitled not dubbed and Isaacs has said he will not censor explicit scenes from films shown on the channel:

> One is always concerned about what one does in three areas which are of enormous concern to a great many citizens, namely language, sex and violence. I am going to be very hard against violence — there will be violent episodes in serious pieces of work, but what we are not going to buy is packaged violence 26 hours at a time. We are not going to buy American cops and robbers series. So I think we'll have fewer people killed a week on Channel Four than on any other British channel.
>
> On language I take the view that sticks and stones may break your bones but names will never hurt you. At the proper time of night there is no difficulty whatever transmitting strong language in a decent piece of work. I think that the way ITV sometimes ties itself in knots over this is a total waste of time and effort. It upsets the public far less than some people believe it does.
>
> The same really with sexuality. The general feeling here is that if you take a film like the latest Godard [*Slow Motion*], and play it in a season and at a proper time of night then there is no difficulty. I am sure that will turn out to be the case. Without touching pornography, of course, British television, if it is to be international and if it is to be conscious of people's tastes and needs in the 80s, has to provide from the best range of movies that is available and not insist that there are films that can never be seen on television.[32]

Whether these sentiments will clash with IBA strictures cannot be known until it happens. But Isaacs's previous stands against intervention by the Authority suggest he will be willing to take risks.

EDUCATION

With one or two exceptions, educational programmes on Channel Four will be for adults, young and old, rather than children. This is partly because of the channel's late opening time — 4.45-5.00 p.m. – and more because of a wish to reach, stimulate and cater for a large educational group generally neglected. Naomi McIntosh, senior commissioning editor for education and former professor of Applied Social Research at the Open University, wants Channel Four to complement the work of the Open University:

> If you believe, as I do, that this is a profoundly under-educated society which has screened the majority of people away from education, then the way to reach those people is to have access to a mass medium . . . I would like to see the 75% of the population who think that education is not for them having their minds changed.[33]

Isaacs has set his channel an even more daunting, some might say presumptuous, challenge. Speaking at the 1981 Edinburgh Festival he declared: 'In the long term we might be judged by our success in turning unemployment into leisure.'[34] Channel Four will seek to avoid ghettoising education. Following on from her work as a member of the Advisory Committee for Adult and Continuing Education, McIntosh questions traditional distinctions of what is and is not education. She favours a broad definition, one that includes anything which causes or stimulates people into further activity:

> What we are doing has to have an outcome — now it can be a private outcome in people's minds, or it can be an outcome measured in terms of voting more at local elections, or going to museums, buying books, joining classes — but there has to be some outcome that we are thinking about as the programme is constructed.[35]

Follow-up to programmes in order to aid such activity is seen as an integral part of educational programming. In general this will be provided through books and other printed materials, but in some cases the channel may work in co-operation with organisations such as the Health Education Council, Age Concern, or the Sports Council. Channel Four's broad definition of educational programming has been endorsed by the IBA's Educational Advisory Committee, so the channel should not find it difficult to meet the IBA's stipulation that 15% of its programmes should fall into an educational category. McIntosh shares responsibility for education with Carol Haslam, a former BBC and Open University producer, who is also a commissioning editor for documentaries. Together the two have planned a weekly output of approximately seven hours of educational programmes, although these will be supplemented by some programmes from other commissioning areas which will be broadly educational in content. By the beginning of 1982 a number of provisional subject areas for the regular strands of educational programming had been decided. These areas include: a regular magazine programme for the elderly; basic numeracy and literacy programmes designed to help the

143

estimated five million adults without adequate basic education; active leisure; access to culture and the arts; a programme 'for people with more time than money', with a special emphasis on unemployed youth; a consumers' report but not confined to purchasing goods in shops; a health programme, but in more than just a medical sense; 'ways of seeing', a visual awareness programme; keeping abreast of new technology; and one children's programme aimed at children with special needs. A contract with the International Broadcasting Trust (formerly the Fourth Channel Development Education Group) was agreed in January 1982 commissioning the IBT to make twenty-two half-hour programmes. At a cost of over £½ million these world development programmes will represent a relatively large proportion of Channel Four's £10 million educational budget.

MULTI-CULTURAL AND YOUTH

In aiming to cater for distinct and neglected audiences, Channel Four has been faced with a strategic choice: either it provides a few programmes specifically designed for those audiences alone, or else it provides programmes that are generally appealing yet in some sense incorporate the interests and perspectives of particular audiences. The former approach guarantees that certain groups are reached, but it can tend to ghettoise the interests of those groups and is open to the charge of tokenism. The latter approach tackles the problem of under-representation across the whole range of output, but it is more ambitious, for it runs the risk of falling between two stools: being attractive neither to the general nor the particular audience.

Channel Four has chosen three different blends of the two approaches in its address to three of its principal target groups – women, ethnic minorities, and youth. In the case of women it has tended towards the latter approach; there are no programmes just for women, nor is there a commissioning editor for women's programmes. The weekly current affairs series produced by women is the most manifest example of an attempt to execute the latter approach in a single programme. Although women are a minority of four in a fourteen-strong commissioning team, it is fair to say that Channel Four's editorial staff are generally more concerned to avoid sexual discrimination than most other media organisations. It is a concern reflected in comments such as Liz Forgan's recent remark: 'Things have now reached the point at Channel Four where it is absolutely impossible for anybody, even the most unregenerate male chauvinist, to utter a sentence which while meaning the world in general uses a male pronoun.'[36]

In the case of ethnic groups Channel Four has decided upon a mixture of the two approaches. There is a commissioning editor for multi-cultural programmes, former *World in Action* producer Sue Woodford, who, being half West Indian, is the only black member of the channel's commissioning team. She has two protected slots in the week's schedule for ethnic programmes, one at peak time. The first is a news/current affairs magazine which will focus alternately on the West Indian and the Indian and Pakistani communities in Britain. Produced by LWT, whose programme *Skin* pioneered television in this area, it is staffed from producer level downwards by West Indians and Asians. The other programme, drawn from a variety of sources, is entertainment-based, featuring music, dance, comedy and drama. But ethnic programming will not be directed solely by the former approach; Woodford is also keen to inject ethnic-based ideas, subjects and individuals into the general output of Channel Four:

> My colleagues are not racial, they are fair-minded liberal people who need to be taught to think of the black perspective. If the supplier strongly disagrees with us on this sort of point, then at the end of the day we shall say 'take your idea somewhere else.' If the commissioning editor feels my suggestion is improper then I will *fight* for a separate series to redress the balance.[37]

While considering multicultural programmes it is worth also noting *Irish Angle,* a half hour slot on Sunday afternoons. The aim is to commission programmes that show the range of Irish life, including politics, in both Northern Ireland and Eire, paying particular attention to the interests of the Irish community in Britain.

Channel Four's programmes for young people, aged 15 to 30, are geared towards the former approach, with two weekly youth programmes and relatively little talk of instilling a 'youth-perspective' into more general programmes, except perhaps in the channel's choice of feature films. Young people at present are not avid television viewers. Isaacs has pinned his hopes for youth programming on his belief that the explanation for this is less to do with any intrinsically passive nature of the medium than the fact that few programmes in the past have been made for them to watch:

> Much for them on radio, something in print, not much on television these days. If, in entertainment and information, we can speak to them by letting them speak to us, we may be able to persuade some who do not watch much television actively to seek out certain programmes they will want to watch. My feeling that I am right about this has been strengthened not just by what is reported back to me, but by the unsurprising news that the BBC will do more of this itself.[38]

Channel Four's commissioning editor for youth programmes is thirty-four-year-old Mike Bolland, former BBC producer of *Something Else* (an access programme by young people) and *Grapevine.* Bolland believes that, as with multicultural programmes, Channel Four should commis-

145

sion work not just *for* a particular audience but made *by* them as well. Thus the suppliers he has commissioned either have young people at the core of their operations or employ young people at researcher level. In two other respects Bolland's task is similar to Woodford's. First, the two weekly youth programmes are also divided into an information/discussion magazine and a music and entertainment programme. Second, both commissioning editors hold regular consultation meetings with *ad hoc* groups that are in some sense representative of their respective target audiences: Woodford with community workers, academics and journalists from the sizeable ethnic press; Bolland with young musicians, youth leaders, 'ordinary' school leavers, and writers for youth magazines such as *Face* and *New Musical Express.*

ARTS AND MUSIC

Channel Four aims to screen more arts and music programmes than any other television channel in Britain and thus, outside the USSR, probably the world. The two commissioning editors for arts and music, respectively Michael Kustow and Andy Park, are both new to television production: Kustow ran the ICA during the 1960s and is former associate director of the National Theatre; Park's background is in radio — he was formerly head of programmes at Radio Clyde. There is obvious overlap between their responsibilities, and they also each individually link up with other members of the commissioning team; e.g. Kustow with Rose for drama, Park with Bolland for rock and pop music.

The centrepiece of Kustow's programming is a two-hour Sunday night performance slot, usually live, which will feature theatre, opera and dance. Kustow wants Channel Four to affect, not just reflect, the arts by co-planning and co-operating on projects that would otherwise not happen, or not so fully, if the channel did not become involved with the relevant theatre, ensemble or artists. He also wants people to think about, not just view, the arts and by means of a regular ninety-minute discussion programme Channel Four will try to provide a sharper, more articulate way of evaluating and criticising the arts than has previously been attempted on television. The fact that Channel Four's hour-long news will, in its efforts to widen the normal news diet, include 'arts news' is something that obviously concerns Kustow. How closely he will work with ITN on this matter has yet to become clear.

Park thinks Channel Four should provide more music for all tastes: for rock fans *The Tube* features live bands; for a vocal minority long disgruntled at their treatment by most broadcasting networks there is a regular jazz programme; and opera-lovers will have the chance to see more full productions. Ashkenazy, Perlman and Zukerman are among the notable performers who appear in productions by Christopher Nupen's company Allegro Films. The quality of film-making, believes

Park, must not, as sometimes happens, come a poor second to the quality of the composition and performance that is being portrayed in a music programme. Music documentaries are another aspect of music commissions; *Music in Time,* presented by the flautist James Galway, is a sixteen-part history of music, and *Deep Roots Music,* which traces the development of reggae from its Jamaican roots, is a good case of a multicultural idea developed in co-operation with another commissioning area.

DOCUMENTARIES

Both single documentaries and documentary series are something of 'catch-all' categories at Channel Four; they refer to those factual programmes, whether 'one-offs' or series, which do not fall into any other commissioning editor's area of responsibility. The diffused manner in which control over documentaries has been given to three commissioning editors, who in each case have other areas of concern, seems to reflect this 'catch-all' approach.

Carol Haslam, whom we have already mentioned in connection with education, looks after documentary series. The extremely high costs involved in major series have meant that most commissions to date have tended to go to the larger, more established companies — both independent and ITV — and their content and style has, to some extent, been tailored to the tastes and expectations of a broad spectrum of international audiences: e.g. *The History of Technology* and *The Arabs* from Video Arts, *The Sixties* from Robert Stigwood, *The History of Africa* from Mitchell Beazley, *The Chinese* from Antelope. It is a tendency that Haslam recognises and she is exploring ways of alternating more experimental series designed for a specifically British audience with these international highly saleable blockbusters.

Paul Madden and John Ranelagh share responsibility for single documentaries. Previously television officer at the BFI, Madden is also commissioning editor for both media (i.e. television and cinema) programmes and community programmes. Ranelagh, who worked with Isaacs on the BBC history of Ireland and is a former member of the Conservative Party research department, is responsible for the Irish programme and religion, as well as being Isaacs's special assistant. Both men believe that the single documentary should be the place where the individual programme-maker's voice should be most clearly heard. It is for that reason that they have chosen a selection policy that concentrates on securing a diversity of tones of voices rather than a diversity of subject matter (which does not mean, of course, that they will all be about the same subject). Thus there will be programmes by experienced documentary makers as well as newcomers, some tough and journalistic, others lighter, more descriptive in flavour.

Re-runs of popular old American comedy series such as *I Love Lucy* and *The Munsters* do not at first sight appear to be particularly innovative. But one of Channel Four's goals is to promote the idea of television being a medium with its own heritage in some ways similar to that of the cinema. Paul Madden has explained:

> Television has acted unwittingly, since its inception, as a living museum of cinema, relying heavily on feature films to bolster its schedules, introducing younger audiences to a cinema heritage (in however an unstructured way) otherwise lost to view. It has never remotely performed the same service for its own output, neglecting its own history. Repeats are a dirty word signifying last year's, last month's, programme which no one wanted to see in the first place. There is [however] a growing audience for 'old' television shows.[39]

Madden is concerned that such 'old' shows should be presented in a structured way with an accompanying discussion/interview element where appropriate. The programmes he selects from the archives are likely to receive such treatment. However, the old US comedy shows have not been bought by Madden but by Cecil Korer, former BBC Senior Editor of Programme Purchasing and now Channel Four's commissioning editor for light entertainment. It is unlikely that these shows will have any accompanying commentary! They have been bought mainly because they are cheap and, it is hoped, they will be popular. Nevertheless, as Paul Bonner has argued, part of their justification for being included in the schedule is to contribute to the point about heritage:

> There was real talent in those old comedy shows, like there is in Marx Brothers or Charlie Chaplin movies. It is crazy to treat television as a once-only, throw-it-away type thing; so we went for certain old shows and, if you remember, *I Love Lucy* was one of the good ones. I think the BBC went through a similar process when they thought of bringing back *Bilko*; *Bilko* is very well written, very well acted, very funny. The fact that Paul Madden will be hauling other, odder things out of the archives and putting them on the screen will provide another source of entertainment. It is a proper use of resources; there is a gold-mine of material out there. *I Love Lucy* is to be seen in that context; it is not a cheap trick, it is part of a broader aim that we are trying to achieve.[40]

Korer is obviously not just relying on old shows for Channel Four's light entertainment. He has brought, from around the world, entertainment programmes not seen on British television before; from lavish Brazilian *Fantastico* spectaculars to brash Australian comedians like Norman Gunston and Paul Hogan. Financially unable to compete for major variety talents in glossy packages, he has gone for recording offbeat comedy performances in cabaret or the one-man or one-woman show; e.g. *Aspects of Max Wall* and *The Comic Strip Presents* . . . Offers from independents for situation comedy have been relatively thin, and nearly all the situation comedies that will be seen on Channel Four will come from the ITV companies, particularly Thames and LWT.

There is no doubt that light entertainment will play an important role in Channel Four's programming. Korer is frank about his objective: 'My brief is to pull big audiences, but not so big as to upset the main ITV channel'.[41] Isaacs is determined that, without reneging on its statutory objectives, his channel should earn its keep as soon as possible. It is a determination demonstrated by the fact that over three hours of 'entertainment' programmes have been planned for Saturday night; something that goes against a prediction Isaacs made just after his appointment that in contrast to other channels, his would be less 'entertaining' at the weekends than during the week.[42]

SPORT

Channel Four has planned for only two one-hour weekly sport programmes. Isaacs confessed from the beginning that sport was not high on his personal priority list: 'there are not going to be hours and hours of jingoistic chauvinism,' he said.[43] The sports viewer is already well catered for, particularly by the BBC. Adrian Metcalfe, who joined Channel Four from LWT to be commissioning editor for sport, therefore wants to screen sports not currently available. This will include basketball, badminton and American football, as well as more conventional sports from less usual locations; e.g. football from Brazil and indoor athletics from the USA. Metcalfe also intends to widen the age range of the sports covered; from English Schools athletics to Masters' (older age groups) athletics.

GRANT-AIDED SECTOR

The commissioning editor for grant-aided independent film and video work that Isaacs mentioned in his letter to the IFA is Alan Fountain. Formerly film officer at East Midlands Arts and a member of the IFA Executive Committee, Fountain has close ties with the grant-aided sector. There will be a regular 'experimental' film slot, *Eleventh Hour*; but from the beginning Fountain has been adamant that work from his corner of the independent market should not be restricted to this slot but integrated across the channel's entire output:

Over the past decade many people working within the grant-aided sector (as well as the BFI-aided cinemas – including the National Film Theatre) have developed methods of programming unfamiliar/ innovative/experimental work alongside the more familiar. This experience

149

can play an important role in aiding the channel to do similar work within a television context.

. . . The best of this work — and the channel will only be interested in the best — will be most productively scheduled across the channel at appropriate points rather than within a separated slot of 'difference'/ 'experimentation'. For the future I believe there can be an important role for me to play in commissioning some of the work from this sector and subsequently devising along with other commissioning editors when and where and, if appropriate, the best way to schedule it. Such a role would not preclude independent film-makers bringing proposals to other commissioning editors — hopefully it would further facilitate it.[44]

Fountain envisages Channel Four being able to draw material from a healthy network of film and video workshops throughout the country. In order to encourage the development of workshop production Channel Four committed itself at the beginning of 1982 to more than the £250,000 originally envisaged by Isaacs: £100,000 was made available for capital expenditure to enable workshops to begin to up-date and improve their facilities; £270,000 was allocated for 'programmes of work' (as opposed to individual scripts for particular programmes). This total of £370,000 has since been further increased to £675,000. This new figure represents the channel's total contribution to the grant-aided sector during the first twenty-six month subscription period from January 1981 to March 1983. Recognising the sector's non-industrial, extended and developmental methods of production, Channel Four has given the workshops considerable freedom to determine the shape and content of their 'programmes of work'. Channel Four has the right to purchase the UK television rights to any work resulting from these programmes, but will generally refrain from doing so until the final product can be seen.

Also in early 1982 the ACTT, the BFI, the English Regional Arts Associations, the Welsh Arts Council and Channel Four agreed upon a declaration covering the practices of various kinds of film workshop. In an imaginative expression of its support for the sector, the ACTT is prepared to allow waging and staffing levels to be well below those for commercial production, but the agreement is firmly restricted to non-commercial, non-profit-making workshops.

One of the problems of integrating workshop production into Channel Four's output is the maintenance of technical standards. Fountain has made it clear that he wants Channel Four to have a 'rougher' look; 'breaking up the sameness of current television.'[45] At present, most video groups work, and indeed wish to work, with light, flexible, ¾-inch low-band U-matic production equipment. This produces an image quality inferior to ¾-inch high-band U-matic tape, which itself has not until recently been acceptable for television since it is not as good as the broadcasting standard one-inch tape. Channel Four has therefore needed to persuade the IBA to accept a 'two-stage' drop in technical standards in order to be allowed to broadcast workshop material. The Authority has agreed in principle to permit a small percentage of the channel's output to originate from low-band equipment, but it is a matter that remains open to review and will probably be reconsidered after the channel has been on the air for a few months.

COMMUNITY

Paul Madden wants Channel Four's community series to escape the worthy but by now 'turn-offable' nature of programmes like *Open Door*. There is no point, he says, in making programmes that people will not watch. Channel Four series will include a wide variety of different kinds of programmes which will have as their common denominator the direct involvement of, and often control by, groups and individuals at a grass roots level. In most cases this will involve a combination of professional expertise and community involvement and support, but in some, probably very few, cases programmes will be made by people who are not principally film or video-makers working without assistance. Locally produced histories will form the mainstay of the programme's initial output. The non-peak time scheduling of community programmes like *Open Door* has in the past signalled to the viewer the relatively low estimation given to such programmes by the relevant channel planners. Channel Four, with its community series tentatively scheduled at 3.00 p.m. on Sunday afternoons, starting early in 1983, does not appear to have broken away from this approach.

MEDIA

A fortnightly magazine slot alternating between a programme on cinema and one on television has been planned by Paul Madden. The cinema programme aims to contextualise the wide range of films and film-making practices that will be seen on Channel Four. The television programme will perform a similar task for television. It also hopes to examine the rapid technological changes taking place in television and allied industries.

The structured presentation of television archive material has already been mentioned. Madden envisages specialised series featuring particular themes, directors, etc.

RELIGION

There is no set slot for religion. John Ranelagh will be pressing for a wide interpretation of 'religious programming'; he wants to challenge the presumption that only religious people and the Churches can be expected to take an interest in religious programmes. Comparative religion is an area that will be explored, and documentaries, debates and lectures, as well as some straightforward worship, will be fitted into slots throughout the schedule. Ranelagh thinks that there should not necessarily be an emphasis on presenting the Christian point of view.

THE COMMISSIONING PROCESS

Although the independent sector has reason to be well-satisfied by the quantity of work Channel Four have commissioned from them, there has been criticism of the operational arrangements between the two parties. By January 1982, Channel Four's commissioning procedures had been sufficiently established for them to be the subject of discussion at the annual general meeting of the IPPA. At the time, the *Channel Four/ Independent Production Sector: Standard Terms of Trade 1982* (for 100% financed productions) had just been published, and these were considered in the light of IPPA members' experience of Channel Four up to that point. Some matters of concern were raised and these were summarised and communicated to Jeremy Isaacs in a strongly worded letter from IPPA Chairman, Michael Peacock. 'It is generally felt,' declared Peacock, 'that the Standard Terms are over-protective and legalistic and, in particular, that the rights of approval, intervention, control and ownership required by Channel Four amount to a negation of the generally accepted meaning of independent production.'[46] The nub of the IPPA's complaint was that Channel Four, in its role as 100% financier of most commissions, was treating the independent producer as a freelancer rather than an independent. Such a distinction seems to rest on a somewhat idealised notion of what constitutes independent production. As Isaacs explained in his reply to Peacock:

> The fact is that the only independent producer who has total control over his programme is one wealthy enough to make the programme without pre-sale having been arranged. Anyone else has to take account of the needs of the purchaser.[47]

If, as we have already implied, the notion of independence is tied to ownership, then in some respects those independent producers whose budgets are entirely provided by Channel Four are effectively freelancers. But they are freelancers in a very different way from the freelancers who work for BBC or ITV. For since Channel Four has no production facilities of its own, they are not required to work within an institutional production organisation and adapt to its particular procedures and practices. Moreover, unlike freelancers in the BBC and ITV, the independent producers commissioned by Channel Four have control over their own budget and take a share in the risks of production. Formally,

152

the independent producer's profit from production is guaranteed in the form of a production fee. This is calculated on a sliding scale, cost-plus basis that varies from a maximum of 10% on large budgets over £1 million to up to 20% on smaller programme budgets of £10,000. But the arrangements for under- and over-spending of the estimated budget have built an element of risk-taking into this production fee. In cases where a production is completed in accordance with the programme specifications for less than the agreed budget, the approved savings (including any unused contingency) are divided: 50% goes to the producer as an additional fee and 50% is returned to Channel Four to be made available to the producer for the development of future projects. The same 50/50 division operates at Channel Four's discretion in cases of overspending, provided that Channel Four believe the reasons for an overspend in excess of any planned contingency is outside the direct control of the producer. (Channel Four has stated, however, that it is only prepared to contribute towards the cost of the overspend on a pound for pound basis up to the total value of the producer's fee; after that point the producer is supposed to bear the full cost of any additional overspend.) Accurate pre-production budgeting is obviously crucial. Consistent over-budgeting by Channel Four will mean fewer commissions in total, while consistent under-budgeting will place the independent producers in an impossible position financially.

In his letter to Isaacs, Peacock concentrated on making five specific points. The first concerned the interpretation of the proper function of the commissioning editors; in particular, the extent to which they were to be allowed to intervene in the production process after the contract for a commission had been signed. He wrote:

> The right of commissioning editors to intervene at all stages of production was viewed with great concern because of independents' experiences during the past year. With only a few exceptions, it was reported that commissioning editors either lacked the television experience necessary to evaluate and respond to offers in a timely and professional manner, or if experienced, were only interested in commissioning 'their sort of programmes' and, in some cases, acting as *de facto* executive producer rather than commissioning editor. The problem is partly one of communication — or a lack of it; but even more importantly, there is a difference of view on the proper functions of commissioning editors.[48]

To which Isaacs replied:

> Commissioning editors must have the right to view programmes as they go along in order to ensure that we are indeed obtaining what we have paid for. However, how much they intervene will depend very much on personal relationships between them and the different

153

producers we commission. This will vary from case to case. Of course, the commissioning editors use their judgment in deciding what to commission and what not to commission. That is what they are there for. They are responsible to me for their contribution to a service whose overall balance is my responsibility. They commission what we want. They reject what we do not want. I agree completely, however, that commissioning editors should act as such, and not as executive producers. That is my instruction to them.[49]

It is too early to assess whether there is a real clash of interests between Channel Four's desire to maximise independent producers' 'creative freedom' and its need to ensure that the millions of pounds of subscription money it is responsible for is spent in the way that it wants. It seems unlikely, however, that the so-called 'executive producer' syndrome is a major problem; there are far too few commissioning editors and far too many commissions made for any commissioning editor to become an executive producer in the traditionally understood meaning of the term. Nevertheless, the precise role of the commissioning editor in the production process remains unsettled and is likely to continue to be controversial. As Isaacs says, it is something that will vary from case to case and will depend on the personal relationships involved. As a condition of the Terms of Trade, changes required by the relevant commissioning editor, in order that a given programme may be made to the 'agreed specifications', have to be carried out by the independent producer. But the necessarily general formulation of the programme specifications laid down in a particular contract leave room for a variety of interpretations on matters of detail. Where commissioning editor and producer disagree in their interpretation, someone has to compromise. Who that will generally be remains an open question, although the fact that the producer is dependent on the goodwill of Channel Four's commissioning team to secure contracts for future work is obviously not something he or she is likely to forget.

Peacock's criticism of the lack of television experience of some commissioning editors cuts both ways. Most independent producers are inexperienced in the skills needed to work outside the two broadcasting institutions and without the administrative back-up they previously took for granted. As David Hewson, writing in *The Times,* put it: 'Creative posts in vast television empires may be demanding but they rarely call for the sort of detailed knowledge of accounting and management which independent groups require.'[50] The point is that independent television production is essentially a new phenomenon in Britain; during this inaugural period *both* the newly fledged independent producers and their principal domestic buyer have much to learn.

Peacock's second point also took little account of the initial greenness of both the new channel and its suppliers. The IPPA Chairman claimed

154

that Channel Four did not understand the 'metabolism' of the independent producer and cited in evidence the channel's 'inefficient and slow decision-taking process.'[51] There is no doubt that Channel Four was somewhat taken aback by the original burst of submissions. As Isaacs has said: 'Plainly, we were sitting ducks when we started for every single one-off idea that anybody had.'[52] Merely acknowledging, let alone considering, all the offers was, at first, a slow process; especially since most of the commissioning team had not then been appointed. But was there any need to go faster? In his reply to Peacock, Isaacs justified his channel's speed of decision-making:

Of course we are aware that on each commissioning decision hinge contracts of employment, and that relationships between producers and technicians are affected thereby. But a quick decision in favour of any one independent producer is a shutout for another. And the decision-taking process now in hand follows precisely the timetable laid down by me when I first spoke to independent producers at the Royal Institution in January last year . . . It would have been unfair to all to have proceeded any faster than we have. Any independent producer who assures his associates that he or she can obtain, magically faster, favoured treatment from Channel Four is deceiving them and calls his or her own credibility into question, not ours.[53]

Peacock's third point remarked upon the importance of accurate and secure pre-production budgeting:

The bases of the commissioning and financing processes appear to be largely insulated from each other. Budgets are being cut arbitrarily, without notice and at a very late stage in the commissioning process, in some cases rendering the production untenable. Members also pointed to the Catch 22 inherent in the need under your Standard Terms to agree a budget in precise detail well before all necessary information is available. Budgets are therefore based in large part on available facts, reasonable assumptions, the independents' experience and market going-rates, all matters of judgement and therefore vulnerable to arbitrary reduction. The end result of under-budgeting is usually overspending and will put the independent in an impossible position financially. Finally, it was noted those concerned with approving budgets had no previous experience of building budgets (i.e. had only controlled production expenditure within budgets prepared by others).[54]

Isaacs replied:

I do not accept that the commissioning and financing processes at Channel Four are, as you suggest, insulated from each other, or that budgets are being cut arbitrarily. We have limited funds and must manage them as efficiently as we can. But we wish to make merit and interest the criterion of programme commissioning, not cost.

. . . We are aware, of course, that we are cutting budgets as tight as possible. That too is inevitable; fatter budgets for some mean fewer commissions for others. But we are also aware that under-budgeting can mean over-spending. We shall monitor carefully what transpires, and take that properly into account for future years. In the meantime, however, I cannot stress sufficiently our need for programmes to be made at minimal cost.[55]

Some budgets have been assessed during the contract negotiation stage at a level substantially lower than that initially requested by producers, something which has upset a few of them. Conversely, however, other producers have, in Channel Four's opinion, underestimated their costs and have received more than they asked for. Prior estimation of costs is obviously not easy. Once again, it is something' that will become more refined as the channel's budgeting team gain more experience. Which is certainly not to say that at present the channel is calculating its figures wildly inaccurately; in fact, most productions so far have come in close to budget.

Streamlining Channel Four's financial operations has been a main concern of Justin Dukes. In his efforts to maximise the channel's cost-effectiveness he has encouraged the channel to employ sophisticated computer-based systems. To help independent producers keep within their budgets, portable radio-contact computer terminals are made available, enabling them, and the channel, to monitor expenditure at all stages of production and give early warning of any over-spending. Dukes is convinced that this reliance on modern technological hardware is saving Channel Four considerable expense:

We are processing the financial and contractual arrangements as well as the programme scheduling arrangements for a portfolio of programming substantially in excess of that of any single ITV contractor, even the biggest. We are doing it with a fraction of the staff that they employ, and we are doing it with computer-driven systems. If we were not to have those systems I am absolutely sure we would be looking for between 75–100 additional staff in this company. That is where the savings are coming from.[56]

Channel Four's attempt to minimise its costs is matched by its desire to maximise the generation of revenue from the efficient exploitation of all its productions. Such exploitation does not only include sales of programmes to overseas broadcasting organisations, but also cable, books, video cassettes, records and other merchandising ventures where appropriate. The channel's intention of centralising this exploitation and retaining, in the case of productions which it has wholly financed, 70% of all net revenues (the remaining 30% being payable to the independent producer) was the subject of Peacock's fourth point:

> The insistence by Channel Four on receiving 70% of all net revenue from exploitation of programmes was heavily criticised, and instanced as evidence that Channel Four was more concerned to build its own business empire than to respect the customary rights of independents to manage their own exploitation arrangements and to retain at least 50% of net revenue.[57]

There are essentially two views on this matter. The first holds that since independent producers are required to meet at least half the cost of overspends, and thus share the risks of production, they should be entitled to an equal share of the benefits from exploiting their programmes; programmes which after all were their ideas in the first place and were realised by their production skills. The second view rests on the details of ownership; if Channel Four pays for the entire cost of production then it owns the relevant programmes and should be free to dispose of them in whatever manner it deems appropriate. Giving the independent producers 30% of exploitation revenue, in addition to their production fees, is therefore seen as an act of generosity made in recognition of the producers' talents and the fact that they have taken some of the risks. Originally, Channel Four wanted a 75/25 division in its favour, but during the course of negotiations this was changed by 5%. In his letter to IPPA's Chairman, Isaacs pointed out that the percentage figure remained open to review:

> We at Channel Four believe that our proposed Terms of Trade, which are in every individual case open to negotiation, and which we specifically state may be varied to 60:40 in certain circumstances, are fair and the right ones on which to base our first year's operation. The Terms of Trade are, as you know, subject to annual review. In that review we shall, each year, have very much in mind not just the Channel's own revenues, but the viability and prosperity of the independent sector, which we have already decided will receive the benefit of growth through re-investment of Channel Four's share of the net benefits of exploitation.[58]

Peacock's final point was to note that there was a strongly voiced suspicion among his members that Channel Four was not treating independent producers and the ITV companies even-handedly. The fact that Channel Four was likely to agree upon bulk supply deals with the ITV companies — as opposed to the single contracts for individual programmes which characterised commissions with independent pro-ducers — was taken to be indicative of this discrimination in favour of ITV. Isaacs rejected the charge. He stressed that the volume of trade the channel was undertaking with the independent sector was far greater than either the ITV companies or Channel Four had anticipated. Regarding the terms of trade, he explained that he had always said Channel Four would deal evenly, but not identically, with the two sectors. Channel Four has been obliged to agree to bulk supply deals with the ITV companies, for the economies of scale implied by such large deals makes programme production for Channel Four attractive, despite the relatively low unit price the channel is paying. Yet the most apposite point has to be that out of Channel Four's total 60-hour week the independent sector is supplying the same as, if not slightly more than, the ITV companies. Depending on the particular week's schedule, both are providing 15–20 hours a week; feature films represent a further 15 hours; four-and-a-half hours come from ITN; and about five hours a week is foreign material.

The successful selling of those 60 hours of airtime, or, to be precise, the short commercial breaks interspersed between them, has now begun in earnest. The question for the ITV companies is, of course, how long they will have to wait before the revenue they derive from the channel is equal to, or preferably greater than, the subscription they have paid to maintain it. That subscription was set by the IBA in July 1981 at £104 million; to cover the fifteen month period between January 1982, when the new ITV contracts started, and April 1983, the end of Channel Four's full financial year. Because of the special circumstances of 1982, a year when advertising revenue from the channel was not available until November, the ITV companies have actually only had to pay £35 million of their 1982 subscription immediately. The remainder has been met by the IBA, who have raised loans from the financial money markets. Since the subscription for future years will include provision for the interest and repayment of those loans, this makes no difference to the ITV companies' desire to see Channel Four succeed as soon as possible, but it is an indication of the uncertainty that accompanied the preparation of Channel Four's launch. As Peter Fiddick commented:

> Even by the opaque standards of television accounting, it will prove a remarkable footnote in British broadcasting history that the state of nerves in ITV in 1981 was so twitchy that the newly franchised commercial companies were asked to cough up less than half the budgeted cost of the new Channel Four and its Welsh-language counterpart, while IBA got the rest in the money market at a time of unprecedentedly high interest rates.[59]

However, by early 1982 there were strong indications that Channel Four would be able to attract sufficient advertising support. ITV's net revenue leapt by 15% in 1981 to £611 million, in spite of the economic recession. This sum is equivalent to about £800 million in 1983 prices, allowing for annual inflation in the television industry of 15%. To recover their £100 million subscription to Channel Four the ITV

158

companies therefore require a 12.5% increase in revenue in real terms during 1983, perhaps nearer 15% to pay for the costs of repaying the IBA's loan. A forecast by the advertising agency J Walter Thompson published in January 1982 was optimistic about the prospect of the ITV contractors securing this extra revenue:

This is just about possible if (i) Channel Four and ITV's joint share of television audiences exceeds 55%, in contrast to ITV's current 50% share; (ii) airtime on Channel Four is fully sold; (iii) there is a slight increase in total weekly viewing as a result of the introduction of a fourth public broadcasting service.[60]

Subsequent market surveys by other advertising agencies have supported JWT's assessment, although it has been suggested that there are likely to be marked regional variations. Channel Four's up-market schedule will probably be much harder to sell in the North than in the South.

With each of the ITV companies responsible for selling the channel's airtime in their regions, Channel Four has effectively fifteen different sales and marketing departments; all with their own sales planning and pricing policies. Dukes and Isaacs are concerned that there should be 'no disharmony in the way the channel is presented.'[61] At first, favouring the idea of a single central sales force, they attempted to re-open the debate about how the channel's airtime would be sold. But the ITV companies were resolved that they should keep control and there was no doubt that Parliament and the IBA had endorsed their view. In January 1982 three contractors — LWT, Anglia and TVS — announced their intention of providing a halfway house by agreeing upon a joint introductory rate for new advertisers. They proposed a joint 40-spot Channel Four package to advertisers whose products were new to television, or had not been aired since 1980, for £140,000. Those who were willing to book before September 1982 would receive a £21,000 rebate towards the cost of producing their commercials. But, in the end, the channel's success will depend on the popularity of its programmes and not the price of its airtime. As Torin Douglas, *The Times* marketing and advertising columnist, remarked in February 1982:

Ultimately, however, it will be the quality of the programming that will determine whether or not Channel Four meets its audience targets and, as a result, attracts sufficient advertising revenue to pay its way. By the beginning of November, there will be no one in the country left unaware of the launch of the new television channel, but if it does not screen programmes that sufficient people want to watch, it will go the same way as the vast majority of other new products launched each year: it will fail.[62]

159

Within the television and advertising industries there is great confidence that Channel Four will not fail. To inform the public of its arrival, the channel spent about £2 million during the immediate pre-launch period on a nationwide advertising campaign. Now, after so many years of discussion, months of preparation, and millions of pounds have been spent on programmes and films, it has finally arrived. And now, only after the Fourth Channel Debate is finally over, the public is, *for the first time*, fully aware of the existence of a fourth television channel. It is an important point: the one group who have notably not featured in the story of Channel Four are the people who will now judge its performance — the television-viewing public. Despite attempts to excite public interest in the subject, there has been no widespread public demand for a fourth channel and the long debate over its allocation has been conducted almost solely by professional broadcasters and film-makers, politicians and civil servants, advertisers and academics. Which is not to say, of course, that there will be no public interest in the channel now that it is available. If Channel Four succeeds in achieving its aim to be engagingly different, to cater for particular audiences traditionally neglected, it will be popular. A channel 'for all of the people — some of time', it hopes to reach 80% of the population over the course of a complete week. The stakes are very high, for virtually the entire nation has the opportunity to assess Channel Four's output. Eighteen years ago when BBC2 was launched only a few people were able to receive the new service. Those that could, turned to see it out of curiosity. Many did not return. With its national reach, the same curiosity will give Channel Four initially a healthy audience. The question is whether this audience will still be watching by mid-1983 and beyond.

What if it is not? Despite the fact that Channel Four is not directly dependent on the income earned from the sale of its advertising space, it is under considerable indirect pressure to attract a sizeable audience. Not only would the ITV companies 'lean' on an unpopular Channel Four, but, since four-fifths of any gap between Channel Four's subscription and the income it generates is effectively met by the Treasury in the form of lost levy, the Government would also be concerned. But above all, it is the channel's own Board and staff who want it to pay its own way; they would like a larger subscription to work with, and they know that they are most likely to achieve this if the ITV companies are making a profit out of their channel. Nevertheless, as Isaacs repeatedly stressed in all his public statements prior to the channel's launch, Parliament has charged Channel Four with various programming objectives and it will strive to meet them. As he says, it is a question of balance:

If we go hell for leather for mass audiences we will fail in our obligation to cater for minorities and special interests. On the other hand, if we keep all our promises and attract no advertising, we will also fail, and so there must be an acceptable balance.[63]

While the financial forces that will prevent a neglect of advertising revenue are clear enough, the forces that will ensure that the channel fulfils its other obligations are a little less clear. The 1980 Television Act specifically requires the IBA in its annual report to demonstrate how Channel Four has fulfilled its statutory obligations:

> 7(2) The report shall include the following information, that is to say . . .
>
> (b) an account of the way in which the Authority have discharged their duty under section 3(1)(c) as regards the encouragement of innovation and experiment in the form and content of programmes for broadcasting in the Fourth Channel Service;
> (c) a description of the sources from which the programmes broadcast in ITV and the Fourth Channel Service respectively were obtained, and an account of the extent to which the Authority have discharged their duty under section 4(3)(b) as regards the sources of programmes broadcast in the Fourth Channel Service.[64]

Much will depend on the attitudes of the personalities directly involved, for in terms of formal structures Channel Four is less 'accountable' than other television channels. There are very few sanctions hanging over it. It does not have a franchise contract which can be withdrawn. It does not have a licence fee which needs to be raised to keep pace with inflation. It does have, in the words of the IBA, 'a considerable degree of independence.'[65] The Authority exercises its control over Channel Four through the appointment of the channel's Board members; by establishing the annual budget; and approving the programme schedules. If it is dissatisfied with the channel's performance it cannot disenfranchise the Channel Four Company, but will have to change the composition of the Board of Directors. At present, however, there is nothing to suggest that such dissatisfaction is likely. In fact, there are many indications that the channel's Board and staff, aware of the balance they must achieve, will ensure that the channel will meet its criteria for success.

On the subject of changing personnel, it is worth noting that the concept of a continual rejuvenation of the channel has been accepted by the Board and its executives. In devising his scheme for a National Television Foundation that would avoid imposing its own 'house-style' on the material it transmitted, Anthony Smith envisaged a small organisation with a rapid turnover of staff. 'It would be the kind of place,' he explained, 'where a few talented people would spend a few years of their lives and then move on; having helped to build this very flexible, lively and innovative organisation.'[66] Much of that idea seems to have carried over into Channel Four. It will probably be expressed in the pension scheme the channel is designing for its staff, which will aim to ensure that its employees' pension rights are not diminished despite relatively short periods of employment. The question is how long that 'in-out' period is likely to be. Paul Bonner estimates it could be less than ten years:

> I do not think that any of us here believe that we have a right or duty to stay beyond a period that allows us to contribute everything we can contribute. If I can take the analogy with film-making, you do not lock a film-maker into a certain strand of film profitably for more than a certain period of time, and I would say the same is true of the channel. Of course, not everyone can leave at once, so it has got to be phased. But I would think that certainly by 1990 there would be very few of the original people here, and most of them would be technical and operational rather than commissioning editors or the so-called executives.[67]

By the 1990s it will be possible to assess fully the impact of Channel Four. By then the BBC/IBA duopoly will probably have been broken, cable and satellite television having been introduced. For the immediate future, however, British television will remain limited to four UHF 625 line terrestrially transmitted television channels. The two VHF 405 line channels are shortly to be finally phased out, and it would be possible to squeeze a fifth 625 line colour national network into the vacated VHF Bands I and III. But such a channel is unlikely, for there are many other groups, such as the police and other civilian services, who would like to use those frequencies. Thus, Channel Four is almost certain to be the last of its kind.

Although it is obviously too early to say what will be the impact of Channel Four, it is possible to ask some questions. For instance, what effect will the channel's 'distinctive' output have on the other three services? BBC2 has already attempted to pre-empt some of Channel Four's programming aims by providing more programmes for youth, more foreign drama, a new ethnic magazine and a new Saturday-night current affairs programme which is likely to clash with Channel Four's weekend politics slot. But will the arrival of Channel Four lead the BBC and ITV to recognise new modes of programming, such as changes in the presentation of news, or the showing of grant-aided independent film work? Assuming Channel Four pays its way and generates advertising revenue equal to or more than its £100 million subscription, and assuming the total level of all forms of advertising expenditure in the United Kingdom remains roughly constant, other advertising media must suffer. With its cheaper airtime (sometimes as much as two-thirds cheaper) and address to particular audiences, Channel Four hopes to attract advertisers who have not, up till now, been able to afford to advertise on television. Will a successful Channel Four pose a serious threat to the Press, particularly the 'quality' press? What effect will Channel Four have on the broadcasting and film industry? An independent television production sector has flourished since January 1981. But, as Peter Fiddick has pointed out, the inaugural boom is over.[68] Never again will so much be commissioned so quickly. How will the independent sector develop over the next few years? Will the emergent international cable and satellite market lead to a further expansion of the seed Channel Four has sown? And what of the impact of Channel Four on British society in general? Will the film and video workshops, now that they are properly funded, have an effect on the local communication of social tensions? What will happen to women's politics, given the advent of a high level of women's participation in a national television channel? What will be the effect on ethnic communities? How will the groups that continually agitate over Third World questions develop, now that they have direct access to a national television channel?

At the end of the last chapter we noted the great expectations that have accompanied the setting up of Channel Four, and asked who, if anyone, would be disappointed? Remarkably, there have been relatively few malcontents so far. But now that the channel's programmes are being seen, to what extent can those expectations be fulfilled will become an increasingly pertinent question.

Notes

1. *The Fourth Channel: Production Facilities,* an edited summary of a consultation held at the IBA, 20 May 1980 (IBA, 1980), p. 6.
2. Ibid., p. 7.
3. Ibid., p. 37.
4. 'Aims and Objectives of the Association', IPPA statement, June 1980.
5. 'Isaacs: the independents' favourite son', *Broadcast,* 26 January 1981, p. 10.
6. Ibid., p. 11.
7. 'The Aims of the WBFL', WBFL publicity statement, 1980.
8. 'Sticking pins into wax dolls', *Guardian,* 1 December 1980.
9. Letter from Jeremy Isaacs to Anne Cottringer of the IFA, 7 April 1981.
10. 'Tickets to ITV2? — Companies ready to take on the Beeb', *AIP & Co,* Number 29, October/November 1980, pp. 3-5.
11. Isaacs, J., speaking to the Broadcasting Press Guild, 20 February 1981, unpublished transcript.
12. Personal communication.
13. Justin Dukes (personal communication).
14. 'Thames agree 80 hours for Channel Four', *Broadcast,* 8 February 1982, p. 3.
15. 'Channel Four — The story so far', *ADP Newsletter,* Issue 33, November 1981.
16. Justin Dukes (personal communication).
17. Douglas, T., 'Finding the contrast in Channel Four advertising', *Marketing Week,* 13 August 1982, p. 47.
18. Lippmann, W., *Public Opinion* (New York: Macmillan, 1922).

19. Glasgow Media Group, *Bad News* (London: Routledge & Kegan Paul, 1976), p. 1.
20. *Report of the Committee on the Future of Broadcasting* (Annan Report) (HMSO, 1977), Cmnd 6753, para. 17.29.
21. Griffin-Beale, C., 'ITN in at the deep end with Channel Four', *Broadcast*, 30 November 1981, p. 3.
22. Ibid., p. 4.
23. 'New views on news views', *Broadcast*, 19 April 1982.
24. Forgan, L., 'News and current affairs on Channel Four', a Channel Four internal background position paper, January 1982.
25. 'Channel Four's current affairs programmes break new ground,' Channel Four press release, 7 April 1982, p. 4.
26. Ibid., p. 5.
27. 'Channel Four's very own soap opera', *The Times*, 23 November 1981.
28. Isaacs, J., 'Channel Four — A different sort of television?' a lecture by the Chief Executive of Channel Four at the National Film Theatre, 19 January 1982, unpublished transcript.
29. Rose, D., & Donohue, W., 'Fiction on Four', a Channel Four internal background position paper, January 1982.
30. Hill, D., open letter to Jeremy Isaacs, 17 July 1981.
31. Isaacs, J., letter to Derek Hill, 22 July 1981.
32. 'Channel Four unveiled', *Campaign*, 5 February 1982, pp. 25-6.
33. 'Switching the nation on to education after tea', *Guardian*, 9 February 1982.
34. *Broadcast*, 7 September 1981, p. 16.
35. McIntosh, N., 'Channel Four — A different way of learning?' a lecture by Channel Four's senior commissioning editor for education at the National Film Theatre, 16 February 1982, unpublished transcript.
36. Forgan, L., 'Channel Four and factual programmes — A role for women?', a lecture by Channel Four's senior commissioning editor for actuality at the National Film Theatre, 2 February 1982, unpublished transcript.
37. *Guardian*, 23 November 1981.
38. Isaacs, J., 'In what way will Channel Four provide a distinctive service?', *Listener*, 5 November 1981, p. 527.
39. Madden, P., 'Media programmes on Channel Four', a Channel Four internal background position paper, January 1982.
40. Paul Bonner (personal communication).
41. 'The wonderful people who will bring you Channel Four', *Sunday Times Magazine*, 24 January 1982.
42. Isaacs, speaking to the Broadcasting Press Guild, op.cit.
43. *Sunday Times Magazine*, op.cit.
44. Fountain, A., ' "Independent" Film and Video', a Channel Four internal background discussion paper, January 1982.
45. Fountain, A., 'A very different sort of television?', a lecture by Channel Four's commissioning editor for grant-aided film and video at the National Film Theatre, 9 February 1982, unpublished transcript.
46. Peacock, M., open letter from the Chairman of IPPA to the Chief Executive of Channel Four, 29 January 1982.
47. Isaacs, J., open letter from the Chief Executive of Channel Four to the Chairman of IPPA, 2 February 1982.
48. Peacock, op.cit.
49. Isaacs, letter to Peacock, op.cit.
50. Hewson, D., 'Giving TV independents elbow room', *The Times*, 22 September 1981.
51. Peacock, op.cit.
52. Isaacs, NTF lecture, op.cit.
53. Isaacs, letter to Peacock, op.cit.
54. Peacock, op.cit.

55. Isaacs, letter to Peacock, op.cit.
56. Justin Dukes (personal communication).
57. Peacock, op.cit.
58. Isaacs, letter to Peacock, op.cit.
59. Fiddick, P., 'Channel Four on the never-never', *Guardian*, 8 August 1981.
60. *Financial Times*, 14 January 1982.
61. Douglas, T., 'Selling £100 million worth of air', *The Times*, 2 February 1982.
62. Ibid.
63. *Broadcast*, 7 September 1981, p. 16.
64. *Broadcasting Act 1980*, Eliz. 2, Ch. 64, 1980.
65. *The Fourth Channel: The Authority's Proposals*, IBA statement, 12 November 1979, p. 5.
66. Anthony Smith (personal communication).
67. Paul Bonner (personal communication).
68. Fiddick, P., 'Chock-a-block at Channel Four', *Guardian*, 10 June 1982.

Appendix 1

This 1973 submission from Jeremy Isaacs to the Minister of Posts and Telecommunications has not previously been published. It is reproduced here for historical interest. It shows what the future Chief Executive of Channel Four believed, *at that time*, the fourth channel should look like. It does not, of course, represent in any sense a statement of current Channel Four policy. The author would like to thank Mr Isaacs for his permission to use the submission.

A SUBMISSION TO THE MINISTER OF POSTS AND TELECOMMUNICATIONS

1. The fourth television channel is a public asset which should be used and not wasted.

2. ITV has a strong claim to the fourth channel on simple grounds of parity with the BBC, and to enable it to provide complementary programmes on two channels. But ITV's interest is not necessarily the public's interest.

3. The Government should only make available a fourth channel for use if by doing so it will lead to a wider choice of programmes, add to the services which broadcasting provides, and offer the possibility of a genuinely new experience on British television.

4. All these conditions could be fulfilled by allocating the channel not directly to ITV but to the IBA, provided the IBA defines more clearly the purposes to which it would wish to see a fourth channel put, and provided it can satisfy you that it will see those purposes fulfilled in its regulation of the channel.

5. The IBA should finance the channel by a levy upon the television companies.

6. The IBA should appoint a Controller of the Channel who, while working in harness with the Programme Controllers Committee which schedules programmes for ITV1, would nevertheless have sole authority, under the IBA, to schedule programmes for ITV2. It is essential that this authority should reside in one person. Only if this condition is fulfilled will it be possible to select programmes strictly on merit, and to build into the system the flexibility the BBC possesses, and which is markedly absent in ITV's schedules today.

7. The Controller of ITV2 should invite offers of programmes for his schedules from all the ITV companies, and from independent producers, in broad proportions agreed with the IBA, and subject to periodic review.

8. ITV2's schedules should contain some entertainment programmes. But there should be a heavy emphasis, heavier than has yet been suggested in submissions to you by the Television Companies or by the IBA, on 'service' programmes catering for the interests of minorities of viewers. I have in mind programmes for viewers as consumers of goods and of services, and with interests in health, education, the upbringing of children, business and trade union practice, the environment, Parliament, and an endless list of hobbies and sports.

9. ITV2 should carry nightly an extended programme of background news analysis and a Parliamentary Report, both provided by ITN.

10. ITV2 should regularly, once a month or once a fortnight, devote an entire

166

evening to one event. Not just plays, operas or ballets, but lengthy debates and discussions on matters of public importance, including, should Parliament ever decide to allow cameras into the House of Commons, Parliamentary debates.

11. The ITV companies should continue to receive all the advertising revenue for transmission in their areas, but the showing of commercials should be less dispersed through the evening's programmes than is the case on ITV1. There would be a considerable further source of revenue available on ITV2 from advertising aimed at viewers with specialist interests.

12. Many of the programmes would, deliberately, be less expensive per hour than the programmes presently provided on BBC1 and BBC2 or on ITV1. All the same the programme service I am describing would cost something of the order of £25 million a year. But this revenue is available in the ITV system today, and it continues buoyant.

13. It may be asked why the ITV companies should be expected to provide a 'service' channel of this sort. The answer is that they enjoy a monopoly public franchise and earn a more than reasonable return on their investment. As the price for the continued enjoyment of that monopoly, the Government is entitled to ask them to provide this new service.

14. To sum up. ITV should have access to ITV2, but only on terms that guarantee the public not a mirror image of BBC1 and BBC2, but a widening of the range of broadcasting. In making it possible and obligatory for them to do so you, Minister, would be authorising the provision of an additional service to the British viewing public, while exacting a proper price for the enjoyment of a public franchise. A Government which effected this extension to British television would convey a lasting benefit of which it might be properly proud.

Jeremy Isaacs
25 June 1973

Appendix 2

The following terms of reference and programme policy statement were issued by the IBA to the Board of Channel Four upon its incorporation in December 1980.

CHANNEL FOUR TELEVISION COMPANY LIMITED
TERMS OF REFERENCE

1. *Preliminary*

The purpose of this Memorandum is to define and describe the activities to be performed by the Channel Four Television Company Limited ('the company') as the subsidiary formed by the Authority for the purpose of Section 4(2) of the Broadcasting Act 1980 ('the 1980 Act').

This Memorandum has been adopted by a Resolution of the Authority passed on 5th December 1980 and noted by the Company by a Resolution of its Directors passed on 17th December 1980 and will remain in force until cancelled by and subject to any variations made by any subsequent Resolution of the Authority, notice of which is given to the Company.

2. *Functions of the Company*

The principal function of the Company shall be to acquire and supply to the Authority the programmes other than advertisements ('programmes') to be provided by the Authority on the Fourth Channel from the date fixed by the Authority for commencement of that service.

For this purpose the Company shall:

i) arrange for the production and supply of programme items by programme producers (which may include, as appropriate, the Authority's programme contractors and Independent Television News Limited) and to the extent (if any) for the time being approved by the Authority produce programmes itself; in particular the Company shall itself produce all programme items and material required for continuity and for information as to other programmes to be broadcast on the Fourth Channel or on ITV; and for those purposes enter into such contracts as it may consider appropriate;

ii) prepare and submit programme schedules for approval by the Authority (in such detail and at such intervals as it may require) and for that purpose liaise and consult with the Authority and its programme contractors in relation to the programmes to be provided by them on ITV;

iii) engage such staff and professional and other services as it considers necessary provided that such senior staff as the Authority may from time to time determine and notify to the Company shall be persons for the time being approved by the Authority itself;

iv) acquire such offices, studios and other premises and such equipment and furniture as it needs;

v) liaise with the relevant programme contractors and with the appropriate officers of the Authority to enable the programme service broadcast by the

168

Authority on the Fourth Channel to include advertisements supplied by programme contractors in accordance with the provisions of the relevant programme contracts;

vi) ensure that the programmes on the Fourth Channel provided to the Authority by the Company comply with the approved programme schedules; accord with the broadcasting hours and times and technical requirements specified by the Authority from time to time; and that at all times such programmes comply with the duties and obligations of the Authority under the Independent Broadcasting Acts and the Broadcasting Act, and with codes and guidelines laid down by the Authority from time to time;

viii) consult with and report to the Authority on such of its activities as the Authority may from time to time specify.

3. *Finance*

The Authority will agree with the Company from time to time the provision of the funds (which will be related to amounts received in the form of subscriptions from television programme contractors) necessary to meet the Company's approved needs, and will agree arrangements to ensure the best use of money and resources available to both bodies. The Company shall conduct its financial affairs in accordance with such agreements and in a manner which reflects the Authority's statutory responsibilities, and shall:

i) submit, for the Authority's approval, budgets for capital and revenue expenditure and cash flow projections at such times and in such detail as the Authority may request;

ii) have power to authorise expenditure within approved budgets in accordance with powers of delegation which shall be decided by the Company and notified to the Authority;

iii) not borrow or give any security or guarantees except within such limits and on such general terms as may from time to time be agreed with the Authority;

iv) agree with the Authority the general form of contracts and arrangements for inviting tenders and selecting contractors in areas of the Company's business where such arrangements would be appropriate;

v) supply such financial information as the Authority may require to enable the Authority to discharge its duties, including the provision of such information to the Home Secretary;

vi) agree with the Authority the form of its accounts and the arrangements for their publication;

vii) make use of the Authority's financial facilities upon such terms and to such extent as are agreed between the Authority and the Company as practicable and reasonable.

4. *Remuneration*

The arrangements for the remuneration, expenses, etc. of Directors of the Company shall be as fixed by the Authority from time to time. The remuneration and terms of service of such of the senior executives of the Company as shall be determined by the Authority shall be fixed by the Company with the prior approval of the Authority.

169

5. Policy

i) In planning its programmes and activities the Company shall conform with any statements of the Authority's policy on the Fourth Channel declared by Resolution of the Authority or by any directive signed by the Chairman, Director General or Secretary of the Authority.

ii) There shall be consultation between the Authority and the Company from time to time about the policies to be adopted, particularly as regards giving the Fourth Channel a distinctive character of its own.

iii) Within the terms of any statements of policy as in i), and subject to the preceding sections of these Terms of Reference, the Board of Directors of the Company shall have full responsibility and discretion for formulating the Company's policies and for conducting its affairs.

THE FOURTH CHANNEL
PROGRAMME POLICY STATEMENT

In the spirit of the Authority's statement in November 1979, the Channel Four Television Company in providing the Fourth Channel service will have as a particular charge the service of special interests and concerns for which television has until now lacked adequate time.

The Fourth Channel is expected by providing a favoured place for the untried to foster the new and experimental in television. The search for innovation whether in style or content or perspective is not itself new, but the availability of additional broadcasting hours and the lesser importance of ratings provide the chance to introduce new talent, to reaffirm creative alliances or bring together fresh ones, and to develop ideas for which the existing services have not so far found a place.

The Fourth Channel is intended to complement and to be complemented by the present Independent Television service. Complementarity means two things; the provision of reasonable choice between two schedules, with a number of common junctions, and the co-ordinated use of the schedules in the best interest of the viewer. The availability of two schedules in this way makes possible greater variety in subject matter, in the pursuit of serious themes, and in the treatment and length of programmes.

The development of a properly complementary service will take time, and the nature of the appropriate balance between different kinds of programme will change as time passes. The Company's planners will need to take acount of the strengths of the IBA's existing service; its regional characteristics, its broad popular appeal and the trust which it commands amongst its audience. The needs and interests of that audience should be served not only by programmes directed to minorities but also by some aiming to attract larger numbers.

There are three areas in which collaboration between the Fourth Channel and the existing service will help to establish a complementary Independent Television service. The first is the purchasing of some programme material, but the Fourth Channel would not be expected to deal exclusively through the companies' Film Purchase Group. The second is sport, where a common approach to the acquisition of rights and the scheduling of events may sometimes be advantageous.

170

The third is repeats; there will need to be a policy for the repeat on one channel of programmes which were initiated on the other.

The Broadcasting Act recognises no distinction between the two channels in the requirements laid upon the Authority in its regulatory role; nevertheless, as the statement in November 1979 indicated, the coming of a wider choice of programmes brings with it the possibility of presenting a wider range of opinions and assumptions.

The Authority requires the Fourth Channel to devote about fifteen per cent of its broadcasting time to educational material. With its commitment to innovation and experiment the Fourth Channel must respond to educational needs as they emerge in the next decade. An important part of this response will lie in finding styles of programming to attract audiences not so far drawn to educational programmes.

The same considerations should influence religious broadcasting. The November statement laid down a minimum of one hour a week of programmes recognisably religious in aim and the Authority looks for distinctive work to enlarge the scope and reach of religious programmes.

The Authority hopes that the Company, through ITN, will evolve a distinctive style in presentation of news and background reporting. The Company will be expected to take current affairs coverage from other quarters, including independent producers. The Fourth Channel Service as a whole is expected to reflect the continuing debate on a wide range of issues of social policy.

The Authority will expect to apply to the two channels the same limits on the use of material made abroad.

The additional hours of broadcasting made available by the Fourth Channel increase opportunities for programmes directed to different kinds of minority groups within the community, whether ethnic, cultural, or occupational distinctions mark them off from their neighbours. There should be a place for an increase in the making of such programmes from within the group rather than from outside.

In achieving an appropriate balance of output, the Fourth Channel will observe a balance between different sources of supply. The Authority welcomes the positive injunction given to it by Parliament to encourage the work of independent producers, and will want to have early and regular assurances that this is being done. It will also expect the regional companies within ITV to make a due contribution to the schedules of the Fourth Channel. Though a national network, the Channel should reflect regional diversities.

In making its financial arrangements, the Fourth Channel will need to ensure that so far as possible the same terms apply to all programme suppliers. The Authority recognises that the making of such arrangements is not an easy task, but the Company will need to make the best use of its limited resources and to ensure the acceptance of its fairness by all concerned.

These are not times when high ideals are fashionable. Survival, rather than expansion and development, may seem to have priority. But that cannot be a lasting mood. It is the Authority's conviction that the Fourth Channel, in the form in which it is being launched, can contribute no less than its three predecessors, to the enlargement of the public's knowledge and experience and can make a real contribution to the society of which broadcasters and non-broadcasters alike form part.

EXECUTIVE STRUCTURE

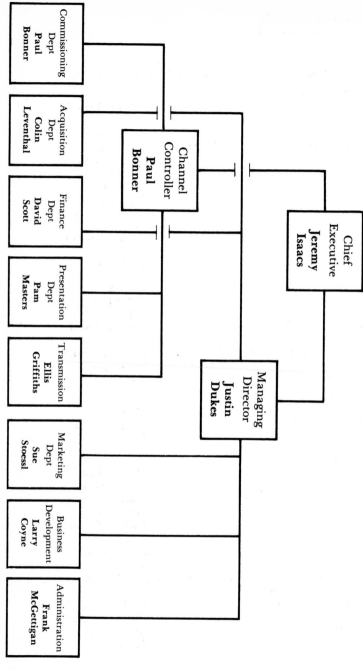

Chief Executive Jeremy Isaacs

Managing Director Justin Dukes

Channel Controller Paul Bonner

- Commissioning Dept **Paul Bonner**
- Acquisition Dept **Colin Leventhal**
- Finance Dept **David Scott**
- Presentation Dept **Pam Masters**
- Transmission **Ellis Griffiths**
- Marketing Dept **Sue Stoessl**
- Business Development **Larry Coyne**
- Administration **Frank McGettigan**

Appendix 3

CHANNEL FOUR PERSONNEL AND ORGANISATIONAL STRUCTURE

The Board of Directors

Chairman	The Rt Hon Edmund Dell
Deputy Chairman	Sir Richard Attenborough
Chief Executive	Jeremy Isaacs
Managing Director & Deputy Chief Executive	Justin Dukes
	William Brown, CBE
	Roger Graef
	David McCall
	The Hon Sara Morrison
	Anthony Smith
	Anne Sofer
	Dr Glyn Tegai Hughes
	Brian Tesler
	Joy Whitby

Executives

Channel Controller	Paul Bonner
Chief Engineer	Ellis Griffiths
Head of Programme Acquisition	Colin Leventhal
Head of Presentation	Pam Masters
Head of Administration & Industrial Relations	Frank McGettigan
Controller of Finance & Company Secretary	David Scott
Head of Marketing	Sue Stoessl

Senior Commissioning Editors

Actuality	Liz Forgan
Education	Naomi McIntosh
Fiction	David Rose

Commissioning Editors

Youth	Mike Bolland
Independent Grant-Aided Sector	Alan Fountain
Education & Documentary Series	Carol Haslam
Light Entertainment	Cecil Korer
The Arts	Michael Kustow
Single Documentaries, Media & Community	Paul Madden
Sport	Adrian Metcalfe
Music	Andy Park
Ireland, Religion, Single Documentaries, & Special Assistant to the Chief Executive	John Ranelagh
Multicultural Programmes	Sue Woodford
Script Associate	Walter Donohue
Film Purchaser	Leslie Halliwell
Film Purchaser	Derek Hill

173

Index

175

177